"McGann provides us with theology and our liturgical planet and to true justice for tne dispossessed and the hungry. Along the way she has given us a very accessible account of the complex global food crisis that we face."

> —John F. Baldovin, SJ
> Professor of Historical and Liturgical Theology
> Boston College School of Theology & Ministry

"Mary McGann's *tour de force* brings together two substantial topics. An inspirational and pastoral handbook of places to start based on the reality of engaging with a meal that reconnects all of this through the simplicity of real bread, real wine, real community, real meals, real conversations, and the real and imminent crises in the world for which we have been called to care in response to the 'cry of the earth and the cry of the poor.'"

> —Lizette Larson-Miller, author of *Sacramentality Renewed:*
> *Contemporary Conversations in Sacramental Theology*

"Rarely does one find a work that so clearly integrates the ancient symbols of Christian faith with contemporary scientific assessment of the fundamental need for food and drink. In *The Meal That Reconnects*, Mary McGann offers a well-documented and articulate presentation of the relationship between the meals of Jesus as expressions of God's reign of justice and peace and how this life-giving practice is thwarted and deformed by industrialization of food systems in which we all participate."

> —Fr. Samuel Torvend
> Professor of Religion
> Pacific Lutheran University in Tacoma, Washington

"While forthrightly exposing the global food economy's degradation of bodies and environments, this book offers an account of food justice that never abandons the sumptuous flavors and joys of the meal itself. This is a food-forward spirituality of the Eucharist to savor and share in an ecological age."

> —Benjamin Stewart, PhD
> Gordon A. Braatz Associate Professor of Worship
> Lutheran School of Theology at Chicago

"Today we face a crisis regarding food and know that we need to change our ways of food production and consumption if we, and the planet, are to survive. Likewise, as Christians, we are in a crisis in our understanding of the Eucharist. Eucharist is an activity. An activity that supposes an awareness of our dependence . . . this book helps us develop that awareness."

—Thomas O'Loughlin, author of *Eating Together, Becoming One*

"Mary McGann invites readers into a eucharistic vision of justice, care, and reverence: food as an interspecies paschal event knitting together all that is. Critical and profoundly connective, this book is a passionate invitation to eating well and wisely, reverently and thankfully, ethically and joyfully on our good Earth."

—Lisa E. Dahill, PhD
Professor of Religion
California Lutheran University

"McGann plumbs essential sources from ecology, food studies, agriculture, economics, health and wellness, social ethics, liturgical studies, and theology—and then in very accessible terms, shows the hope-filled potential of the Christian Eucharist as a paradigm to counter the vast injustices of the current global corporate food industry. A 'must read'!"

—Dawn M. Nothwehr, OSF, PhD
The Erica and Harry John Family Professor of Catholic
Theological Ethics
Catholic Theological Union

The Meal That Reconnects

Eucharistic Eating and the Global Food Crisis

Mary E. McGann, RSCJ

LITURGICAL PRESS
ACADEMIC

Collegeville, Minnesota
www.litpress.org

1	2	3	4	5	6	7	8	9

Library of Congress Cataloging-in-Publication Data

Names: McGann, Mary E., author.
Title: The meal that reconnects : Eucharistic eating and the global food crisis / Mary E. McGann, RSCJ.
Description: Collegeville : Liturgical Press Academic, 2020. | Includes bibliographical references and index. | Summary: "Discusses the sacredness of eating, the planetary interdependence that the sharing of food entails, and the destructiveness of the industrial food system, presenting the food crisis as a spiritual crisis. The author invites communities to reclaim the foundational meal character of eucharistic celebration while offering pertinent strategies for this renewal"—Provided by publisher.
Identifiers: LCCN 2019032400 (print) | LCCN 2019032401 (ebook) | ISBN 9780814660317 (paperback) | ISBN 9780814660324 (epub) | ISBN 9780814660324 (mobi) | ISBN 9780814660324 (pdf)
Subjects: LCSH: Dinners and dining—Religious aspects—Catholic Church. | Lord's Supper—Catholic Church. | Hunger—Religious aspects—Catholic Church. | Food supply—Moral and ethical aspects. | Food supply—Religious aspects—Catholic Church.
Classification: LCC BR115.N87 M378 2020 (print) | LCC BR115.N87 (ebook) | DDC 234/.163—dc23
LC record available at https://lccn.loc.gov/2019032400
LC ebook record available at https://lccn.loc.gov/2019032401

For all the hungry people in the world,
especially the women and children

Contents

Preface

Eating is a foundational human act, one that ties us to all other living and nonliving creatures and to the complex processes of exchange that characterize the planetary community. Meeting more than the biological need to survive, eating affords a sense of pleasure, an experience of nurture, and an invitation to celebrate the goodness of life, the faithfulness of Mother Earth, and the graciousness of a God whose creative life flows through the web of creaturely existence.

But today food is in crisis and with it the Earth and her peoples. Food production at the hands of a corporate, multinational food industry[1] is exacerbating hunger, poverty, and inequality; creating ill health; contributing to climate change; destroying ecosystems; and poisoning Earth's resources. More profoundly, the market forces driving this system have estranged human beings from the sources and processes by which food comes to our tables. They insulate us from the devastating effects of industrial food production. Food has become a product to be consumed rather than a living relationship between the Earth and the human community. To eat in ignorance of this is to live a distortion of our foundational relationship with the world and ultimately with God who created Earth and became incarnate in the biological web of earthly being.

---

1. Documentation for these claims can be found in the remainder of the book, especially in part 2. In this book, the terms "corporate agriculture," "industrial farming," "agribusiness," and "corporate/industrial food system" will be used somewhat interchangeably.

Although industrial agriculture is not the sole provider of the world's food,[2] its influence has negatively impacted conventional and subsistence farmers around the globe, exacerbating the exodus of people from rural habitats to sprawling urban centers[3] and forcing an abandonment of centuries-old, ecologically sound ways of farming and keeping the land. Touted as the most efficient way to feed the world, such efficiency is a mirage that masks destructive and life-threatening practices.[4] In 2013, several United Nations agencies declared industrial farming unsustainable and urged that it be replaced by organic, regionally based agriculture.[5]

Given the financial and political power of corporate agribusiness, this transition will come about only from the ground up, through human choices, increased awareness, and renewed commitments to health, sustainability, justice, and human happiness. It is my contention that the spiritual resources of the many faith traditions that

2. See Vandana Shiva, *Who Really Feeds the World* (Berkeley: North Atlantic Books, 2016), 111–24. Shiva estimates that 70 percent of the world's food continues to be supplied by small farmers, especially women.

3. See Timothy Gorringe, *The Common Good and the Global Emergency* (Cambridge: Cambridge University Press, 2011), 192. Gorringe notes that the cause of this urban migration is that "agricultural livelihoods have been destroyed by neoliberal economic policies." Gorringe references the United Nations report, *The Challenge of Slums: Global Report on Human Settlements 2003* (London: Earthscan, 2003), 40.

4. See, for example, Andred Kimbrel, ed., *The Fatal Harvest Reader: The Tragedy of Industrial Agriculture* (Washington, DC: Island Press, 2002).

5. Several UN agencies have jointly stated that food security, climate change, poverty, and gender inequality can all be addressed by a radical change from the current industrial agricultural and globalized food system to a conglomerate of small, biodiverse, ecological farms around the world and a localized food system that promotes consumption of local/regional produce. See "Paradigm Shift Urgently Needed in Agriculture," Science in Society Archive, first published September 17, 2013; accessed June 17, 2019, http://www.i-sis.org.uk/Paradigm_Shift_Urgently _Needed_in_Agriculture.php.

cherish rituals of eating, sharing food, and blessing God—most especially Christian Eucharist—are critical to this process.

This volume asks: How can eucharistic eating create an alternative paradigm and effect a prophetic healing of relationships with the Earth's abundance and all who share it? How can eucharistic practice strengthen relationships of justice, solidarity, and reciprocity between human communities and the rest of the web of life?

To answer these questions, part 1 focuses on eating as relationship. Chapter 1 explores eating as a foundational human act that situates us in a vast web of social, economic, political, ethical, ecological, and theological relationships. In light of this complexity, chapters 2 and 3 explore Jesus' table fellowship and the legacy of this meal practice in early Christian eucharistic practice. Part 2 explores the emergence of a global, corporate food industry, focusing first on the circumstances of its origins (chap. 4) and then examining in more detail its current practices (chaps. 5 and 6), including a closer look at four critical areas: seeds, life's miracle betrayed; soil, farming's critical matrix; hunger, a human tragedy; and farmworkers, laborers with little justice. The last chapter of part 2 focuses on new regenerative agricultural practices that will contribute to the healing and reconciling of human relationships with the life-giving Earth (chap. 7).

Part 3 returns to the eucharistic table, exploring how a revitalization of eucharistic eating can make a unique contribution to healing broken relationships within the human community, with Earth, and with the One whose life pulses through all creation: first, through reclaiming the foundational meal character of eucharistic celebration (chap. 8) and, second, by reinvigorating the vital connections between Eucharist and the ecological, social, and economic forces that shape global society today (chap. 9).

This volume grows out of deep personal concern and scholarly interest in the future of food, the justice by which it is available to the human-biotic community, and the contribution that Christian meal practice can make to shaping an equitable future. It is written across multiple fields of study—ecology, food studies, agriculture, economics, health and wellness, social ethics, liturgical studies, and theology—all of which contribute to the composite picture of both the crises and the promises and hope we find in today's global food situation. The literature for such a study is vast, and I draw only lightly on the enormous wealth of resources available. But the specific task of making connections between Christian eucharistic practice and the food crises is just beginning and has not been widely taken up by scholars in liturgical studies. My hope is that this book will invite and encourage others to follow, building on what they find here, and that all readers will be inspired to reimagine the gift of Christian Eucharist to a global society in need of healing and hope for a future of abundance.

In completing this volume, my heart is full of gratitude. To my associates in the Ecology and Liturgy Seminar of the North American Academy of Liturgy and to members of *Societas Liturgica*, who responded to early drafts, my sincere gratitude. To my colleagues at the Graduate Theological Union, Berkeley, and especially to the faculty at the Jesuit School of Theology of Santa Clara University, who gave feedback on an early draft and whose interest and encouragement has accompanied me along the way, my deep thanks. A special word of gratitude to Mary Dern Walker for her excellent editorial assistance, to Catherine Holcombe for assistance in checking references, and to Dianna Gallagher and Mey Saechao for technical assistance. Finally, my special thanks to the Religious of the Sacred Heart, especially my own community members at Sophia House, who have supported and accompanied me through the research and writing process, celebrating each stage along the way. And to the One whose love sustains each moment of life in this amazing world, eternal gratitude!

part one

Eating as Relationship

Eucharistic eating is deeply rooted in the human sharing of food, in the provocative meal fellowship of Jesus' public ministry, and in the earliest gatherings of Christ's followers who recognized his continual presence among them in the breaking of the bread. The three chapters that follow invite communities to remember these roots, allowing them to engage their imaginations as to the role eucharistic eating might play in healing the broken relationships caused by today's industrial food system.

chapter one

Eating Matters

Food: Communication, Identity, Gift

Eating matters: what we eat, with whom we eat, where the food is grown, who is left out and who decides—these are all questions with ecological, ethical, and theological significance. Eating matters for Christian liturgy as well, and the complexities of growing, preparing, and sharing food are likewise pertinent to contemporary liturgical renewal and practice.

Eating is an expression of one's vision of the world and of one's faith in a God whose abundant life is poured out in creation. How we eat manifests our relationship with the world as consecration or desecration. In the words of Wendell Berry, "To live, we must daily break the body and shed the blood of Creation. When we do this knowingly, lovingly, skillfully, reverently, it is a sacrament. When we do it ignorantly, greedily, clumsily, destructively, it is a desecration. In such desecration, we condemn ourselves to spiritual and moral loneliness, and others to want."[1]

Food is a "system of communication revealing what we believe and value about people, things, bodies, traditions, time, money and

---

1. Wendell Berry, "The Gift of Good Land," in *The Gift of Good Land: Further Essays Cultural and Agricultural* (New York: North Point Press, 1981), 281.

places."[2] Eating negotiates personal and communal identity, the cultivation of memory and the maintenance and creation of tradition. For this reason, eating can also keep persons and groups separate from each other, lest identity markers on which people depend be disturbed.[3] Patterns of fasting and feasting, of blessing God and giving thanks and of gathering around festive tables to feast with special foods enable communities to mark time, hallow space, and claim the meaningfulness and deeper anamnetic[4] significance of the moment while joining generations past and to come in a vast liturgy of life and celebration of divine fidelity.

To eat is to enter a realm not under human control, to admit that we are not self-sustaining gods but finite creatures, dependent on a graced universe of soil, sunlight, seed, and photosynthesis.[5] Ecologically, food entangles us in intricate food webs too vast to map and in the lives of creatures too numerous to count. Hence, the decontextualization of food by industrial processes that dissociate it from its biological origins and relationships is a spiritual impoverishment of our understanding and experience of food.[6]

Food comes to us at a price. Eating invites us into a daily life-and-death drama in which some creatures give their lives so that others

2. Norman Wirzba, "Food for Theologians," *Interpretation: A Journal of Bible and Theology* 67, no. 4 (2013): 375.

3. Ibid., 381.

4. The term *anamnetic* is based on the Greek term *anamnesis*, referring to the making present, or "reactualizing," of an event, object, or person from the past. The term is used in reference to remembrance of Christ's paschal mystery in liturgy—the making present his action at the moment of the church's prayer.

5. David Grummett, Luke Bretherton, and Stephen R. Holmes, "Fast Food: A Critical Theological Perspective," *Food, Culture and Society* 14, no. 3 (September 2013): 379.

6. Norman Wirzba, *Food and Faith: A Theology of Eating* (Cambridge: Cambridge University Press, 2011), xvi.

may survive and thrive.[7] Within this paschal economy of creation, planetary interdependence is rooted in sacrificial giving, whereby God's providential, sustaining love is mediated through the death of some creatures for the life of others. To eat is to accept the costly gift of another's life; to enter a mystical union in which another being becomes part of us, its molecules now part of our human tissue.[8] In this light, some speak of our union with other creatures in terms of "natural communion."[9]

Today, this organic cycle of death enabling life is exacerbated by food systems that bring premature human death (hunger, malnutrition), termination of lives (farmer suicides),[10] ecocide (destruction of soils, rainforests, and arable land), and violent systems of animal husbandry. A major cause of these unnecessary deaths is the vastly increased consumption of meat by communities around the world, which entails an unprecedented clearing of rainforest land for grazing, the feeding of two-thirds of all grain exported from the United States to livestock rather than to hungry humans, and brutal practices in American slaughterhouses that are concealed from public view.[11] Awareness of these unnecessary and merciless deaths invites

7. Ibid., 76. Fritjof Capra, *The Web of Life* (New York: Anchor Books, 1996), 179. In "Food for Theologians," Wirzba notes that the food industry does a masterful job of hiding death from us. See p. 379.

8. See Michael Schuet, "Why Food? Spirituality, Celebration and Justice," in *Food, Faith and Sustainability* (Seattle: Earth Ministry, 1997), 9.

9. Sergi Bulgakov, *Philosophy of Economy: The World as Household* (New Haven: Yale University Press, 2000), 103. As noted in Wirzba, *Food and Faith*, 2.

10. See Vandana Shiva, *Seeds of Suicide: The Ecological and Human Cost of Globalization of Agriculture* (New Delhi: Research Foundation for Science, Technology and Ecology, 2000).

11. John Robbins and Jia Patton, "A Bite Felt 'Round the World,' " in *Food, Faith and Sustainability*, 27. See also Wirzba, "Food for Theologians," 379. Animal husbandry, although closely interwoven with other aspects of industrial farming, will not be a major focus of this volume.

a commitment to a sacrificial understanding of eating, one that commits eaters to promote the health and flourishing of whatever creatures they consume.[12]

Eating today engages us in conflicting paradigms: food as gift or food as commodity.

Food as gift implies a posture of receptivity and gratitude toward the One who is the source of the gift. An abundant Earth is assumed, an abundance that is meant to be fostered, sustained, nurtured. Human engagement with the Earth's produce is seen as a continuation of God's creative work, a cooperation with the regenerative forces of nature, with soil, seed, and sun. The fruits of this cooperative process are meant for the health and mutual well-being of all people. Hence, justice, concern for the common good, and sharing rather than hoarding food are essential responses. Equity becomes the aim of common life. Acknowledging food as gift implies an honoring of the organic limits of the Earth's productivity, honesty about the true costliness of food, respect for seasonal cycles and growth processes, and a commitment to sustainability so that future generations may also eat. Most especially, acknowledging food as gift issues in thankfulness and gratitude, returning grace for grace, engendering trust, contentedness, and a will to live in harmony with other creatures.

The contrasting paradigm of food as commodity implies a posture of ownership and the right to control. Scarcity rather than abundance is assumed: the Earth is deemed incapable of providing for all and must be brought under human expertise and domination so as to force a greater yield. Human intervention is meant to improve on God's created order: to design, alter, expand, and repackage the fruits of the soil so as to make up for Earth's imagined deficit and to produce value-added products intended for selected markets and those with sufficient purchasing power.

In this paradigm, profit is the goal of economic life. Expanded markets rather than nature's limits become the norm; growth of

---

12. Wirzba, "Food for Theologians," 379.

sales, as well as the acquisition and accumulation of foodstuffs, requires overstepping the natural limits of plants and animals so as to satisfy the imagined needs of consumers. In this process, the costliness of food is masked by failing to account for damage done to the Earth and to living beings. Sustainability is jeopardized and, with it, the feeding of future generations. The fruit of this paradigm is anxiety rather than satisfaction, the loss of a grateful spiritual relationship with food, and a preoccupation with individual needs and preferences rather than a concern for the well-being of all.

Given the dominance of a corporate food system and its ideals and motivations, these conflicting paradigms face people today in much of the world, requiring informed choices, a strong sense of justice and care for fellow creatures, and a commitment to the flourishing of the future generations who will inherit the fruit of our choices.[13]

Growing, Preparing, and Sharing Food at Table

Growing Food

To grow food is to enter an intricate web of relationships at once cosmic and microscopic. It is to engage in the miracle of interdependence, the mystery of Earth's synergy, and the awesome truth that we were made for relationship. The intensity of the sun,[14] the movement of the planets, the tilt of the Earth, and the patterns of climate,

---

13. See Alice Waters, "The Ethics of Eating: Why Environmentalism Starts at the Breakfast Table," in *The Fatal Harvest Reader* (Sausalito, CA: Foundation for Deep Ecology, 2002), 283–87. Pope Francis writes strongly in *Laudato Sí* (LS 159–63) that all people have a moral responsibility to provide for future generations. All further references from *Laudato Sí* will be indicated with paragraph numbers in the text.

14. According to biologist Christopher Uhl, the amount of solar energy intercepted by Earth every hour exceeds the total amount of fossil fuel energy humankind uses in a year. *Developing Ecological Consciousness: The End of Separation*, 2nd ed. (Lanham, MD: Rowman and Littlefield, 2013), 14.

rainfall, and soil composition work together to make growth possible. Tiny microbes, too small for the human eye to see, create dense feeding webs within the soil itself by which plant roots are nourished and protected, all the while sequestering carbon from the atmosphere and restoring it to soil and plants.[15] The opening hymn of Genesis reminds us that in all this, Earth is the primary acting subject, second only to God.[16] To grow food is to recognize that, as humans, we are receivers and beneficiaries of the Earth's bounty, thus putting to rest any inflated notions that it is we who produce food or the misguided assumption that money is the source of food.[17] Rather, gardening and farming involve a humble midwifing of the universe's productivity.

Nature's economy involves an intricate balance of laws, seasons, and rhythms, one that humans enter into when growing food. Virtues of anticipation and hope, longing and waiting, fasting and celebration accompany a gardener's endeavors—quite in contrast to the twenty-four-hour society fostered by today's fast-food culture, where waiting is unnecessary and immediate satisfaction is the norm.[18] Growing food invites what Wendell Berry calls "kindly action," a graceful cooperation with the Earth's patterns, allowing them to instill in us wisdom, respect, patience, and care.

Growing food teaches us that Earth's treasures are not simply resources to be plundered but integral parts of a vast, living organism—a global commons, a precious treasury intended for the nour-

15. See David R. Montgomery and Anne Biklé, *The Hidden Half of Nature: The Microbial Roots of Life and Health* (New York: W. W. Norton & Co., 2016); Vandana Shiva, *Soil Not Oil* (Berkeley: North Atlantic Books, 2015); and Courtney White, *Grass, Soil, Hope: A Journey through Carbon Country* (White River Junction, VT: Chelsea Green Publishing, 2014).

16. Ellen F. Davis, *Scripture, Culture, and Agriculture: An Agrarian Reading of the Bible* (Cambridge: Cambridge University Press, 2009), 57.

17. Ibid., 75. Davis calls the notion that we make the food the "fundamental delusion of agricultural industrialism."

18. Grummett, et al., "Fast Food," 383.

ishment of all peoples and creatures and not to satisfy the greed of a few. To grow food with reverence is to encounter creation as "one vast symbol of grace" that reflects the divine self-giving that we glimpse in Christ, a "grace that inheres in the world by virtue of a gracious God."[19] Growing food is thus a collaboration with "God's own primordial sharing of life."[20]

Preparing Food

To prepare food is to engage in a world of artistry and alchemy, of culture and cuisine. Be it an elaborate banquet or a simple meal, food prepared with care involves a process that might be described as "priesting" creation—enabling human food to be healthful, not harmful, a source of human solidarity and fellowship.[21] It is one of the most human ways to create beauty, a beauty unleashed by a creative combination of colors, shapes, and tastes, one providing physical and spiritual nourishment for the whole person, not only the palate. In contrast to contemporary fast foods that create an illusory abundance—oversized and larger portions that promise to be more fulfilling than they prove to be—artistically prepared food offers more than meets the eye. It provides an entry into the boundlessness of divine fecundity and a reassurance that despite the destructive forces that mark our planet today, God's creation is indeed very good!

The profound interplay of the "fruit of the Earth and work of human hands"—imaged in the prayers of the Eucharist—is clearly evident in the artful preparation of food; indeed, this foundational cooperation between the forces of nature and human creativity are essential for creaturely flourishing. In a world where convenience

19. Timothy Gorringe, "Grace and the Built Environment," in *The Common Good and the Global Emergency* (Cambridge: Cambridge University Press, 2011), 44.

20. Wirzba, *Food and Faith*, xiii.

21. Grummett, et al., "Fast Food," 380.

and cheapness often rule the day, a patient, sensitive, resourceful collaborating with the Earth's fruitfulness affirms human work as a spiritual discipline offered for the thriving of others.

Preparing food is intricately bound up with culture and one's place of origin: with crops that flourish in a particular locale, culinary preferences honed over generations, cultivated tastes, and well-loved fragrances. Food is a kind of language. The one preparing it employs vocabulary (ingredients), grammatical rules (recipes that transform ingredients into dishes), and rhetoric (social protocols) that create and communicate a world of shared meaning and identity.[22] In today's world of migration, where movement rather than stasis marks much of the world's population, foods can, with a surprising suddenness, bring a sense of home, of family, and of a shared vision of life. At the same time, new locales can be a springboard for both preserving tradition and for culinary experimentation and creativity—for fusion, hybridity, and inculturation.

Sharing Food at Table

Finally, growing and preparing food culminate in the art of sharing food at table. More than simply eating, sharing food around a table of hospitality allows nurture to accompany nourishment and fellowship to suffuse feeding. A shared table is, ideally, a place of welcome, of making room for another, of being both host and guest. Eating together invites one to enter into communion with others, to receive their visions of life and horizons of meaning, while welcoming their points of view with respect and openness. At table, diners practice habits of attention and reflection, of listening, and of reimagining their perceptions of the world from another's point

---

22. Massimo Montari, *El Mundo en la Cocina: Historia, Identidad, Intercambios*, trans. Yolanda Daffunchio (Buenos Aires: Paidós, 2003), 11. Angel M. Montoya quotes and translates this passage in *A Theology of Food* (Oxford: Wiley Blackwell, 2009), 5.

of view. These processes are never easy, never without challenge, but require self-offering, openness, and genuine love.

Sharing food provides both an occasion and a paradigm for shared life and human solidarity. To be gathered around an abundant table, fed and nourished from common bowls and platters, is to recognize that Earth's plenty is a common good, belonging to all and requiring just distribution and radical care. Sharing the pleasure of eating, attracted by flavor and fragrance, satisfied by conviviality and bodily nourishment, spirits and bodies are rejuvenated. As beneficiaries of the generosity of the living Earth, eating at one table underscores that life in not a possession to be jealously guarded but a participation in the mutual giving and receiving foundational to planetary interdependence.

Sharing food is invariably accompanied by conversation; table and word are essential partners.[23] Both humanize, nurture, and increase the pleasure of eating; both have the potential to create communion. The gospels liken word to seed: to generative life, to biological fecundity, entrusted to human care and wise distribution. Conversation can likewise be a source of fertility and new life, of speaking one's truth with honesty, of listening others into speech, of discovering shared passions and commitments, and of resolving to take common action.

Speech and shared food find their natural fulfillment in gratitude: in the humble acknowledgment that all life is gift, that we are graced daily by more abundance than we can conceive, that we live indebted to an Earth and cosmos that seek our flourishing, and that all good things flow from a Creator whose generosity knows no telling. Saying grace, giving thanks, is perhaps one of the most profound and honest expressions of our humanity.[24] Engaging in this ancient Christian practice rooted in Jewish ancestry bears witness

---

23. Joaquin Racionero Page, "Foreword," in Montoya, *Theology of Food*, vi.
24. Wirzba, *Food and Faith*, 179.

to a God who, for the sake of love, continues to create the world as a delectable expression of divine self-giving.[25] It invites one into deeper knowledge of God, the intimacy of communion with the very center and heartbeat of all that exists.[26] And from this point of thankful union, saying grace aligns those who give thanks with God's healing, reconciling, and justice-instilling mission within the terrestrial community.

But no matter how eloquent our thanksgiving or how honest our gratitude, those who share food at a graced table are left with more to say than can be articulated, with a surplus of meaning that defies full expression, and with an intuition of the cosmic banquet—the superabundance of God in whose awesome presence one can only be silent.[27] Beyond words, we are invited to "taste and see that the LORD is good" (Ps 34:9), to enter the multisensory experience of shared eating and sense the promise of a future fulfillment in the great messianic banquet. Wine and bread, rice and beans, millet and palm wine, face-to-face encounter, shared laughter, tears, and stories—here in this humble human gathering we are caught up in a unique way in the "terrible and sublime liturgy . . . which God celebrates and causes to be celebrated in and through human history."[28] We sense, if only by the slightest, unarticulated intuition, that this great liturgy flows into the fullness of the kingdom, into the eternal feast of love where every tear will be wiped away by the divine host who washes feet and offers himself as the bread of eternal life.

25. Ibid., 199.
26. Ibid.
27. Montoya, *Theology of Food*, 3, 149–55.
28. Karl Rahner, "Considerations on the Active Role of the Person in the Sacramental Event," *Theological Investigations* 14 (New York: Seabury, 1976), 161–84. As quoted in Michael Skelley, *The Liturgy of the World: Karl Rahner's Theology of Worship* (Collegeville, MN: Liturgical Press, 1991), 93.

Eucharistic Eating

All that we have seen so far invites us to understand Christian eucharistic practice as more closely related to our broader experiences
of food and shared meals than is normally acknowledged.[29] It situates
the daily and weekly celebrations of this ancient and ever-changing
rite within the vast intersecting worlds of planting and harvesting,
fasting and feasting, preparing food and table fellowship, and con-
textualizes eucharistic eating within the conflicting paradigms of
food as gift or commodity, of Earth as resource or abundant giver,
of choices about food based on convenience or on companionship
and conviviality.[30]

   At the same time, theological reflections on Eucharist invite us to
plumb new depths in how we interpret, appreciate, and live the
human processes that surround eating. Already signaled by terms
such as anamnetic, paschal, word and table, sacrifice, hospitality, and
thanksgiving, eucharistic understandings move one's appreciation
of human table fellowship toward deeper awareness and appreciation
of all eating as eating with Christ. We participate in Christ's serving
and reconciling ways, engage in trinitarian life and perichoretic[31]
hospitality, make room for every other creature as precious and valu-
able in God's sight, and respond to the Spirit's call to a common life
of justice and responsibility, building up the Body, affirming its many
gifts, and caring for the precious Earth. In turn, the experience of

29. See Norman Wirzba's excellent chapter on "Eucharistic Table Manners:
Eating Toward Communion," in *Food and Faith*, 144–78.

30. These two words—companionship and conviviality—have roots that imply
shared life and table fellowship: a companion is one who shares bread, and "to
convive" implies "one who shares life: a table companion."

31. The term "perichoretic" is based on the Greek word *perichoriesis*, a term used
to image the divine self-giving, the love poured out among the persons in the
Trinity, the flowing of life, divine hospitality, and energy from one to another. See
Catherine Mowry LaCugna, *God for Us: The Trinity and Christian Life* (San Francisco: HarperSanFrancisco, 1991), 270–78.

deep human and creaturely exchange apprehended in ferial or festive table fellowship can challenge our complacent expectations of the eucharistic meal and revitalize our eucharistic imagination. To this task we will return in part 3. Our focus turns now to the life and ministry of Jesus: to his entanglement in the foodways of his time and the implications this might have for our contemporary food crisis.

Questions for Reflection

1) How do you distinguish between food as commodity and food as gift? Which dominates in your life and choices?

2) How might a deeper engagement with growing, preparing, and sharing food at table bring greater satisfaction to your life and a more profound appreciation for the Earth and her abundance?

3) Do the needs of future generations influence your current choices about food: what, where, and how much you eat? If not, what new insight and responsibility emerge with more awareness of their potential needs?

chapter two

Food in the Life and Ministry of Jesus

The gospel narratives, both Synoptic and Johannine, are filled with stories of Jesus sharing food, eating and drinking, and offering parables of food and feasting to his followers. Clearly, eating mattered to Jesus: stories of where and with whom he ate, of who had access to nourishing food, and of how food and shared meals became revelatory of the reign of God he came to proclaim are threaded throughout the gospel accounts. Jesus' meal fellowship became the legacy of the early church and served as one of the most important ways Christianity would spread. In what follows, we explore Jesus' engagement with the foodways of his time as recounted by two of the evangelists, Luke and John.

Meals of Jesus in the Gospel of Luke

The Synoptic Gospels are full of meal stories. Luke's narrative especially, in which the "aroma of food issues from every chapter,"[1]

---

1. Robert J. Karris, "The Theme of Food," in *Luke: Artist and Theologian* (New York: Paulist Press, 1985), 47. See also Robert J. Karris, *Eating Your Way through Luke's Gospel* (Collegeville, MN: Liturgical Press, 2006).

situates Jesus' earthly birth in Bethlehem—literally the "house of bread" (2:4)—and structures the whole gospel around ten meals.[2] From intimate tables to large, impromptu meals in a desert place, meals were parables enacted by Jesus to teach his disciples about reconciliation, inclusion, service, forgiveness, covenantal love, and redemptive hospitality.[3] Jesus came "eating and drinking," (7:34), inviting all to "rejoice with the bridegroom" (5:34), and in extravagant scenes of feeding, sharing food, and uncovering abundance in the face of scarcity, Jesus demonstrates God's fidelity to his hungry creation by feeding it.[4]

Three aspects of Jesus' engagement with food in Luke's narrative are significant for our exploration. First, Jesus' inclusive table fellowship was essential to his mission and the mission of those he called to follow him. Second, Jesus' engagement with food—through meals, parables, and teachings—inaugurated a new economy of food, a radical economy of abundance in the face of the oppressive practices of Roman occupation. Third, followers of Jesus are called to a justice-oriented and egalitarian meal fellowship, in which the hungry are fed and outcasts are welcomed in memory of Jesus and in anticipation of the great messianic banquet in the end time.

Inclusive Table Fellowship as Mission

Perhaps the most provocative aspect of Jesus' sharing of food in Luke's account is the inclusivity of his meal fellowship and the

---

2. Eugene LaVerdiere, "The Eucharist in Luke's Gospel," in *Dining in the Kingdom of God* (Chicago: Liturgy Training Publications, 1994), 1–32. LaVerdiere situates three of these meals in Jesus' Galilean ministry, four on his journey to Jerusalem, one is the "Last Supper," and two are postresurrection meals: Emmaus and with the Jerusalem community. See also Dennis E. Smith, "The Philosophical Banquet: Meal Symbolism in Luke," in *From Symposium to Eucharist: The Banquet in the Early Christian World* (Minneapolis: Fortress Press, 2003), 253–72.

3. See LaVerdiere, *Dining*, for an exploration of these themes.

4. Karris, "The Theme of Food," 52.

boundary crossing it entailed. Deemed by some a "glutton and a drunkard" (7:34), Jesus ate with Pharisees and sinners alike, with rich and poor, with tax collectors, Samaritans, and those considered outside the orbit of grace. He sought out their tables, invited them to follow him, and called them to conversion. Moreover, in meeting them at table, Jesus became a friend to these religious and social outcasts, a companion on their journey, one who enjoyed sharing food and life with them, reclining at table in their presence.[5] These choices put Jesus in constant conflict with the religious authorities, who saw his association with unrighteous "sinners" as apostasy (Deut 21:18-21).[6] Moreover, at a time in the sociopolitical life of the world in which he lived, when eating together was a primary way in which group boundaries were established and inner-group loyalties were solidified, Jesus' crossing such boundaries to create an inclusive table was a provocative act.

Food became the medium of Jesus' proclamation of justice, and the sharing of food at table an enacted parable of the arrival of the kingdom of God.[7] Levi the tax collector, despised by fellow Jews as a sinner because of the dishonesty associated with this trade, is invited by Jesus to follow him (5:27). In the banquet that ensues in Levi's home, Jesus challenges those who are grumbling about his

---

5. Smith, in *From Symposium*, 268, underscores the primacy of friendship in the ethical categories of meal fellowship of the time. He also notes Luke's use of the Greek word for "reclining" in most of the meal stories, a clear reference to *symposia* practice and the ethical demands of friendship.

6. See Karris, "The Theme of Food," 58, and 74n36. Deuteronomy 21:18-21 instructs parents of unruly offspring to bring them to the elders, saying, "This our son is stubborn and rebellious, he does not obey our voice; he is a glutton and a drunkard." The punishment for such rebellion was stoning to death.

7. Smith in *From Symposium*, 261, 269, underscores that "a central theme for Luke's theology is that salvation has come for the poor, a term he uses as a symbol for social outcasts in general." This theme is expanded proleptically in Luke 14, where Jesus' eating with tax collectors and sinners is a direct parallel to the "poor, crippled, blind and lame" who will inhabit the messianic banquet (14:21).

association with sinners, saying, "I have come not to call the righteous but sinners to repentance" (5:27-32). Likewise, at a celebratory meal in the home of Zacchaeus, the chief tax collector, Jesus announces, "Today salvation has come into this house!" (19:9). Zacchaeus, in turn, witnesses to fellow tax collectors and guests alike that his life will now be marked by Jesus' ways of justice, giving half his possessions to the poor and rectifying any defrauding he might have done (19:8).

Throughout Luke's gospel, Jesus searches for and finds those who are rejected and despised, reclining with them at table and teaching all who would follow him to do likewise. In a provocative table encounter in the home of a Pharisee, Jesus criticizes the manner in which the religious leaders present seek out places of honor and status and, in so doing, turn a meal that celebrates God's gift of food and life into an occasion of celebrating themselves.[8] He challenges his listeners: "When you give a banquet, invite the poor, the crippled, the lame and the blind. And you will be blessed; because they cannot repay you, for you will be repaid at the resurrection of the righteous" (14:12-14).[9] In both Greco-Roman and Jewish society, these vulnerable persons were outcasts beyond the pale of any religious leader's care or concern. For Jews, as for the community of Qumran, the maimed, the lame, and the blind were not only forbidden access to common meals but were believed to be excluded from the great messianic banquet. Yet in a great reversal, one typical of the eschatological reversals envisioned by Luke, Jesus proclaimed and embodied a God who eats and shares life with society's disabled and despised and declares righteous a person who does the same.[10]

---

8. Karris, "The Theme of Food," 61. See also Smith, *From Symposium*, 260–63, on Luke's portrayal of reversals as characteristic of the messianic banquet.

9. See Smith, *From Symposium*, 270–71.

10. Karris, "The Theme of Food," 61.

A New Economy of Food

In announcing the kingdom of God through his provocative meal fellowship, Jesus likewise ushered in a new economy of food, a radical economy of abundance and sufficiency for all in the face of the oppressive practices that characterized the Roman occupation of much of the Mediterranean world.[11] Food in first-century Palestine was in crisis.[12] Roman emperors, intent on keeping the price of bread low in imperial cities and providing for their legionnaires, pressed small Palestinian farmers and landholders to surrender their surplus grain, often leaving them without adequate provisions for daily consumption. Many who were drawn to Jesus' ministry and preaching suffered from sickness, hunger, and diseases associated with malnutrition. Within this context, Jesus' preaching about seeds and growth, harvests and banquets, as well as his dining with those considered unrighteous and sinful, took on a messianic significance: a new society was in the making, forged around an egalitarian table where there was not only enough for all but food to spare (John 6:12-13). Eating with Jesus became a way of tasting, feeling, and discovering one's place in the economy of grace.

At the outset of Luke's gospel, the prophetic words of Mary's *Magnificat* proclaim this new economy of grace, announcing that, in Jesus, God "fills the hungry with good things, while the rich are sent empty away" (1:53).[13] This promise to fill the hungry is reiterated in one of the Beatitudes Jesus proclaims to his followers: "Blessed are you that hunger now; for you shall be satisfied" (6:21).

11. See Barbara Rossing, "Why Luke's Gospel? Daily Bread and 'Recognition' of Christ in Food-Sharing," *Currents in Theology and Mission* 37, no. 3 (June 2010): 227–29.

12. What follows is taken from Michael Northcott, "Faithful Feasting," in *A Moral Climate* (Maryknoll, NY: Orbis Books, 2007), 248–50.

13. Karris in "The Theme of Food," 52, states that the *Magnificat* is an "advance interpretation of who Jesus is; . . . a song of God's fulfillment of all that he has planned for creation and humankind" seen as beginning with Jesus' conception.

While to be fully realized only in the messianic banquet, this promise is proleptically fulfilled in the extravagant scene of Jesus' feeding some five thousand hungry people in a desert place (9:10-17). Seeing that those who have followed him are hungry and tired, Jesus' disciples encourage him to send the crowd away so that they might secure food for themselves. Instead, Jesus hosts a great impromptu banquet, inviting all to recline[14] and then offering them food. From the simple provisions available—five loaves and two fish—Jesus provides enough for all to eat their fill, with some to spare. Jesus, Luke tells us, took the bread and the fish and, blessing God, broke and gave them to the disciples to feed the crowd. All were satisfied, and the leftover fragments filled twelve baskets. So significant was this narrative for the early church that all three Synoptic evangelists link Jesus' actions in this desert banquet with the final meal Jesus ate with his disciples on the night before he died. In both cases, Jesus took bread, blessed, broke, and gave it. . . .[15]

The new economy of abundant food inaugurated by Jesus in feeding the five thousand echoes the "manna economy" described in the post-exodus wilderness narrative. Here, the fledgling community of Israelites was taught how to live as God's people (Exod 16:1-36).[16] Having escaped their lives of slavery in Egypt and the iron fist of Pharaoh, the Israelites sojourned in a desert place where they were schooled by God in a new economy of food: "God gives. Enough

14. Reclining at table in first-century society was a mark of status and dignity. In noting that those gathered were invited to recline, Luke is indicating that this meal is indeed a banquet, a festive meal of freedom, respect, and equality.

15. Scenes of the feeding of the five thousand predominate imagery for Christian Eucharist in early iconography. See "Early Symbols of the Eucharist," New Advent, accessed January 31, 2019, http://newadvent.org/cathen/05590a.htm.

16. See Ellen F. Davis, "Leaving Egypt Behind: Embracing the Wilderness Economy," in *Scripture, Culture, and Agriculture* (New York: Cambridge University Press, 2009), 66–79.

for all. No surplus is to be hoarded."[17] The Israelites yearned for the food of Egypt, which was a nutritious and varied diet. "No people would eat so well again for thousands of years."[18] Yet the abundance and diversity of Egypt's cuisine was based in Pharaoh's economy of scarcity.[19] Overcome with anxiety about not having enough to maintain a lifestyle of wealth and luxury, Pharaoh imposed an economy based on accumulation and monopoly, one that forced the maximum production of food from the land, amassed huge harvests, and hoarded this abundance in militarily protected places of storage. All of this was made possible through Pharaoh's ceaseless demand for slave labor, especially from the resident alien community in the land, the Israelites.[20]

Against this background, the wilderness narrative in Exodus portrays a people charged by God to cultivate a radically different way of life in community on the land.[21] In their liminal wilderness sojourn, food is no longer either an end in itself or a source of self-serving profit or gain. Rather, it is an expression of God's sovereignty over creation and generosity toward humankind, God's immediate presence and promise. Food is ultimately a gift: in the morning God provided manna and in the evening, quail (Exod 16:13). Israel is invited to depend on God for this gift, to recognize God as source of sufficiency and abundance, to share what is received, and to avoid hoarding. In this economy, eating is worshipful and even revelatory;

17. David Erlander, *Manna and Mercy: A Brief History of God's Unfolding Promise to Mend the Entire Universe* (Order of St. Martin and Theresa, 1992), as quoted in Rossing, "Why Luke's Gospel?," 227.

18. Davis, "Leaving Egypt Behind," 70.

19. Walter Bruggemann, "Food Fight," *Word and World* 33, no. 4 (Fall 2013): 320.

20. Davis, "Leaving Egypt," 66–79, and Bruggemann, "Food Fight," 320–24.

21. Davis, "Leaving Egypt," 69.

it engenders both nourishment for the body and healthful knowledge of God for the soul.[22]

The Lukan Jesus invites his followers into such an economy of food. In contrast to the hoarding policies of the Roman occupation of his time that echoed the "pharaoh ideology" of accumulation and monopoly described in Exodus, Jesus teaches his disciples an economy of abundance, trust, sharing, and neighborliness. Creation is seen as God's partner and vehicle for wellness, and his disciples are called to generosity and gratitude.[23] "Consider the ravens," Jesus teaches; "they neither sow nor reap, they have neither storehouses nor barn, and yet God feeds them. Of how much more value are you than the birds! . . . Do not keep striving for what you are to eat and what you are to drink, and do not keep worrying. . . . Instead strive for God's kingdom and these things will be given to you as well" (12:24, 29). These attitudes suffuse Jesus' feeding miracles and parables. The new creation he inaugurates "is a gift that keeps on giving, and there is no excuse now for parsimony toward the neighbor."[24]

Two of Jesus' most vivid parables, unique to Luke's gospel, warn of the foolishness of hoarding food rather than sharing the abundance with all.[25] In one, a rich landholder misperceives the abundance of his land as his private possession. Intending to build more barns in which to store the overflow, he settles in to enjoy his just reward: to "relax, eat, drink, and be merry" (12:16-28). Yet, as Jesus teaches, the hoarding of his assumed possessions will "this very night" cost him his life.[26] In yet another parable about greed and food injustice, Jesus portrays a rich man who, feasting sumptuously, feels no obli-

---

22. Ibid., 73–74.

23. Bruggemann, "Food Fight," 330.

24. Ibid., 339.

25. See Rossing, "Why Luke's Gospel?," 227–29.

26. Ibid., 227. Rossing proposes that the best translation of the passage implies it is the man's very possessions that demand his life, since his possessions have possessed him.

gation to provide food for Lazarus, the poor beggar at his door. Vindication comes after the death of both men. Lazarus can be found reclining on Abraham's bosom while the rich man suffers torment in Hades, besieged by an insatiable thirst. Despite the rich man's cries to send a warning to his living brothers, Abraham reminds him that the Scriptures already teach God's economy of abundance and sharing and that hearts hardened to one's hungry neighbor will not be turned, "even if someone rises from the dead" (16:31).

Jesus' Followers Called to a Justice-Oriented Meal Fellowship

In the Lukan narrative, followers of Jesus are called to an egalitarian meal fellowship in which the hungry are fed, outcasts are welcomed, and disciples become servants of all "in memory of [him]" (22:19). Jesus' last meal with his disciples before his death embodies this invitation, gathering together all his prior table fellowship with friends and foes alike.[27] Jesus declares that he has "eagerly desired to eat this Passover" with them before he suffers; indeed, he will not eat it again "until it is fulfilled in the kingdom of God" (22:15-16). Seated at table, he sums up his earthly ministry as one of servanthood and invites his disciples to continue this same ministry: "The greatest among you must become like the younger, and the leader like one who serves. For who is greater, the one who reclines at table or the one who serves? Is it not the one who reclines at table? But I am among you as one who serves" (22:25-27).

The Lukan account of the Last Supper creates a historical transition: from Jesus' service at table to that of his followers.[28] Jesus' entire ministry, characterized as one in which he feeds the hungry and has compassion on those who are marginalized, is now handed over to his disciples for generations to come.[29] Not only are they called to

---

27. See LaVerdiere, *Dining*, 121–42. Also Andrew B. McGowan, *Ancient Christian Worship* (Grand Rapids, MI: Baker Academic, 2014), 20.

28. Smith, *From Symposium*, 263.

29. Ibid., 271.

feed and clothe the needy, a theme that is pervasive in the Lukan account, but they are invited to share meal fellowship with others as Jesus has done before them, a fellowship of the most intimate kind, around a table at which is shared not only food but also friendship.

Meals and Metaphors of Food in the Gospel of John

Turning now to the Gospel of John, we find that meal scenes and related discourses permeate the narrative, demonstrating that communal dining and metaphoric talk about food and drink play a significant role in John's portrayal of Jesus and the life of those who come to believe in him.[30] While quite distinct from Luke's account, John underscores at several points in the narrative that Jesus provides food for his disciples and that, in accepting and partaking of this food, the disciples come to know Jesus intimately. In stories of unexpected and abundant quantities of food and drink—bread, fish, and wine—Jesus provides earthly nourishment for those who follow him. He likewise speaks metaphorically of offering the water of life that has the power to quench thirst forever and the heavenly bread that bestows eternal life. Meal scenes and metaphoric talk of food and drink are settings for the emergence of true believers in Jesus, whom he forms as disciples who will carry on his work in the world after he has returned to the Father. Throughout the gospel, Jesus is portrayed as the true host, the provider of food and drink, and the center of communities who gather with him at table.

Three aspects of Jesus' engagement with food in John's narrative are significant: (1) miraculous provisions of food and drink, especially those that frame his earthly ministry, serve as epiphanies of God's nourishing, compassionate, and celebratory presence in the world in the person of Jesus; (2) John's portrait of Jesus echoes the

---

30. Esther Kobel, *Dining with John: Communal Meals and Identity Formation in the Fourth Gospel and Its Historical and Cultural Contexts* (Leiden: Brill, 2011), 104. What follows here based on ibid., 104–7.

figure of Woman Wisdom from the Hebrew Scriptures, a gracious provider of food and drink who herself becomes the very food she offers; and (3) meals with Jesus in John are primary contexts for the formation of Jesus' disciples in values of love, friendship, service, and co-abiding.[31]

Miraculous Provision of Food and Drink

Meal stories that recount miraculous provision of food and drink mark the beginning and end of John's account of Jesus' earthly sojourn. At the opening of the gospel, a wedding at Cana in Galilee becomes the setting of Jesus' first "sign"—a miraculous flow of delicious wine from what had previously been jugs of water (2:1-12). At the conclusion of John's gospel, an unfruitful night of fishing on the Lake of Tiberias becomes the occasion for a remarkable catch of fish by his beleaguered disciples, who had toiled all night without a nibble. In each case, the unexpected provision of food or drink becomes an epiphany—a revelation of God's nourishing, compassionate, and celebratory presence in the world in the person of Jesus and an invitation to believe in him.[32]

The wedding meal at Cana unfolds like many miracle stories: the wine runs out, Jesus turns water into wine at Mary's prompting, the steward is astounded at the quality of the wine, and the disciples come to believe. But the text is replete with biblical allusions that enrich and deepen the surplus of meanings.[33] The very occasion, a

---

31. The term "co-abiding" reflects Jesus' command at the Last Supper, "Abide in me, as I abide in you" (John 15:4).

32. These two stories create what Kobel in *Dining with John*, 81–82, terms a "meal inclusio," framing the entire account of Jesus' life, death, and resurrection in images of food and drink.

33. What follows is taken from Jane S. Webster, *Ingesting Jesus: Eating and Drinking in the Gospel of John* (Atlanta: Society of Biblical Literature, 2003), 37–45, and Margaret Daly-Denton, *John: An Earth Bible Commentary* (New York: T & T Clarke, 2017), 48, 90, 221.

wedding banquet, evokes images of the covenant between God and God's people, often described as a marriage (Hos 2:18-20; Isa 54:4-8). Isaiah describes this divine marriage as followed by an extravagant and abundant banquet overflowing with rich food and drink (Isa 54:8; 55:1-5). Wine, in a particular way, evokes the coming of the Messiah and the messianic banquet of the end time, when God will host "a feast of rich food and well-aged wine for all nations" to share (Isa 25:6-8). John's narrative has already identified Jesus as Messiah (1:41), and this miraculous provision of wine at Cana signals that the messianic age has arrived in the person of Jesus. Isaiah's text images this new age as a universal one, in which all nations are invited to share a common table (Isa 25:6) where "God will wipe away the tears from all faces" and "swallow up death forever" (Isa 25:7-8). Moreover, an inadvertent mistake on the part of the steward caring for the banquet in Cana, who assumes that the bridegroom is the one who has provided the superior wine, suggests that Jesus is the true Bridegroom,[34] whose presence is cause for celebration. In sum, this first meal story in John reveals Jesus as guest-become-host, who, in providing wine in abundance, reveals God's covenantal desire for intimacy with God's people. In response, Jesus' disciples come to believe in him and stay with him.

The postresurrection breakfast on the shores of Tiberias in the conclusion of the Gospel of John follows a miraculous catch of fish by seven of Jesus' disciples.[35] Again, the text is replete with biblical imagery. The scene unfolds "just after daybreak," and Jesus, the light that has come into the world (1:4, 9; 3:19; 12:35, 46), addresses the disciples who have failed to catch any fish during the night. As they comply with Jesus' instructions to cast their nets on the right side

34. This designation is later confirmed by John the Baptist, who proclaims Jesus as the true messianic bridegroom (3:29).

35. See Sandra M. Schneiders, *Written That You May Believe: Encountering Jesus in the Fourth Gospel* (New York: Crossroads, 1999), 202, which concludes that chapter 21 is integral to the gospel and its fundamental theological continuity.

of the boat, their nets swell with a miraculous abundance of fish. The scene is evocative of Genesis 1, where, through God's creative power, light appears (1:3) and the waters teem with living things (1:20-21). Meanwhile, Jesus has prepared breakfast on the beach— fish grilled on a charcoal fire and bread—and he invites the disciples to contribute some of their fish to the meal. Jesus then "takes the bread and gives it to them, and does the same with the fish" (John 21:13), an act reminiscent of the feeding of the great multitude in John 6.[36] In this postresurrection context, the disciples "eat the bread that has come down from heaven directly from the source."[37]

In the after-breakfast conversation on the shore of the Lake of Tiberias, Jesus commissions Peter in particular to carry forward his mission of feeding and nourishing his people. In response to a tripartite question posed by Jesus, "Simon, son of John, do you love me?" and Peter's affirmative answer, Jesus commissions him to "Feed my lambs. . . . Tend my sheep. . . . Feed my sheep" (21:15-17). Numerous biblical allusions image God as gathering and feeding God's sheep (Ps 23:1, 5; Isa 40:11; Ezek 34:1-31), and the Johannine narrative describes Jesus himself as the good shepherd who calls, cares for, leads, protects, and provides pasture for the sheep who hear his voice (10:2-4, 14, 27-28). Jesus calls Peter to feed his sheep precisely by leading them to believe in Jesus' life-giving death and resurrection.[38]

Framed within these two accounts of abundant food and drink, other stories of meals and images of food reveal similar patterns, most especially the miraculous feeding of the five thousand near the shores of Tiberias. In each of these miraculous accounts, Jesus manifests himself, inviting those who experience them to believe, to

36. Webster in *Ingesting*, 138, points out that the parallel is very precise in that the same Greek words are used for "Jesus," "take," "bread," "distribute/give," "fish," and "likewise."

37. Ibid., 139.

38. Ibid., 142.

follow, and, through love, to give themselves as food for others. Eating of the abundant food and drink he provides means coming to know and believe in Jesus as both the provider and the substance of food that gives eternal life.[39] Moreover, "believing in him" is, in turn, an invitation to continue his mission: to draw others to encounter him and become witnesses to God's nourishing and compassionate presence in the world.

Wisdom Motifs of Food Provision

John's portrait of Jesus echoes the figure of Woman Wisdom, Sophia, the feminine figure of the Wisdom books of the Hebrew Scriptures,[40] who "was with God at creation and who pitched a tent among a chosen people."[41] Wisdom/Sophia is a gracious provider of food and drink to those who will "come and eat," and she herself becomes the very food she offers.[42]

Wisdom/Sophia is first of all a gracious host who has built her house, slaughtered her beasts, mixed her wine, set her table, and calls out to all who will hear, "Come, eat of my bread and drink of the wine I have mixed" and "walk in the way of insight" (Prov 9:1-6; Sir 24:19-21). In like manner, Jesus, seeing a large crowd coming toward him on the mountain, takes five barley loaves and two fish, and "when he had given thanks . . . distributed them to those who were seated [reclining]," first the bread and then the fish, "*as much as they wanted*" (John 6:5-11, italics mine). Jesus, the gracious host,

39. Ibid.

40. Wisdom, we are told, was with God at creation (Prov 8:22-31) and, like Jesus, pitched her tent among a chosen people (Sir 24:8). Hence, the cosmic significance of both Wisdom/Sophia and Jesus.

41. Dianne Bergant, *People of the Covenant: An Invitation to the Old Testament* (Franklin, WI: Sheed & Ward, 2001), 124, as quoted in Barbara Bowe, "The Divine 'I Am,' " in *The Wisdom of Creation*, ed. Edward Foley and Robert Schreiter (Collegeville, MN: Liturgical Press, 2004), 37.

42. Raymond Brown focuses on twelve "wisdom motifs" in John that "taken together constitute the unique Johannine portrait of Jesus." See Bowe, "The Divine 'I Am,' " 39.

distributes the food directly to the waiting crowd, providing enough to satisfy them and to spare.

Second, the rich fare offered by both Wisdom/Sophia and Jesus includes both food and insight, both bread and divine teaching. Both need to be consumed to be effective.[43] Wisdom/Sophia blesses those who meditate on wisdom, who reflect on her ways and ponder her secrets, promising that she will come to meet them "like a mother," feed them "with the bread of understanding," and give them "water of wisdom to drink" (Sir 14:20-21; 15:1-3). Likewise, in the discourse that follows the great feeding, Jesus teaches that both the bread that he gives and the words that he speaks are life-giving: "I am the living bread come down from heaven. . . . The words that I have spoken to you are spirit and life" (John 6:51, 63). Indeed, John's gospel opens with the proclamation that Jesus is the Word, who was in the beginning "with God"; the very Word that "became flesh and lived among us" (1:1, 14). This "Word," this flesh, when ingested, is source of both life and wisdom.

Third, both Sophia and Jesus speak of themselves as the very food they offer others. Sophia images herself as the tree of life and as a fruitful vine laden with abundant fruit, who becomes food for those who seek her wisdom: "Like a vine I caused loveliness to bud, and my blossoms became glorious and abundant fruit. Come to me, you who desire me, and eat your fill of my produce. . . . Those who eat me will hunger for more, and those who drink me will thirst for more" (Sir 24:17-21). Likewise, in a provocative claim that echoes not only the self-descriptive statements of Sophia but also the "I am" pronouncements of YHWH in the First Testament,[44] Jesus asserts that he *is* food for those who come to him: "I am the bread of life" (John 6:35), a claim that he repeats several times: "I am the living bread come down from heaven. . . . Unless you eat the flesh of the Son of Man and drink his blood, you shall not have life in you" (6:51, 53).

43. Kobel, *Dining with John*, 191.
44. Bowe, "The Divine 'I Am,' " 43.

But unlike those who eat of Sophia and still "hunger for more," those who consume Jesus "will never be hungry," and those who believe in him "will never be thirsty" (John 6:35).

Finally, consuming the food provided by both Woman Wisdom and Jesus leads to eternal life.[45] Wisdom claims that those who have sought her from their youth, and who seek friendship with her and "good counsel," will have immortality "because of her" and "leave an everlasting remembrance to those who come after [them]" (Wis 8:2-18; 6:17-20). Revealing his identity as the "bread of life," Jesus promises that the food he gives "endures to eternal life" (John 6:27). "It is the will of my Father, that all who see the Son and believe in him may have eternal life; and I will raise them up on the last day" (John 6:39-40). While Jesus speaks of resurrection "on the last day," John's gospel underscores that "eternal life" is likewise "the experience of union with the risen Christ in this life," which fills "the believer's present with eternal life."[46]

Meals as Contexts for Community Formation

From the beginning of his earthly ministry, Jesus engages in forming his disciples, teaching them the values that shape his way of life: love, friendship, service, and co-abiding. Meals and the discourses that follow them are primary contexts of this dynamic formation. As the drama of Jesus' life unfolds, the size of the group that surrounds him, having expanded during the first episodes of John's account, becomes markedly smaller.[47] At the same time, Jesus' self-disclosure to his true followers, his invitation to intimacy with him, and the

45. Kobel, *Dining with John*, 191.

46. Schneiders, *Written*, 157–58.

47. The pivotal moment of this decline is the "bread of life" discourse in chapter 6 of John's narrative. Having instructed those following him to seek not perishable food but that which brings eternal life, Jesus invites them to eat and drink his flesh and blood. John records that this caused many to no longer travel with him (6:60-71).

clarity of his formative teaching intensifies around the tables of the latter portion of John's account, especially the supper at Bethany (12:1-8) and the final meal Jesus shares with his disciples before he dies (13:1–17:26).

The supper at Bethany given in honor of Jesus by his beloved friends Lazarus, Mary, and Martha gives little evidence of the actual food served (12:1-8). Nor is there an extensive discourse by Jesus. Yet the meal setting and the gestures of service that take place, most especially the action of Mary toward Jesus during the meal, speak eloquently about friendship, mutuality, and mutual respect. While they are at table in this intimate setting, Mary anoints Jesus, honoring him and adorning him as a guest in the house, wiping Jesus' feet with her hair (12:3-4).[48] This intimate act speaks of Mary's tender love for Jesus and echoes other biblical stories of anointing and anointed women in relationships of love (Ruth 3:3; Song 1:3; Jdt 10:3).[49] Jesus accepts Mary's display of tenderness, noting that she is anointing him for the day of his burial (12:7). Moreover, this celebratory action honors Jesus' messianic identity as the anointed of God, while at the same time anticipates his washing the feet of his disciples at the meal before his death (13:1-30). Mary's servanthood at the feet of Jesus mirrors Jesus' servanthood at the feet of his disciples and anticipates his teaching that his disciples must wash each other's feet (11:2; 12:3; 13:5, 13-17).[50] Moreover, Jesus underscores the relationship of this anointing to his burial (12:7), reminding his followers that he must die in order that others might

---

48. See Webster, *Ingesting*, 92.

49. Implied is that Mary's action "anoints" her as well, as her hair absorbs the overflow of the costly ointment. Theodore of Mopsuestia notes that "it was as if the woman planned this so as to attach the fragrance of our Lord's flesh to her body. For she took care that she should always be with him: she did this in her love so that if she should come to be separated from him, by this she could suppose he was with her still." As cited by Webster, *Ingesting*, 93.

50. Webster, *Ingesting*, 93–94.

"eat him" and live (12:24). Jesus' death, anticipated in the home of his beloved friends in Bethany, is to be celebrated rather than mourned, for his death brings life to the world.[51]

Mary's tender act of love at this meal underscores the centrality of love, friendship, service, and co-abiding at the heart of Jesus' formation of his disciples, values that are redundantly evident in the last meal Jesus shares with them on the eve of his passion (13:1–17:26). As in the supper in Bethany, there is no account of the actual food consumed at this last supper, but the context of shared table fellowship with an intimate number of close disciples sets the stage for Jesus' final invitation to embrace his vision and values. John tells us that Jesus, "loved his own who were in the world" and, loving them "to the end" (13:1), he now gives them a new commandment: "Just as I have loved you, you should also love one another. By this everyone will know that you are my disciples, if you have love one for another" (13:34-35; 15:12).

At the heart of his last meal, Jesus demonstrates his love in an extravagant act of washing the disciples' feet, an act that both incorporates them into his mission (13:8) and invites them more deeply into divine friendship: "I do not call you servants, because the servant does not know what the master is doing, but I have called you friends, because I have made known to you everything that I have heard from my Father" (15:15). Hence, the intimacy Jesus has with his Father he shares with his followers, an intimacy that empowers them for a reciprocal intimacy among themselves.

Themes of mutual love remain at the center of Jesus' last discourse as a whole. Those who love him will rejoice in his departure and welcome the Spirit-Advocate whom Jesus will send to guide them (14:16, 19). They will keep his commandments (4:15, 23) and be loved by the Father (14:21), and Jesus and the Father will come to them and make their home in them (14:23). In an evocative image

---

51. Ibid., 97.

that gathers up this intimate and intricate relationship of Jesus with both his Father and his disciples, Jesus declares, "I am the vine . . . you are the branches . . . and my Father is the vine-grower" (15:5, 1). "Abide in me as I abide in you. . . . Those who abide in me and I in them bear much fruit, because apart from me you can do nothing" (15:4-5). As in the wedding at Cana, images of the vine and of bearing fruit are laden with biblical associations. At this last meal of Jesus' earthly sojourn, the image of an intricately connected vine, with the flow of life that courses through its trunk and branches, bearing fruit that provides nourishment, joy, and festivity for those who eat and drink, images the dynamic process by which the disciples will "abide in Jesus" and co-abide with each other and with all God's abundant creation, while anticipating the joy of the messianic end time (17:24). In all of this, the process by which Jesus becomes food for those who hunger and wisdom for those who receive his word will be prolonged in the world that God has loved so much (3:16) through the ministry of Jesus' disciples, who in bearing fruit, become food for those whom they will serve.

Questions for Reflection

1) How does Jesus' engagement with food in both Luke's and John's gospels invite us to become more involved in issues of hunger and just distribution of food in today's world?

2) How does Jesus' new economy of food, as portrayed by Luke, speak to today's inequality between those with an overabundance of food and the millions worldwide who are robbed by corporate agriculture of their small rations? What can we do to address this situation?

3) How does Jesus' revelation that God comes to God's people as food offer new ways to imagine our relationship with God and with each other? How are we called to bear abundant fruit and so become food for others?

chapter three

In the Beginning Was the Meal

From the beginnings of Christianity, community meals shared in memory of Jesus were central to the life of believers.[1] Gathering for a meal was vital to the formation and maintenance of the early communities of disciples and the manner in which they carried on Jesus' mission in the world.[2] This chapter explores these beginnings: the meal practice of the first generations of Christ-followers,[3] which over time came to be known as Eucharist.

Recent decades have seen a burgeoning of scholarship on meals in first-century Greco-Roman society and specifically in the life of the first Christian communities. At a time when Roman domination

---

1. The chapter title is taken from Hal Taussig, *In the Beginning Was the Meal: Social Experimentation and Early Christian Identity* (Minneapolis: Fortress Press, 2009).

2. Thomas O'Loughlin, *The Eucharist: Origins and Contemporary Understandings* (New York: Bloomsbury T & T Clark, 2015), 86. O'Loughlin points out that while specific information about the earliest Christian meals is both limited and fragmentary, by treating all references to meals and food, including those in the gospels, as "memories transmitted and preserved in early communities," we can learn much about how they understood the significance of their actions.

3. I use this image to indicate that the term "Christian" was not used from the beginning but was a name attributed to followers of Christ during missionary journeys to Antioch, as recorded in Acts 11:26.

was breaking down earlier structures of civic belonging, meal gatherings of friends, associates, and colleagues provided an important sense of membership, allegiance, and social standing within Hellenistic society.[4] Christians participated in this wider tradition of shared meals, and it was here that the emerging eucharistic meal tradition unfolded and claimed its significance.[5]

This chapter explores several aspects of early Christian meal practice that offer points of reflection for the larger concerns of this book: namely, how current eucharistic eating addresses the contemporary world of food, meals, hunger, and human-earthly flourishing.[6] Our focus is on the earliest generations of Christ-followers, who negotiated the transition from Jesus' earthly ministry in Palestine to his risen presence among communities of followers on mission in the larger world.[7]

The Meal and the Stories

The Centrality of the Meal

The earliest chapters of the Acts of the Apostles describe the Christian community in Jerusalem as devoted to "the apostles' teaching and fellowship, to the breaking of the bread and the prayers" (Acts 2:42). While we lack details of what this "breaking of the bread" might have looked like, the passage underscores the centrality of meal

---

4. Taussig, *In the Beginning*, 27. Taussig, among others, employs social history as a cognate field in his research on early Christian meals—using the history of an entire society as context for studying one group within it.

5. Andrew B. McGowan, *Ancient Christian Worship: Early Church Practices in Social, Historical and Theological Perspective* (Grand Rapids, MI: Baker Academic, 2014), 20.

6. See Paul F. Bradshaw and Maxwell E. Johnson, *The Eucharistic Liturgies: Their Evolution and Interpretation* (Collegeville, MN: Liturgical Press, 2012) for a fuller exploration of early Eucharist.

7. My primary focus here will be the period between Jesus' resurrection and the mid-second century, but references to later information will be included.

fellowship. Sharing food and drink was not a social event in addition to worship but the regular form of Christian gathering "where bread was broken, a cup blessed, and various forms of discourse shared among the community and offered to God."[8] Such a shared meal was "not *like* a banquet; it [was] a banquet."[9] Bread and wine were not sacred additions to a more prosaic communal meal that could later be detached and resituated in an attenuated ritual. Rather, the earliest accounts suggest the actual identity of Eucharist and meal as a single event that involved giving thanks to God for Jesus Christ over food and drink. Here, Christ-believers remembered Jesus' expansive meal fellowship, not simply his "last supper," as later interpreted.[10]

Meals were central to the life of the earliest communities. Around the table they offered thanks for food, shared stories and common life, forged their emerging self-understanding, and discerned the meanings that would guide their lives, all the while remembering the risen Jesus, present with them in the breaking of bread. Domestic spaces provided the first context for such sharing: dining rooms of wealthier members, outfitted with couches for reclining that could enable a small group of Christ-followers to share food and fellowship. As communities grew in size, other spaces were borrowed or rented for community meals. In these familial places, disciples of Jesus reflected on his presence and promise and ate together in his name. Meals became a central act around which others—reading, preaching, prayer, prophecy—were arranged.[11]

8. McGowan, *Ancient Christian Worship*, 19.

9. Andrew B. McGowan, "Rethinking Eucharistic Origins," *Pacifica* 23, no. 2 (June 2010): 186.

10. Ibid., 189–90. McGowan proposes that the emergence of a now familiar "token" sacramental meal happened gradually, involving an "attenuation . . . of the basic meal itself into a token form, rather than the separation of an essentially separate rite." This took place, he suggests, not in the first century but was still developing across the third.

11. McGowan, *Ancient Christian Worship*, 20.

Formation of the Gospels within Early Meal Practice

It was precisely this table practice that provided a context for the emergence of written gospel accounts. Stories of Jesus' ministry, death, and glorious resurrection were told and retold in oral form and eventually written down to preserve the memory and meaning of his life for all time. The stories and the communities who heard and retold them at table mutually influenced each other and shaped the way the evangelists would later record the life, teaching, and risen presence of Jesus for future generations.[12]

Clearly, then, the gospels did not provide a script for the early meals or offer instructions for how early meals might unfold. Despite the later interpretation of Jesus' last supper as the paradigm for eucharistic gatherings, this was not the case in the earliest centuries. Rather, these narratives reflect the early communities' sense that their meal practice was a continuation of a whole series of Jesus' suppers and banquets—impromptu meals and unexpected feasts, miraculous feedings and intimate breakfasts—rather than the memorialization of one.[13] In their gatherings, communities kept alive the "memory and meaning of those meals in which Jesus healed the hungry and responded to real human needs through extravagant gestures of loaves and fishes."[14]

---

12. Esther Kobel, *Dining with John: Communal Meals and Identity Formation in the Fourth Gospel and Its Historical and Cultural Contexts* (Leiden: Brill, 2011), 295. See also Taussig, *In the Beginning*, 36–40.

13. McGowan, *Ancient Christian Worship*, 26. The very designation "last" suggests that this supper on the eve of Jesus' passion was one of a whole series of meals that included impromptu meals and large banquets, miraculous feedings and intimate dining for which he served as host, guest, or in some cases both. Nor was this meal before Jesus' death the "last" meal recorded in any of the emerging gospels. Luke, for example, recounts two meals that Jesus shared with his disciples after the resurrection, one at Emmaus with two discouraged disciples (24:13-35) and the other in Jerusalem, where after eating a piece of broiled fish, Jesus commissioned the disciples present to be his witnesses to all nations (24:42, 47-49).

14. Nathan D. Mitchell, *Eucharist as Sacrament of Initiation* (Chicago: Liturgy Training Publications, 1994), 102.

The Shape and Ritual Dynamics of Ancient Meals

The shape and ritual flow of early Christian meals were significantly influenced by the festive meal practice of the surrounding Hellenistic culture, often referred to as *symposia*. Groups bound by kinship or by social, religious, professional, or ethnic ties met regularly for meals to create and express their identity and beliefs. Gentile and Jewish communities alike, from all classes of society—wealthy, poor, elite, merchants, or laborers—gathered to mark personal, familial, or religious occasions. Despite the variety of occasions and groups, these banquets followed similar patterns across social classes in terms of the types of food served, the manner in which invitations were sent, the arrangement of the dining room, the leadership of a president, the placement of guests at table and its social significance, the order in which the event unfolded, and the entertainment or extended conversation that concluded the meal.[15] Reclining, a mark of social status, was the usual posture of participants, and before they reclined, guests had their hands and feet washed by servants, who then served the meal, setting tables for food and drink in front of those reclining.

Banquets and festive meals in Hellenistic society were at once religious and social events, often dedicated to a deity and opening with a hymn and/or prayers. The meal unfolded in two parts: the sharing of food, in Greek the *deipnon*, followed by the *symposium* comprising conversation, teaching, or entertainment, a pattern followed by the earliest Christ-believers. Characteristic of these early Christian meals was the blessing of bread during the *deipnon* or supper. The first-century *Didache* instructed communities to give thanks for the bread at the *deipnon* (9:5), an action attributed to Jesus "during the supper/*deipnon*" in both First Corinthians and the three Synoptic Gospels.

15. Matthias Klinghardt, *Gemeinschaftsmahl und Mahlgemeinschaft* (Tübingen: Francke Verlag, 1996), 253–73, as referenced in Taussig, *In the Beginning*, 26. See also Valeriy A. Alikin, *The Earliest History of the Christian Gathering* (Leiden: Brill, 2010), 27–30, for more information on Jewish banquets.

In the larger social context, the ritual transition from *deipnon* to *symposium* was marked by several actions. After removing the serving tables, servants brought in a bowl of wine, which was then mixed with water and a libation offered to the gods or to the emperor, most often accompanied by a hymn. The diners then shared the wine in individual cups.[16] For Jewish communities, this ritual transition was marked by a formal *berakah* or blessing: "Blessed are you, Lord our God, King of the universe, Creator of the fruit of the vine."[17] As emerging Christian communities negotiated their unique identity as Christ-believers, they too replaced the expected libation with a "cup of blessing" shared among participants, which in Paul's imagery was a cup that remembered Jesus' action at table. In First Corinthians 11:25, Paul writes: "Jesus took the cup after the *deipnon*, saying, 'This cup is the new covenant in my blood.'"

For early Christians, the *symposium* that followed the meal might include singing, prayers, readings, and teachings that supported their faith in Jesus and remembered his presence in their midst while celebrating their shared values and common commitments.[18] Ephesians 5:19 instructs its hearers, "Do not get drunk with wine . . . but be filled with the Spirit, as you sing psalms and hymns and spiritual songs among yourselves, singing and making melody to the Lord in your hearts." Singing might have included newly composed songs, as well as sung or chanted "readings"—texts or stories that were intoned to add volume and gravity to their performance. Paul mentions "speaking in tongues" as a distinctively Christian activity, and this may well have happened at Christian meal celebrations, although ecstatic expressions have been noted in the *symposia* of other groups of the time as well.

---

16. McGowan, *Ancient Christian Worship*, 21.
17. Mitchell, *Eucharist*, 74.
18. McGowan, *Ancient Christian Worship*, 22.

Food and Creativity

Food at Ancient Banquets

Bread and wine were central to festive meals precisely because they were the everyday food of first-century Greco-Roman culture. Bread held primacy of place, providing over half of most people's daily intake of calories. Barley bread, darker and coarser than wheat bread, was the fare of all but the elite strata of society and most likely was used by Christian communities for communal meals. We note that in John's account of Jesus' feeding the five thousand, the loaves provided by a small boy were made of barley. Wine was likewise a source of nutritional benefit, especially for poorer communities. Along with bread and wine, everyday fare included some cooked relish made from fish bits or vegetables and occasionally cheese.[19] The food menu at banquets could be considerably more elaborate, although bread remained the center of the meal, accompanied by "smaller amounts of highly seasoned food such as fish (often in preserved form), salt, vegetables, legumes, oil, cheese and sometimes meat."[20] Olives were likewise characteristic of simple or festive meals, and olive oil was used for anointing. Christian documents from the second and third centuries mention that various foods were blessed at Eucharist along with bread and wine, which may have been the case from the beginning. The *Apostolic Tradition* describes a newly ordained bishop giving thanks to God for oil, cheese, and olives and

---

19. Graydon F. Snyder, *Inculturation of the Jesus Tradition* (Harrisburg, PA: Trinity International, 1999), 146. Note that bread was a primary staple; some estimates say that 53–55 percent of people's calories came from bread or other grain products.

20. Meat was expensive and, given its association with religious sacrifice, was particularly problematic for Christians. Meat was an integral part of Greco-Roman sacrifice. At some Greco-Roman banquets, the meat used in sacrifices was eaten right after its ritual slaughter. See McGowan, *Ancient Christian Worship*, 20.

notes that milk and honey were consumed at a celebration associated with baptism.[21]

Bread not only was a source of sustenance for early communities but also was used as a metaphor for their corporate life and meal sharing. Writing to the Corinthians, Paul claims that "because there is one loaf, we who are many are one body, for we all partake of the one bread" (1 Cor 10:17). This image of a single body, a community at once diverse and united, takes on an eschatological significance in the *Didache*: "As this broken bread was scattered upon the mountains and having been gathered together became one, so may your church be gathered together from the ends of the earth into your kingdom; for yours is the glory and the power through Jesus Christ for evermore."[22]

The sharing of a full meal was assumed throughout the first century and remained the ideal, as well as the actual practice of some communities, well into the third or even the fourth century.[23] As noted earlier, the eucharistic elements of bread and wine were not distinctive sacral additions to a prosaic communal banquet that could be readily resituated in a setting apart from the full meal.[24] Rather, the emergence of a "token" eucharistic meal came gradually, involving the reduction of the basic meal itself into a token form, rather than the detachment of an already separate rite. An early example of this transition is seen in Carthage around 200 CE, where the renowned Tertullian maintains an evening meal as the main

---

21. *Apostolic Tradition*, 6–7, 22. We note as well that some ascetic communities abstained from wine, either using a cup of water only or omitting the cup altogether. See Andrew McGowan, *Ascetic Eucharists: Food and Drink in Early Christian Ritual Meals* (Oxford: Clarendon, 1999), 89–142. McGowan dates this document to around 300 CE.

22. R. C. D. Jasper and G. J. Cuming, *Prayers of the Eucharist*, 4th ed., ed. Paul F. Bradshaw and Maxwell E. Johnson (Collegeville, MN: Liturgical Press, 2019), 42.

23. See, for example, Bradshaw and Johnson, *Eucharistic Liturgies*, 25–36.

24. McGowan, "Rethinking," 185.

communal gathering but provides a separate opportunity for members to "receive the Eucharist" in the morning.[25] Given the diversity of practice that marked early communities spread throughout the Mediterranean world, however, the transition to a briefer eucharistic service and its relationship to the continuing banqueting tradition happened gradually over a few centuries.[26]

The emergence of bread and wine as "holy food" within the variety of other foods shared at Christian meals, and the association of these foods with the actual body and blood of Christ, likewise happened gradually.[27] The *Acts of Thomas*, for example, mentions bread, oil, vegetables, and salt as "blessed and as shared in an unmistakably 'eucharistic style'; [yet] there is no hint that these other elements were thought of as the body and blood of Jesus."[28] Rather, in blessing all, "these worshipers were ensuring that all their eating, especially their eucharistic food, reflected the purity and holiness to which they had been called."[29]

The striking development of metaphoric language for bread and wine found in John 6, where Jesus speaks of the necessity of "eating his flesh and drinking his blood," indicates at least one trajectory of interpretation that associated the bread and wine with Jesus' sacred body.[30] But interestingly, Jesus' directive in this passage is associated not with his "last supper" but with the feeding of five thousand people in a deserted place, where he "took, blessed, broke, and gave" the five barley loaves and few fish to feed a crowd of hungry people.

25. Tertullian, *De Corona* 3.3I. See McGowan, "Rethinking," 189.

26. McGowan, *Ancient Christian Worship*, 47–52.

27. See also Bradshaw and Johnson, *Eucharistic Liturgies*, 24.

28. McGowan, *Ancient Christian Worship*, 42.

29. Ibid.

30. Ibid., 45. The familiar "words of institution" recited as a matter of course in contemporary eucharistic prayers, that identify the bread and wine as Jesus' Body and Blood, are notably missing from most of the earliest prayers that are extant today.

By the mid-second century, Justin Martyr speaks of the sacred character of the bread and cup specifically, noting that after the presider has offered thanks for these foods, they are received by all and sent to those who are absent. He comments, "For not as common bread or common drink do we receive these things . . . [but] the flesh and blood of that incarnate Jesus."[31]

Ritual Creativity

The common pattern of Greco-Roman festive meals (a shared supper followed by discourse of some kind) and the range of ritual gestures that communities might employ (libations, prayers, hymns, teaching) allowed ample room for early Christian assemblies to engage creatively in expressing and negotiating their emerging identity as followers of Christ. In the absence of a common script, diverse communities gave expression to the cultural, social, and theological perspectives that shaped them locally.[32] Such mutual creativity was encouraged by Paul in his missive to the Corinthian community: "When you come together, each one has a hymn, a lesson, a revelation, a tongue, or an interpretation" (1 Cor 14:26). Such a collaboration was likely a regular part of early meals, most especially during the *symposium*.

Meal prayers, especially prayers of thanksgiving over the food and drink, were at first improvised by the president of the assembly.[33] One of the earliest accounts of a eucharistic meal, written by Justin Martyr in the mid-second century, states that the one presid-

31. Justin Martyr, *First Apology* 66, in Jasper and Cuming, *Prayers of the Eucharist*, 26.

32. See Paul Bradshaw, *The Search for the Origins of Christian Worship: Sources and Methods for the Study of Early Liturgy*, 2nd ed. (Oxford: Oxford University Press, 2002). Also McGowan, "Rethinking," 190–91.

33. See Allan Bouley, *From Freedom to Formula: The Evolution of the Eucharistic Prayer from Improvisation to Written Texts* (Washington, DC: The Catholic University of America Press, 1981).

ing prays "at considerable length," offering "prayers and thanksgivings, according to his ability, and the people assent, saying 'Amen.'"[34] While Jewish prayer forms most likely served as a source for this improvised praying, those in leadership crafted the unfolding prayers in light of the community, the context, and the overarching awareness of the power and presence of the risen Christ.

Given that New Testament scholars have for some time identified hymns, songs, and hymn fragments imbedded within the texts of the gospels, letters, and the book of Revelation, a question arises about if and how these poetic texts might have been performed during Christian *symposia*. The hymn of Jesus' self-sacrificing *kenosis* found in Philippians 2 is a well-known example, with its poetic climax describing the raising up of Jesus as Lord, to the glory of God the Father (Phil 2:6-11). Paul invokes this hymn when encouraging the Philippians to "put on the mind of Christ" (Phil 2:5). Without direct evidence, one can only wonder if and how such a hymn might have been sung or chanted at an early Christian gathering, especially when Paul's letter was read.[35]

Apart from questions of performance, one marvels at the effusiveness of the poetry and cosmic vision of these compositions. Clearly, expansive understandings of the role and mission of Christ had emerged among the earliest generations. In the words of a hymn found in Paul's letter to the Colossians, Christ is the "image of the unseen God; the firstborn of creation." Indeed, "all things have been created through him and for him. . . . In him all things hold together . . . [and] will be reconciled through and in him" (Col 1:15-20). Moreover, this cosmic sovereign is in dynamic relationship to the community gathered for a meal: "He is the head of the body, which the assembly is" (Col 1:18).[36] Other hymns echo these cosmic

---

34. Justin Martyr, *First Apology* 65, 67. Jasper and Cuming, *Prayers*, 28, 30.

35. Taussig, *In the Beginning*, 37.

36. Translation taken from Taussig, *In the Beginning*, 106. The NRSV translation reads: "He is the head of the body, the church."

images. The opening of John's gospel speaks of Jesus as the Word, the divine Logos, who "was with God in the beginning" and "through whom all things came into being. In him was life, and that life is the light of all people" (John 1:2-4). A hymn in Paul's letter to the Ephesians states that according to God's design for the world, "when the times had run their course to the end . . . [God would] bring everything together under Christ, as head, everything in heaven and everything on Earth" (Eph 1:10).[37]

Visions, Ethics, and Resistance

Vision, Values, and Ethics of the Table

Integral to the spiritual and social ferment of early Christians at table was the process of imagining themselves as an alternative society with distinct values, visions, table ethics, and future hopes. Images such as "the realm of God," "the body of Christ," "*koinonia* with God," "the heavenly court," or "the heavenly city"[38] suggest that despite their lack of status or power, early believers saw themselves as belonging to a new social order, a kingdom far better than the kingdoms of this world and with a Lord more exalted than any emperor.[39] Although an insignificant social group, early Christians relied on Jesus' words, remembered in Luke's gospel, that captured a vision for the future: that many would "come from the east and west, north and south, and recline at the feast of the kingdom," in the empire of God (Luke 13:28-30). From such a vision flowed the values and ethics that marked their table fellowship.

Three values, highly cultivated within the larger Hellenistic banqueting tradition, would have influenced these communities: *koinonia* (community), *isonomia* and *philia* (equality and friendship),

---

37. New Jerusalem Bible translation (Garden City, NY: Doubleday, 1985).
38. Taussig, *In the Beginning*, 54.
39. Ibid., 54.

and *charis* (grace, generosity, beauty).[40] While these values converge on an expectation of mutuality, rapport, and familiarity among those gathered, they were in conflict with the actual social stratification of participants that typified Hellenistic banquets: guests reclined according to their respective social rank and were served different kinds and quantities of food based on their social ranking.[41]

Early Christian communities embraced these three values but interpreted them in an expansive and inclusive way in light of their experience of Jesus and of one another.[42] *Koinonia*, for example, was closely associated with sharing a common loaf and drinking from a common cup. The Gospels of Mark, Matthew, and Luke, as well as 1 Corinthians, portray the drinking of a common cup as an act of "covenant in Christ's blood" among those drinking. This act of sharing the one cup binds those eating together to one another and evokes Jesus' loyalty to them to the point of death.[43] Likewise, the shared loaf. Paul makes this clear to the Corinthians: "The bread that we break, is it not a sharing in the body of Christ?" (1 Cor 10:16b). To share the same loaf or cup was thus an ethical commitment to *koinonia*—to be and to live as one body.

Koinonia likewise affected how service at table was practiced at Christian meals. The gospel stories reflect the reversal of status proclaimed by Jesus: "For who is greater, the one who reclines or the one who serves? . . . Behold I am among you as one who serves" (Luke 22:27). Among early communities, performing service at table became as important as reclining, valued as a mark of dignity and status in the *koinonia* of God. Likewise, this *koinonia* meant reimagining who was eligible to recline at table. Traditionally only males could recline, although that tradition was in flux, and women were more

40. Klinghardt, *Gemeinschaftsmahl*, 153–73, identifies this trilogy. Used by Taussig, *In the Beginning*, 26–32.

41. Taussig, *In the Beginning*, 26–32.

42. What follows is drawn from Taussig, *In the Beginning*, 49–56.

43. Ibid., 50.

and more included, especially in Christian communities. Paul signaled that exclusiveness of any kind was not compatible in Christian discipleship: "There is no longer Jew or Greek, . . . slave or free, . . . male or female for all of you are one in Christ Jesus" (Gal 3:28).

Philia, friendship, was an integral part of the supper teaching of Jesus recorded in John's gospel: "I do not call you servants any longer, because the servant does not know what the master is doing; but I have called you friends, because I have made known to you everything that I have heard from my Father" (15:13-15). Friendship, in this Johannine perspective, is rooted in the intimacy of Jesus and his beloved "Abba" that spills over into a depth of friendship between Jesus and each disciple and into the love they have for one another—a bond so strong that, for the sake of the other, one would be willing to lay down one's life (John 15:13). Moreover, Jesus became "friend" to tax collectors and sinners (Luke 7:34), stretching the meal ethic of *philia* beyond his immediate followers to include the undesirable and "unworthy" members of society. Hospitality, both given and received, was likewise critical to Christian understandings of *isonomia/philia*. Within the larger society, hospitality—*xenia* in Greek—involved extending welcome to a stranger or foreigner by inviting them to one's table.[44] Jesus taught that hospitality must not only be offered but likewise include receiving the ministrations of others. In sending out his disciples for mission, he urged them to carry little with them, so as to experience the hospitality offered by those they would meet.

The third value, *charis*, imaged Hellenistic meals as participation in an ideal society marked by generosity, beauty, elegance, and grace. In contrast, Jesus described the great eschatological assembly as including the poor, the crippled, the blind, and the lame, and he invited his followers to embody this in their table fellowship. Rather than the genteel society of Hellenistic banquets, Christians were called to envision a community of "the least of these," the undesir-

44. Ibid., 30

ables—the beloved children of God gathered from the ends of the Earth around the messianic banquet table. The earliest extant example of a prayer used over bread at Christian meals, as recorded in the *Didache*, reverberates with this expansive imagery: "As this broken bread was scattered over the mountains, and when brought together became one, so let your church be brought together from the ends of the Earth into your kingdom."[45]

Given these values, it is easy to understand Paul's chiding the Corinthians for their behavior at community meals: "When you come together, it is not really to eat the Lord's supper. For when the time comes to eat, each of you goes ahead with your own supper and one goes hungry and another becomes drunk" (1 Cor 11:20-21). In contrast, Paul calls this Corinthian community to discern the true nature of their new identity as the Body of Christ—one of common fellowship, friendship, and mutual care among all, in which "the weak are respected alongside the strong, the rich eat and drink alongside the poor,"[46] and care is taken that no one is lacking either food or dignity.

Implied in the ethics of such a table is the "new economy of food" that Jesus embodied in his table fellowship. God is the provider of all that is needed for human flourishing: food, drink, and mutual care. There is enough for all, and everyone is welcome at this banquet of life. Among early communities striving to be Jesus' disciples, table ethics must have reflected, with varying success, the challenging task of ensuring that all experienced the generosity, abundance, and sustaining love poured out in Jesus' presence in their midst.

Ritual Resistance to Roman Imperial Power

One of the most provocative aspects of early Christian meals was their role as ritual resistance to the imperial domination of Rome. Recall Rome's pervasive control over Palestinian life, including the

---

45. *Didache* 9. Jasper and Cumming, *Prayers*, 23.

46. Michael Northcott, "Faithful Feasting," in *A Moral Climate: The Ethics of Global Warming* (Maryknoll, NY: Orbis Books, 2007), 252–53.

extraction of food grown by local farmers to fill imperial storehouses that fed elite Roman urbanites and the huge imperial army. Beyond this crippling system of agricultural extraction and taxation, which left massive hunger, poverty, malnutrition, and disease in its wake, Roman enslavement, cultural domination, and military occupation were all coupled with religious claims of the godly identity of the emperor and his divine right to rule the world.[47]

Current scholarship finds extensive evidence of resistance to imperial power and policies, both in emerging Christian literature, including incipient New Testament texts, and in the behavior of the early communities.[48] Both coalesced in meal gatherings. Here, in the relatively private yet politically significant setting of a meal, communities could experience an alternative society to that of Rome, strengthened by the bonding of meal fellowship and prodded by explicit evocations of the memory of Jesus' resistance on the cross. Common meals elicited two strategies of resistance against Roman imperialism: meal behavior that embodied the ideals of a counter-society—inclusion, service, hospitality, and justice—and specific ritual practices that celebrated the death of Jesus by crucifixion at the hands of the Roman Empire and his now cosmic reign as Lord of heaven and Earth.

Inclusive table practices were serious challenges to the hierarchical structures and inequalities of Roman society; Christian slaves, freedmen, and slave owners reclined together; men, women, Jew, Greek, and Gentile shared food. Viewed as a new world order by gathered Christ-followers, these customs would have been judged by local Roman agents as seriously disordered practices.[49] The description in Acts 2 of communities of mutual support in which food is shared and resources held in common (2:44-47) challenged the indebtedness and dependency of imperial patron-client relation-

47. Taussig, *In the Beginning*, 116, 125.
48. See ibid., 115–43.
49. Ibid., 116.

ships and represented "a nearly explicit political and economic challenge to Roman rule."[50]

References to Jesus' crucifixion at the hands of Roman authorities were significant at many early meals, as in the New Testament texts themselves. Since crucifixion was an imperial punishment for insurrection, Christian emphasis on Jesus' death might well have been interpreted as an explicit challenge to Rome.[51] Reiterated among communities at various moments in the meal, remembrance of Christ's crucifixion could be interpreted as a self-conscious, if somewhat hidden, challenge to imperial authority.

Recall, for example, the libation that marked the transition from the initial *deipnon* to the subsequent *symposium* in Hellenistic banquets. Roman emperors had decreed that this libation be poured in their honor or in honor of another Roman deity. Yet most Christian communities associated this libation with Jesus' death, as noted in Pauline and Synoptic texts. Paul claims a "tradition received from the Lord," that links the libation cup with Jesus' blood: "the cup of blessing that we bless, is it not a sharing in the blood of Christ?" (1 Cor 10:16). Drinking this cup, Paul asserts, proclaims Jesus' death until he returns (1 Cor 11:23-26). Moreover, Jesus' blood represents a new covenant, a term with overtones of social and political solidarity and loyalty to Jesus, the executed one.[52] Engaging in such a libation in memory of Jesus strengthened the anti-Roman character of the act: Christian communities hereby evoked the death of Jesus as source of a new sociopolitical bonding among Christian diners.[53]

Hymns and songs likewise claimed Jesus to be both Lord and Savior, titles reserved for Caesar alone, who was widely celebrated as having "saved the world as an act of his own divine benevolence."[54]

---

50. Ibid., 117.
51. Ibid.
52. Ibid., 131.
53. See ibid., 131–35.
54. Ibid., 136.

They praised the cosmic outcome of Jesus' ignominious crucifixion and death. The hymn quoted in Paul's letter to the Philippians contrasts Jesus, who endured "even death on a cross," with the now glorious Christ whose name is "above all other names," and at whose name "all beings in the heavens, on Earth, and under the Earth bend a knee" (Phil 2:10). Such poetry creates an ironic tension between Jesus' cosmic reign and his execution as an enemy of the empire, suggesting that the meal at Philippi was at least implicitly a meal of resistance to Roman rule and that the *kosmos* envisioned stood in deep opposition to imperial rule.

"We Call This Bread Thanksgiving"[55]

Finally, we ask, how did the earliest Christians image their meals? By what names and metaphors did they describe the practice of eating together in the Lord's name? The Acts of the Apostles refers to "the breaking of the bread" (2:42, 46), and Paul, addressing the Corinthian community, writes of "the Lord's supper" (1 Cor 11:20). But neither of these images became a characteristic designation for Christian table fellowship. On the other hand, despite a great diversity of practice, the term *eucharistia*, "thanksgiving," emerged somewhat early, becoming a term that referenced the distinctive practice of Christians, their specific actions at table, and the elements of food shared.[56] Hence emerges our term, Eucharist.[57] Justin Martyr, in one of the earliest written descriptions of a Christian gathering, speaks of prayers and thanksgivings prayed over bread and cup and likewise

55. Justin Martyr, *First Apology* 66:1. Jasper and Cuming, *Prayers*, 29.

56. McGowan, *Ancient Christian Worship*, 33–34. Scholars have pointed out that thanksgiving became the predominant mode of Christian prayer, in contrast with the emphasis on blessing found in earlier Jewish prayers. See ibid., 28–29.

57. Ibid., 33. McGowan points out that the term *eucharistia* referred to the prayer offered over the bread and cup but was quickly extended to mean the food and drink for which thanks were given, as well as the event itself.

describes the bread itself as thanksgiving. But the meanings he finds in these acts of *eucharistia* are indeed expansive. In a beautiful passage from his *First Apology*, Justin links the posture of thanks offered to God, who feeds humankind, with three experiences that flow from such gratitude: a use of these created gifts for the well-being of the community, an attentiveness to the needs of all, and thanksgiving not only for personal existence but for the variety of the Earth's creatures and its changing seasons.[58] This expansive understanding of thanksgiving, encompassing all human-earthly existence, acknowledging as gift all we have to eat, and remembering those in need and the responsibility of the community to care for them, implies an attitude of life that flows well beyond meal gatherings into all aspects of Christian existence.

Questions for Reflection

1) How does the realization that the tradition of Eucharist began in the sharing of a full meal impact your understanding of the tradition, and how it might be celebrated today?

2) Can we imagine Eucharist today as resistance to oppressive political systems? If so, what aspects of current eucharistic practice might express this resistance?

3) Providing sustenance for the poor and hungry was an essential part of the shared life and meals of the earliest Christ-believers. How is this part of eucharistic ways of living in the world today?

4) Diversity preceded uniformity in early Christian eucharistic practice, and the church's unity was not dependent on a single

58. Justin Martyr, *First Apology* 13:1-2, as quoted in McGowan, *Ancient Christian Worship*, 8.

way of engaging in the action. Given the cultural diversity of the global church today, can diversity of expression be reclaimed as a means to unity rather than feared as a path to destruction?

part two

Broken
Relationships

Dining in
the Industrial Food System

The values implicit in Jesus' table fellowship and the meals of the earliest Christians—hospitality, shared resources, co-abiding, gratitude—find little resonance with the current global food system. The state of food production, distribution, and consumption at the hands of corporate industrialized agriculture, which dominates the current market, can be summed up in a single word, crisis: a crisis based in broken relationships. We eat today in exile estranged from the ecological, social, spiritual, economic, and bodily relationships that constitute deep human nourishment and health.[1] Moreover, this alienation involves a more massive

---

1. Norman Wirzba, *Food and Faith* (New York: Cambridge University Press, 2011), 71–109.

degradation of the Earth and a more widespread violence toward animals than the human community has ever before known.[2] Although the crisis remains invisible to many Americans, whose supermarket shelves are lined with a glut of food products,[3] its effects are quite evident. Most people eat today without knowing where their food comes from, by whom it was grown, and under what conditions—a situation that invites rampant food injustice. Small conventional and organic farmers are severely challenged to compete with large corporate agriculture. Hunger abounds in the richest country in the world, leaving one in six Americans not knowing where their next meal is coming from. Soil and seed, primary sources of life, have been relegated to the economic goals of giant chemical companies. The majority of available food has been commodified—removed from any obvious connection with the life-giving Earth, processed often with the addition of nonfood sources, packaged and sold as objects of desire, tailored to the highly individualized tastes of each consumer.[4] Eating is often done in haste, alone, on the run—a practice fostered by individually portioned foodstuffs, "reinforced" to contain all the nutrients one might gain from a well-balanced meal. Families rarely eat together; indeed, the practice of family meals in the United States has been largely lost in a single generation.[5] The art of cooking has been replaced in many

2. See Michael Northcott, "Faithful Feasting," in *A Moral Climate: The Ethics of Global Warming* (Maryknoll, NY: Orbis Books, 2007), 258.

3. As we will see, inner-city and rural communities often do not experience this excess but are situated in industry-created food deserts. Such is the injustice of the food system.

4. Wirzba points out that our consumer economy trains people to be discontented, ungrateful, and separated from each other. In a system dedicated to consumer fulfillment, we remain perpetually unfulfilled, making it "very difficult for any of us to live deeply, or with affection and responsibility, into the places where we are." Wirzba, *Food and Faith*, 102.

5. See Miriam Weinstein, *The Surprising Power of Family Meals: How Eating Together Makes Us Smarter, Stronger, Healthier and Happier* (Hanover, NH: Steerforth Press, 2005).

instances by microwave "warm-ups," and food is marketed to meet these expectations. People's bodies tell the whole tale: disease has dramatically increased in the last twenty years—obesity, diabetes, cancers of every type, cardiovascular disease, to name a few—due in large part to the high sodium, highly sweetened, and processed diet consumed by many Americans.[6] Obesity, in a word, is "good for the economy."[7]

While a full accounting of the industrialized food system is beyond the scope of this volume, a closer look at its origins, goals, and strategies, as well as its impact on Earth's ecosystems and people, is important if we are to identify how renewed eucharistic eating can reconnect and heal our broken relationships with the Earth, with the human family, and with God.

---

6. The National Institutes of Health estimates that two-thirds of Americans are either overweight or obese. See Wirzba, *Food and Faith*, 105. Obesity, he comments, has political, medical, and financial ramifications, including the multibillion dollar healing and dieting industries. Also Paul Roberts, *The End of Food* (Boston: Mariner Books, 2008), 95. Roberts quotes Tomas Philipson, a University of Chicago economist specializing in obesity, who wrote: "The obesity problem is really a side effect of things that are good for the economy."

7. Roberts, *The End of Food*, 95.

chapter four

The Corporate Industrial Food System

Origins, Goals, Outcomes

Scholars place the origins of human agriculture some ten thousand years ago. They stress that the growing of food crops, as opposed to the acquisition of edibles through hunting and gathering, began in different parts of the world at different times and using different technologies. Although the origins of today's corporate industrial food system can be situated in the early 1940s, its roots reach back into this entire history of agriculture. Implements to break up the soil, for example, from simple digging sticks to an infinite variety of ploughs pulled by humans or animals, are the ancestors of the massive tractors capable of ploughing the interminable cornfields of the US Midwest, so typical of today's industrial agriculture. Hybridization, methods of fertilization, systems of irrigation, and use of a specialized labor force were likewise introduced in farming practices long before they became strategic tools of a corporate food system.[1]

1. New World Encyclopedia contributors, "History of Agriculture," *New World Encyclopedia*, accessed June 20, 2019, //www.newworldencyclopedia.org/p/index .php?title=History_of_agriculture&oldid=1008693, for this citation and what follows.

From the first engagement of human communities with the soil through processes of planting and harvesting, human relationship with the food-producing Earth has been paradoxical, a relationship that could sustain human life or destroy it. Only through cooperation, mutuality and the ensuring of mutual benefit for both the Earth and the human-biotic community could this relationship flourish. Over the centuries, a pool of common wisdom about successful ways of growing food emerged among farmers in many parts of the world. Described today as "traditional methods," these common strategies are based on long-term cooperation between farmers and the land they cultivated. Traditional farming mirrored the natural nutrient cycles of Earth's soils, by which organic and inorganic matter are constantly recycled into the production of new food crops. Plant growth was enabled by the abundant solar energy reaching the Earth daily, creating the miracle of photosynthesis. Farmers were part of a natural food web, gathering seeds from one year's crop for the next sowing and sharing their excess seed with neighboring farmers. This ensured that the seeds were appropriate to the local soil and climate and that the food produced was aligned with the tastes cultivated by their local community. Domesticated animals were integrated into areas of plant cultivation, providing natural fertilizer for plants and food for animals. Multiple crops were interspersed in the same fields, enabling natural pest and weed control, and fields were allowed to rest fallow for periods of time or planted with cover crops to restore fertility. Most important, food was grown for local communities and sold directly to them, ensuring the food's freshness and delectability and building local economies.

Conceiving the Industrial Agricultural System

The close of World War II in the mid-1940s marked a significant turn in US and global agricultural practice that would call into question the traditional methods just described. Designed by a group of powerful American economists and businessmen, food and farm policies were formulated that over the ensuing years would become the operative food and farm policy of the US federal government. As businessmen and economists, rather than agrarians or farmers, the designers of this new food system focused on profit rather than on human nutrition and care for the food-bearing Earth. As powerful and well-positioned white males, they had access to high-ranking politicians and government officials who were shaping the country's postwar strategies. Notably, two of their associates served as US Secretary of Agriculture: Ezra Benson, who served under Presidents Truman, Eisenhower, Kennedy, Johnson, and Nixon; and Earl Butz, who served during the presidencies of Ford, Carter, Reagan, and George H. W. Bush.[2]

The system was launched in 1942 by Paul Hoffman, president of Studebaker; William Benton, inventor of modern consumer research and polling practices; and Marion Folsom, an executive of Eastman Kodak, who joined forces to found the Committee for Economic Development (CED), a think tank where business leaders could develop economic policy and then "use new techniques of public relations to promote their agreed-upon agenda."[3] This cadre of businessmen began mapping a post-war program for a chemically-intensive and financially lucrative agriculture. They opposed the prevailing New Deal farm measures, policies that ensured parity for farmers and prevented a glut of farm produce from flooding the market, driving down prices precipitously.[4] Instead, they lobbied for a reduction of the number of farmers, fearful that the political power and influence

---

2. Benson was a "far-right ideologue trained as an agricultural economist . . . who served simultaneously in the governing hierarchy of the Mormon Church— a multi-million dollar agribusiness corporation to this day." See Wenonah Hauter, *Foodopoly: The Battle over the Future of Food and Farming in America* (New York: The New Press, 2012), 21.

3. Ibid., 14.

4. Ibid., 16. Hauter notes that parity was a policy that ensured that "farm income would keep up with the cost of farming."

of organized farmers might initiate "a reorganization of the economy and a more socially, economically and racially egalitarian society."[5] The future of food envisioned by these economists and businessmen involved several interwoven strategies.[6]

- First, a small number of corporately owned, industrialized farms would control the entire food market. Implied in this goal was that most young rural men would abandon farming and become a cheap labor force for the manufacturing sector.

- Second, food production would become more globalized for the sake of economic efficiency. Imports and exports of farm produce would become standard and expected, bringing wealth to both the "agribusiness" corporations that would control the system and the transportation industry that would ship these goods around the world.[7]

- Third, processed food would come to dominate the market, increasing the number of stakeholders and profit makers involved in the "production" and transportation of food products.

- Fourth, a deregulated, free-market system would enable corporations to produce the cheap food and goods necessary to supply the global market. From its inception, the CED lobbied for governmental cooperation with free-market strategies and

5. Ibid., 17. New Deal economics, and especially the care for the well-being of American farmers, were considered "socialism."

6. The CED's strategy for agriculture culminated in the publication of "An Adaptive Program for Agriculture" in 1962. The report was prepared by fifty influential business leaders and eighteen economists from leading universities. See Hauter, *Foodopoly*, 20; Paul Roberts, *The End of Food* (Boston: Mariner Books, 2008), 120.

7. Hauter, *Foodopoly*, 23. The United States was regarded by these businessmen as having a "comparative advantage" in the export of grain and producing "capital-intensive crops, while the developing world was better suited to growing labor-intensive fruits and vegetables."

for the removal of trade barriers so as to allow large food companies and grain traders to obtain crops from countries and locales where prices were lowest.[8]

Implementing these strategies through the joint efforts of corporate and governmental leaders brought numerous shifts in the ensuing decades. Smaller farms were consolidated into major corporate food enterprises, leaving many fewer persons across the United States directly engaged with soil and seed. Large farm machines for ploughing, planting, fertilizing, and harvesting were employed, and transportation systems developed to move food to its new destinations. Monoculture, the growing of fields of single crops such as corn and soybeans, became an efficient means of managing expansive fields and maximizing output. Chemical pesticides and insecticides, developed during the first decades of the twentieth century as war weapons, were pressed into service to control weeds and insects no longer controlled by traditional methods of intercropping diverse species. That these pesticides also have the ability to kill birds, fish, reptiles, and mammals, as well as causing injury to human health, including cancers and neurological, reproductive, and developmental damage, mattered little.[9] Synthetic fertilizer that could increase nitrogen in the soil, also developed for the making of bombs during the world wars, was routinely added to the soil to induce greater fertility, with little attention to the soil's natural processes of regenerating nitrogen.

8. Ibid., 23. Crucial to expansion of food trade were negotiations around General Agreement on Tariffs and Trade (GATT) and later, in 1995, the WTO. The WTO agreement incorporated the CED's "Agreement on Agriculture."

9. Rosemary Radford Ruether, "Corporate Globalization and the Deepening of Earth's Impoverishment," in *Integrating Ecofeminism, Globalization and World Religions* (Lanham, MD: Rowman and Littlefield Publishers, 2005), 17. Ruether notes that pesticides kill insects "by such methods as blocking the nerve-impulse enzyme." She also notes that estimates suggest that "3 to 25 million people are injured by pesticide use worldwide, especially farmworkers who come into direct contact with these substances."

High-yield hybrid seeds were developed that could ensure greater dependability of the crop, but in the process, the rich diversity of food varieties previously grown were replaced by single strains.[10] These newly bred crops were designed not only for larger size and faster growth but for uniformity of size and shape, a requirement that enabled them to be harvested, picked, and processed mechanically.[11] Intensive watering, a requisite of the hybrid seeds, became the norm, drawing more frequently on centuries-old aquifers that held stores of precious groundwater. Moreover, all of these advances were dependent on the cheap and abundant fossil fuel energy that was available at that time.

The Green Revolution

By the 1960s, these strategies had doubled or tripled crop production in the United States. Without any assurance that this initial upsurge could be sustained into the future, the farming techniques developing in the United States were marketed to countries around the world. Labeled the "Green Revolution," this program claimed that these new strategies had the potential to feed expanding populations. Paul Hoffmann, noted previously as a founder of the CED,

---

10. At one time, for example, apple varieties numbered in the thousands, with each strain carrying a unique genetic code. Given the commercialization of apples in the industrial food system, the number of available species has dwindled to a few choices. Deliberately engineered apples like the Red Delicious and the Granny Smith now dominate the market, and the heirloom apples our forbearers loved are now relegated to backyards, community orchards, and extinction. Without diversity, these single apple strains are highly vulnerable today to disease and pests. See Rossi Anastopoulo, "Where Have All the Apples Gone? An Investigation into the Disappearance of Apple Varieties and the Detectives Who Are Out to Find Them," *PIT Journal* (2014), accessed June 11, 2019, http://pitjournal.unc.edu /article/where-have-all-apples-gone-investigation-disappearance-apple-varieties -and-detectives-who.

11. Roberts, *The End of Food*, 21–22.

was among the architects of this "revolution." Hoffman had subsequently been named by President Truman to administer the Marshall Plan for rebuilding war-torn Europe, and while serving as the president of the Ford Foundation in the 1960s, he administered the United Nations Development Programme.[12] Among Hoffman's associates were Norman Borlaug of the Rockefeller Foundation, who later received the Nobel Peace Prize for "saving over a billion people from starvation,"[13] and William Gaud, former director of the US Agency for International Development, who coined the term "Green Revolution." In 1968 Gaud claimed that "these and other developments in the field of agriculture contain the makings of a new revolution." But, he pointed out, "It is not the violent Red Revolution like that of the Soviets, nor is it a White Revolution like that of the Shah of Iran. I call it the Green Revolution."[14] Gaud's implication that this system countered communism was looked on favorably by Cold War Americans, who feared that growing hunger in Asia "would so destabilize Asian countries that they would be easy prey for Communists."[15]

The entire developing world was poised for such a revolution in agriculture.[16] Frightened by crop failures, expanding populations, growing food insecurity, and the predictions of massive famine in many parts of the world made by Paul Ehrlich in his 1968 book, *The Population Bomb*, national governments welcomed the new initiatives. High-yield plant varieties were imported and developed that could resist fungus and insects and tolerate greater quantities of nitrogen fertilizer, increasing the number of crops that could be grown in a single year. By 1965, wheat yields in Mexico had almost

12. Hauter, *Foodopoly*, 14.

13. Roberts, *The End of Food*, 148–49, 208. Also Wirzba, *Food and Faith*, 72.

14. Roberts, *The End of Food*, 147.

15. Ibid., 150.

16. Paragraph based on ibid., 148–52.

tripled. A few years later, Pakistan and India had harvested record wheat crops, and the Philippines brought in a record rice harvest.

But with these remarkable increases, another revolution was taking place: an abrupt transition from diverse and local agricultural systems, based in local economies, to a global industrialization of all that pertains to food and its availability. Food and chemical corporations were now negotiating with governments in the developing world, offering to help them build the infrastructure needed for industrial food production. "Western governments were giving hundreds of millions of dollars for aid projects in African and Asia."[17] The World Trade Organization, which from its inception had embraced the agenda of corporate agriculture, was setting rules that reinforced the dependence of farmers in other parts of the world on giant US corporations.[18] Traditional growing methods honed over centuries by farmers in local settings, in light of their unique soils and climate conditions, were undermined as "primitive" and incapable of meeting current food needs. These were replaced with commercial systems designed for use in the United States that made farmers in vastly different terrains completely dependent on external inputs from large agro-corporations.

Along with the hybrid seeds, petroleum-based fertilizers, pesticides, and large farm machines, industrial agriculture brought with it a whole new attitude toward the Earth and toward the social contacts that exist within the human community.[19] Patterns by which farmers had cooperated with Earth's natural systems and worked within the laws and predilections of local ecosystems, both in the United States and abroad, were replaced with attitudes and practices of subjugation and

17. Ibid., 151.

18. Ruether, *Ecofeminism*, 29.

19. See Debi Barker, "Globalization and Industrial Agriculture," in *The Fatal Harvest Reader: The Tragedy of Industrial Agriculture*, ed. Andrew Kimbrell (Sausalito, CA: Foundation for Deep Ecology in collaboration with Island Press, 2002), 252.

conquest of the land and its plant life, practices that Ron Keoese describes as "industrial agriculture's war against nature."[20] Biodiversity was replaced with a curtailing of the number of crop species, limiting selection to those that could be more efficiently planted, grown, and harvested. Local food crops, grown for local communities, were replaced by crops that were grown for export that could be shipped thousands of miles to their destinations. Not only did this growing of export crops leave local farmers without food security and dependent on imports from other countries, but long-distance transportation only exacerbated the levels of greenhouse gasses that were mounting in the Earth's atmosphere. In sum, farmers' self-reliance was replaced with wholesale dependence on corporate strategies, and the cultural, social, and ecological relationships previously cultivated by local agriculturalists were significantly disrupted.

Almost as soon as it started, Africa's Green Revolution was over. By the early 1990s, Africa's food boom faltered and collapsed.[21] One assessment of the failure points out that heavy reliance on expensive industrial inputs and the dependence of high-yield crops on massive irrigation were grossly unsuited to the physical and social realities of African agriculture. Given the strategic involvement of Western chemical and fossil fuel corporations—DuPont, Dow, Monsanto, BASF, and Exxon—in promoting the industrial system and providing its necessary fertilizer and pesticides, some question whether the primary goal of the Green Revolution was to provide lucrative new markets for US farm inputs rather than to ensure global food security.[22]

20. Ron Kroese, "Industrial Agriculture's War Against Nature," in *The Fatal Harvest Reader: The Tragedy of Industrial Agriculture*, ed. Andrew Kimbrell (Sausalito, CA: Foundation for Deep Ecology in collaboration with Island Press, 2002), 92–105.

21. Roberts, *The End of Food*, 152. At this point, Asian yields continued upward, a trend that would reverse itself in more recent years.

22. Ibid., 153.

We recall, at this point, that the intent of the industrial agricultural system as envisaged by American businessmen in the 1940s was to replace small farmers by deliberately shifting the production of food to large agricultural "fiefdoms" owned by corporations. Earl Butz, US Secretary of Agriculture in the 1970s, spoke this threat to farmers, "Get big, or get out!"[23] The dictum was not intended for US farmers alone. Vandana Shiva recounts the plight of farmers in India, describing the attitude expressed by Butz as a global "war against small farmers," robbing them of their right to livelihood, their dignity as knowledgeable producers and ultimately their right to life.[24] In India, some thirty thousand small farmers who lost their land and their freedom to farm have committed suicide.[25] This is a tragic situation stemming from the indebtedness suffered by farmers because of the steep costs of agricultural inputs and the falling prices of agricultural produce. A study carried out by the Research Foundation for Science, Technology and Ecology shows that "due to falling farm prices, Indian peasants are losing $26 billion annually."[26] As Shiva comments, "The word suicide obscures the social cause of this act."[27] Instead, it represents a cry for a more just system that enables small farmers to provide for their families and live with dignity.

The effects of the industrial food system have been destructive both for small farmers and for the food itself. Physically, food is highly unsuited to the mass production and distribution techniques of industrial farming. Hence, agribusiness corporations have had to

23. Hauter, *Foodopoloy*, 23. See also Darryl Benjamin, *Farm to Table* (White River Junction, VT: Chelsea Green Publishing, 2016).

24. See Vandana Shiva, "Living Cultures," in *Earth Democracy* (Berkeley, CA: North Atlantic Books, 2005), 107–12.

25. See Vandana Shiva, *Seeds of Suicide: The Ecological and Human Costs of Globalization of Agriculture* (New Deli, India: Research Foundation for Science, Technology and Ecology, 2000), 64–110.

26. Shiva, "Living Cultures," 109.

27. Ibid.

reengineer plants and livestock to make them more readily harvested and processed.[28] Paul Roberts points out that the attributes of food that the current system values—mass producibility, cheapness, uniformity of size and shape, and year-round availability—do not support the health of people eating the food, the culture in which it is consumed, the environment in which it is produced, or, most especially, the quality of the food itself.[29] Food priorities such as taste, nutrition, variety, wholeness, and ripeness have been sacrificed to the economic goals of increased productivity, efficiency, and ultimately corporate profit.

Industrial Farming and Manufactured Foods

Paralleling agribusiness's impact on growing food is the emergence of manufactured, "processed foods" that increasingly dominate food sales in developed countries and, to some extent, in developing countries as well. As industrial farming forced more and more people out of rural areas and into crowded cities, these urban dwellers, many of whom worked factory jobs, were left with no means to grow their own food and with little time to even prepare it. Hence the need for foods that were readily available, easily prepared, and quickly eaten. Companies that could produce such prepared foods burgeoned, introducing industrial techniques that could meet these requirements with speed and efficiency: "assembly lines, canning and bottling technologies, mechanical refrigeration and a growing network of rail, trucking, and shipping lines" that allowed food to be "processed *en masse*, quickly, cheaply, and with reasonably consistent quality."[30]

One of the earliest producers of "prepared" foods was Henri Nestlé, a chemist and fertilizer manufacturer, who in the Swiss town of Vevey in the early 1860s "mixed wheat meal, sugar, and 'wholesome

28. Roberts, *The End of Food*, xiv.
29. Ibid.
30. Ibid., 32.

cow's milk' to make *kindermehl* or 'infant cereal,' which he marketed to working-class Swiss mothers whose new factory jobs prevented them from nursing their babies." Today, the corporation that Nestlé founded in 1867 is the world's largest maker of food and beverages, with annual sales globally of $71 billion.[31]

Once "prepared foods" were released on the market, demand for them grew. Over time, companies like Nestlé, General Foods, Kellogg, and Heinz developed "thousands of new products, many marketed as time-saving alternatives to home cooking."[32] Indeed, what was being sold to consumers was not only processed food but, more important, convenience. As early as 1937, Kraft Foods pitched its Macaroni and Cheese Dinner with the slogan "Make a meal for four in nine minutes."

By the 1990s, the billions of food items produced by the Nestlé corporation each year required some fifteen thousand square miles of farmland and pastureland to yield the "raw materials": coffee, cocoa, sugar, milk, oil, wheat, corn, salt, and others. Given the magnitude of Nestlé's purchases of these basic ingredients, the corporation wields considerable power over the whole chain of suppliers who provide them. Hence, the company can bargain down the prices paid to farmers and can outsource the growing of foods used in its processed products to "parts of the world where they can be most cheaply produced."[33]

The production of processed foods is predicated on values of efficiency and convenience, qualities welcomed in the United States as more and more women were drawn out of the home and into the workforce. Moving beyond efficiency and convenience, food companies have developed strategies of "value adding," by which natural food products are transformed into novel and adventuresome new

31. Ibid., 30, 32. What follows is taken from 29–35.

32. Ibid., 33.

33. Ibid., 34. This power extends to dictating how grocery stores will shelve, market, and price their products, thus making Nestlé and other giant food corporations "the rulers of a supply chain that stretched from farmers to consumers."

commodities, attractive in every way to consumers—taste, fragrance, color, shape, and clever packaging—and marketed with giant advertising campaigns that are essential to the success of their sale. These value-added products have been swelling the coffers of food corporations for decades, bringing in profits far beyond what natural food products could have secured.

Ironically, one reason for the invention of this "value-adding" process was a glut of food products on the market, which lowered prices and created deep losses for farmers and for food companies. In the 1930s, coffee prices fell so low in Brazil that farmers were actually burning the beans to fuel locomotives. Nestlé capitalized on this cheap commodity to create its instant coffee, which sold at much higher prices than the raw beans themselves. Prior to this, consumers had not clamored for an instant version of their morning cup of coffee! But Nestlé seized the opportunity to "add value" and novelty to a failing market that could capture the imagination of susceptible customers. While coffee drinkers were intrigued and happy with the innovation, the initiative created an inverse relationship between the plummeting profits of farmers and the rising earnings of the food industry, a relationship that has only increased over time. Today, about twenty cents of every dollar spent on processed food goes to pay for the promotions, celebrity endorsements, clever packaging, event sponsorship, coupons, and massive advertising of the product.[34] And, the greater the advertising, the greater the sales.

What is masked in processed foods, tailored as they are to the trendy tastes of consumers and often filled with the addicting foodstuffs of sugar, fat, and salt that keep the eaters eating, is that the foods themselves have been reengineered, often significantly changing their basic composition, to enable them to both tolerate the process and emerge with a longer shelf life than natural foods.[35]

34. Ibid., 38.
35. Ibid., 45.

Indeed, the contingencies of processing foods have "required the development of a whole new job description—the food engineer— to actually change the molecular structure of the food."[36] Vegetable oils, for example, can be thickened and preserved by injecting them with hydrogen atoms, flours and powders are kept from lumping with anticaking agents, and moist food can be kept from drying out with an injection of glycerin or sorbital.[37] Color, flavor, and, to some extent, the nutrition of the food itself that is lost in the necessary heating process can be boosted synthetically, often with chemical substitutes. Lost vitamins can be replaced synthetically, creating such items as "fortified" breakfast cereals. The taste of vanilla can be infused or heightened with the addition of a single synthetic compound—4-hydroxy-3-methoxybenzaldehyde, better known as "vanillin"—a common ingredient in vanilla ice creams sold today in the American market. What consumers may miss, however, is that vanillin is a substance "synthesized from paper-manufacturing residues," used by food processers because it is much cheaper than its natural counterpart, vanilla. Indeed, with the right chemical additives, the global "flavor industry" can now synthetically duplicate nearly any taste experience imaginable, an effort that brings them profits of nearly $18 billion a year. One novel way of preserving desired flavors in factory produced cookies is to spray the flavoring on after baking them. Moreover, in contrast to traditional foods, which can only be made from specific ingredients—an apple pie requires apples, butter, sugar, flour, salt, and spices and must be baked in an oven—the "reengineered version" of this American favorite has no such requirements. It can be created synthetically with whatever ingredients and processes give consumers a relatively similar experience of the original taste and texture, no matter what

---

36. Ibid., what follows is from this source, 45–47.

37. Ibid., 45. Roberts also notes that diacetyl became "butter" in microwave popcorn production, until "it was taken off the market in mid-2007 as a possible cause of lung disease." Ibid., 47.

ingredient substitution or preparation process might be used.[38] As Roberts comments, as long as a company's "brand remains strong and the products themselves continue to deliver their explicit and implicit promise of taste, texture, convenience, status, health, purity, cost or any of a myriad of 'added values,' companies are free to produce those products in the most economic and profitable way possible," with or without actual food.[39]

Eating in the Industrial Food System

With corporate agriculture and the processed food industry came significant transformations in what, when, where, and with whom people eat. Food companies are well aware that people's relationship with food has changed dramatically over the past decades and are happy to exploit these changes.[40] Time and speed are critical factors. Roberts notes that when Nestlé was founded in 1867, most of the world's calories were processed at home or in local shops, with the average household spending half its labor hours preparing meals. Today in developed countries like the United States, most families have cut that time drastically by outsourcing the preparation and cooking tasks to companies like Kraft, Unilever, Tyson, Nestlé, Kellogg, or Danone and thousands of others.[41]

Food companies have calculated that an average family devotes some thirty minutes a day to cooking, down from an hour in 1970, and they project that it will fall precipitously to some five to fifteen minutes by 2030.[42] One study asserts that "sandwiches are now the most commonly served dinner entrée, ahead of beef and chicken

---

38. Ibid., 47. For an extensive exploration of processed foods and their impact on how and what people eat, see ibid., 29–56.

39. Ibid., 48.

40. Ibid., 42.

41. Ibid., 30.

42. Ibid., 43.

entrées."[43] Skipping meals and eating on the go, patterns that mark the lives of many in the United States, have provided one more opportunity for lucrative food sales, this time of "snack food." Today, snacking accounts for nearly half of all eating occasions. Industry produced snacks, we note, are one of the most highly processed food sources available and bring corporations some of their highest profit margins.[44]

What, then, of meals, of those foundational social and spiritual practices with which we began this volume? Lisa Graham McMinn in her book *To the Table* describes the significant discrepancy that exists between long-standing affirmations of the value of meals in American culture and the reality of how and when they take place. She notes, for example, that while most families portrayed on TV seem to value eating together, the commercials that punctuate the programs reflect the reality that "we are mostly a culture that eats fast food—that is, food on the run or food-for-fuel."[45] While Americans seem to long for something like family dinners, many hold to a firmly entrenched belief that work, sports, drama, music, and other civic- or church-related activities are far more self-fulfilling and personally enriching than a "family-cooked dinner enjoyed at leisure with the entire family."[46] Moreover, when families do sit down to a meal with some regularity, members engage each other much less than they once did. Television is often an accompaniment to the meal—at times the main focus—and family members may engage with cell phones or other devices by which to text friends, answer email, or follow a sports events.

The losses that flow from these evolving practices of meal fellowship are many. Research has demonstrated that in families who eat

43. Ibid.

44. Ibid., 44.

45. Lisa Graham McMinn, *To the Table: A Spirituality of Food, Farming, and Community* (Grand Rapids, MI: Brazos Press, 2016), 19.

46. Ibid.

together, children do better both socially and academically and are less likely to abuse alcohol or drugs or to suffer depression.[47] Family members tend to be physically and socially healthier. But perhaps most important, eating together can enable participants to experience that "they belong to something bigger than their isolated selves."[48] It is a source of communion, of that felt knowledge that we are part of a community that makes a claim on our lives and our choices, while at the same time affirming who we are. It can underscore a felt sense that "these are my people, and I belong here."[49] The gift given and received in shared meals goes beyond what most polls and research studies reveal, namely, a sense of co-responsibility for each other's lives and well-being. Meals can offer "scaffolding," a support that can help participants negotiate the trials of living in a consumer-driven, postmodern, postindustrial, individualistic culture.[50] "Eating with others," McMinn notes, offers a daily opportunity "to engage ideas, troubleshoot conflicts, encourage, inspire, correct, love and be loved—both in body and soul."[51]

In the next two chapters we will explore in more depth the severe and multidimensional crisis that marks the industrial food system today (chaps. 5 and 6) and then propose a vision of what a more promising food and agriculture culture might look like in the future (chap. 7).

47. Ibid., 20.

48. Ibid., 21.

49. Rachael M. Stone, *Eat with Joy: Redeeming God's Gift of Food* (Downers Grove, IL: InterVarsity, 2013), 76, as quoted in McMinn, *To the Table*, 21.

50. McMinn, *To the Table*, 21.

51. Ibid.

Questions for Reflection

1) What new insights have you gained about the origins, ideals, and practices of corporate agriculture, and how do they affect your relationship with food?

2) How do speed, efficiency, novelty, and your many commitments affect your choices of what to eat?

3) With whom do you eat on a regular basis? How does this experience shape your sense of belonging in the world and your purpose in life?

chapter five

Industrial Agriculture Today
The Ecological Cost

In the first decades of the twenty-first century, the corporate industrial food system is in crisis. What was once described as the Green Revolution is now recognized as neither green nor a revolution.[1] Strategies implemented through the mid- and late twentieth century that produced high yields and seemed able to feed an ever-expanding world population are now clearly unsustainable.[2] Moreover, they are a major contributor to ecological destruction and looming climate chaos, responsible for the destruction of some 75 percent of the world's soil, water, and biodiversity and 40 percent of the climate distress.[3] The cost of these breakdowns has been severe, both to Earth's ecological systems and to human health and well-being. This chapter will address

1. Vandana Shiva, Keynote Address (Soil Not Oil Conference, Richmond, CA, September 4, 2015).

2. United Nations Food and Agriculture Organization, "UN Agencies Call for an End to Industrial Agriculture & Food System," Science in Society Archive (September 17, 2013), accessed September 12, 2016, http://www.i-sis.org.uk/Paradigm_Shift_Urgently_Needed_in_Agriculture.php.

3. Vandana Shiva, *Who Really Feeds the World* (Berkeley, CA: North Atlantic Books, 2016), 126.

two key dimensions of a failed food system's cost to Earth: the betrayal of seeds and the destruction of soils. Chapter 6 will then address two aspects of how the crises affect human life: the tragedy of hunger and the suffering of farm laborers.

But first, we turn to the larger picture, offering an overview of six of the intersecting crises that mark industrial agriculture today and that must be addressed if Earth's peoples and creatures are to be nourished into the future.

Crop yields, a critical factor for the future of human nourishment, have been in decline since the late 1980s. Despite the seeming abundance that meets a shopper in major grocery stores across the United States, food crops are in serious decline. Global grain harvests, which produced 285 kilograms per person in 1961, peaked at 376 kilograms in 1986 but have been falling ever since, even as population increases.[4] A major contributor to this decline is the depletion of soils due to intensive crop growth and the use of synthetic fertilizers that destroy the natural biology of fertile soil. Today, greater and greater amounts of nitrogen fertilizer must be applied to counteract soil degradation and erosion, and increasing amounts of pesticides must be sprayed to overcome newly developed resistances by pests. Yet despite these measures, crop yields continue to diminish.

Second, the ecological costs of the corporate system—damage to water, climate, and soil—have never been factored into the cost of food and are seldom acknowledged. In addition to direct pollution of water and soil, chemical runoff from agricultural practices travels downstream, creating large "dead zones" in major waterways where aquatic life is suffocated.[5] Moreover, critics of the system note that

---

4. Bill McKibben, *Eaarth: Making a Life on a Tough New Planet* (New York: St. Martin's Griffin, 2011), 153–54.

5. According to Jay Tomczak, "crops only absorb about half the nitrogen they are exposed to, much of the rest runs off the fields with water flow, saturating the environment and polluting aquatic ecosystems." See "Implications of Fossil Fuel Dependence for the Food System," Resilience (June 11, 2006), accessed June 21, 2019,

"chronic human-induced imbalances in major biological systems" are even more serious than pollution and are producing nonreversible destruction of the ecosystems on which growing food ultimately depends.[6]

Third, human hunger in the United States and worldwide continues to rise at an alarming rate. Nevertheless, food crops such as corn and soybeans that could help address this crisis are being sold and traded as biofuels or livestock feed, both lucrative commodities.[7] The value of grain as fuel has become far more financially profitable than its value as food.[8] Lester R. Brown comments that this "epic competition between cars and people for the grain supply is leading to a political and moral issue of unprecedented dimension."[9]

Indeed, all food, processed or otherwise, is treated by agribusiness as a "commodity." Within the last decades, food commodities have become "financialized," seen as investments that can be traded, bought, and sold for more than the cost to plant and harvest them. "The higher the price, the better the investment," notes journalist

www.resilience.org/stories/2006-06-11/implications-fossil-fuel-dependence-food-system.

6. See E. Matthews and A. Hammond, "Critical Consumption Trends and Implications Degrading Earth's Ecosystems," World Resources Institute, 1999. Accessed June 1, 2019. www.wri.org/publications/critical-consumption-trends-and-implications.

7. Lester R. Brown notes that there is an insatiable demand for crop-based automotive fuels. Yet even if the entire US grain harvest were dedicated to supplying fuel for cars, it would meet at most 18 percent of automotive fuel needs. "The grain required to fill a 25 gallon SUV tank with ethanol could feed one person for a year." See Lester R. Brown, "Could Food Shortages Bring Down Civilization?" *Scientific American* (May 2009): 53.

8. Ibid. Brown comments that "this double demand is leading to an epic competition between cars and people for the grain supply, and to a political and moral issue of unprecedented dimensions. The U.S., in a misguided effort to reduce its dependence on foreign oil by substituting grain-based fuels, is generating global food insecurity on a scale not seen before."

9. Ibid.

Frederick Kaufman. "The better the investment, the more costly the food. And those who cannot pay the price, pay with hunger."[10]

Fourth, the entire system of industrial agriculture is highly dependent on fossil fuels, especially oil and natural gas.[11] Some 1,500 liters of oil equivalents are needed to feed each American per year.[12] The current decline in availability of fossil fuels and the necessary cessation of their use due to climate change are in stark contrast to the cheap, abundant supplies that were available in the mid-twentieth century.[13] Perhaps the most vulnerable part of the current agricultural system vis-à-vis fossil fuels lies in its dependence on an elaborate transportation system for getting food to global markets. Without such transportation, the current food system would fail.[14] It is estimated that the ingredients for an average American meal travel some 1,500 miles from farm to table.

Fifth, climate change is seriously affecting the world's ability to feed itself. Hotter temperatures are diminishing crop yields, and excess CO_2 in the atmosphere is threatening the quality of foods grown.[15] Bill McKibben notes that wheat grown under the levels of

---

10. Frederick Kaufman, *Bet the Farm: How Food Stopped Being Food* (Hoboken, NJ: John Wiley and Sons, 2012), 37. The author notes that, in 2008, farmers produced more grain than they had ever grown before, enough to feed twice the global population. That same year, for the first time in history, a billion people went hungry and the price of the world's most basic foods doubled, then doubled again.

11. The system is "dependent on fossil fuels for powering irrigation pumps, petroleum-based pesticides and herbicides, mechanization for both crop production and food processing, fertilizer production, maintenance of animal operations, crop storage and drying, and for the transportation of farm inputs and outputs." Tomczak, "Implications of Fossil Fuel Dependence."

12. Ibid.

13. The creation of synthetic nitrogen fertilizer, for example, is extremely energy intensive, relying on large amounts of natural gas.

14. Tomczak, "Implications of Fossil Fuel Dependence." Furthermore, "Data from 1977 show that 2,892 million gallons of diesel fuel and 411 million gallons of gasoline were consumed for the purpose" of transporting farm inputs and outputs.

15. McKibben, *Eaarth*, 154. What follows is taken from this source.

CO_2 expected by midcentury will contain markedly less protein and iron and 14 percent more lead. Moreover, the stripping of rain forests to create cheap agricultural land, especially in the Amazon, is increasing the carbon in the atmosphere and contributing to a hotter, drier planet.

Sixth, of all the goals of the agribusiness system projected by its conceivers in the 1940s, what has been most successful is the corporate control of all facets of food production. Today, a handful of massive monopolies control the food system from seeds to dinner plates.[16] Twenty food corporations—among them Pepsi, Nestlé, Kraft, Tyson, General Mills, ConAgra, and Cargill—produce most of the food eaten by Americans, even organic brands.[17] Four large chains—Walmart, Kroger, Costco, and Target—control more than half of grocery store sales, while "one company dominates the organic grocery industry, and one distribution company has a stranglehold on getting organic products into communities around the country."[18] Given the economic power, prestige, and profit of these corporations, it is unlikely that positive changes in the food system will flow from their leadership.

In 2013, several United Nations agencies, including the Food and Agriculture Organization (FAO), declared the globalized system of industrial farming to be unsustainable and urged that it be replaced

---

16. Wenonah Hauter, *Foodopoly: The Battle over the Future of Food and Farming in America* (New York: The New Press, 2012), 2.

17. Ibid., 3. See pp. 42–43 for full list of corporations and list of brands controlled by each.

18. Ibid., 3, 107–15. Hauter notes that Whole Foods, after aggressively acquiring all its competitors, has dominated the organic grocery industry for several years. Its strategy has been to "sell conventional foods under the false illusion that they are better than products sold at conventional grocery stores." Yet most of its products are neither healthier nor even organic, and their meats are raised by standards that are clearly welfare-negative. In 2017, Whole Foods was purchased by Amazon for $13.7 billion. How this acquisition will affect market strategies is yet to be seen. "Amazon plans in terms of decades," notes one commentator.

by regionally based, organic agriculture.[19] Again in 2015, the Sustainable Development Goals adopted by the United Nations included a threefold commitment to "sustainable food production systems and resilient agricultural practices . . . equal access to land, technology and markets [and] . . . international cooperation on investments in infrastructure and technology to boost agricultural productivity."[20] Accomplishing these objectives depends on the essential cooperation of national governments, as well as changes in the policies of the international lending organizations, the World Bank, and the International Monetary Fund.

What is most lost in the crises that engulf the industrial food system today is the recognition that food is a gift, given from the depths of divine love and sourced by the cosmic generosity of the universe; that food is relationship, an invitation to participate in the relationships that mark our identity as members of a global community of life: relationships with the Earth, with each other, with the poor and suffering of the world, and with the divine Source of all being. Rebuilding the food system, as we will explore in chapter 7, is thus a holy endeavor, a true *leitorgia*.[21] We begin this sacred work by coming to better awareness of the nature of seeds and soil—

19. United Nations Food and Agriculture Organization, "End to Industrial Agriculture." Several UN agencies have jointly stated that food security, climate change, poverty, and gender inequality can all be addressed by a radical change from the current industrial agricultural and globalized food system to a conglomerate of small, biodiverse, ecological farms around the world and a localized food system that promotes consumption of local/regional produce.

20. This commitment is part of Goal 2, to End Hunger. Accessed June 1, 2019. www.un.org/sustainabledevelopment/sustainable-dvelopment-goals/.

21. The term *leitorgia*, translated today as "liturgy," was used by ecclesiastical writers of antiquity to refer to the cultic service of God but also with reference to the term's broader meanings, such as spiritual sacrifice or charitable works. The term was more widely used to refer to a "public service," a political, religious, or technical function "that was exercised in the interests of the people as a whole." This interplay of meanings has direct relevance to rejuvenating the food system.

two of the foundational elements in Earth's food-producing process—and of the severe threats to their fruitfulness for future generations. Each section concludes with a short reflection on its connection with Eucharist.

Seeds: Nature's Miracle Betrayed

Seed is the first link in the food chain,
and the repository of life's future evolution. . . .
Every seed is an embodiment of millennia of nature's evolution
and centuries of farmers' breeding.[22]

Seeds are sacred, indeed one of Earth's most precious gifts. Seeds hold the entire cycle of life, its beginning and its end. They carry the collective memory of their species, including patterns of growth and adaptation.[23] Seeds manifest nature's intelligence, carrying within them the wisdom and life force of Earth itself.[24] Seeds are evolutionary wonders, having coevolved with the human community over the ages, while the plants they bear provide the food we eat, the fibers we weave, the shelters we build, and the medicines that support our health. Seeds carry the miracle of life from one generation to the next, ensure the biodiversity of plant species, and are key to the regenerative capacity of Earth. Whatever happens to seeds affects the whole web of life.[25]

See A. G. Martimort, *The Church at Prayer: Principles of the Liturgy*, vol. 1 (Collegeville, MN: Liturgical Press, 1989), 8–9.

22. Vandana Shiva, *Who Really Feeds the World? The Failures of Agribusiness and the Promise of Agroecology* (Berkeley, CA: New Atlantic Books, 2016), 67, 70.

23. Acharya David Frawley, "The Power and Importance of the Seed: The Heritage of Nature's Intelligence," in *Sacred Seed* (Point Reyes, CA: The Golden Sufi Center, 2014), 63.

24. Ibid., 64.

25. Vandana Shiva, "Introduction," in *Sacred Seed*, 1.

Yet today, corporate control of seeds and the manipulation of their genetic makeup are altering our relationships with Earth, with its implicit drive toward biodiversity, and indeed with the very cycle of life that seeds embody. This is happening through processes of hybridization of seeds, often to create high-yielding varieties (HYVs), through their genetic modification using recombinant DNA technology,[26] through patenting of these altered seeds by corporations who claim ownership of them as intellectual property, and through the consolidation of seed companies under the ownership of a few agrochemical corporations.[27] In each case, Earth's natural proclivity to produce life and biodiversity is thwarted; the food produced is judged by many to be dangerous to human health and to Earth herself; and farmers, who are forced to pay high prices year after year to purchase new seed, become enslaved to the profit motives of the corporations.

Altering Seeds for Profit

Hybrid and HYV seeds were introduced during the "Green Revolution" along with fossil-fuel fertilizers and chemical pesticides, all of which farmers had to purchase from corporate sources.[28] Farmers were pressured by agribusiness representatives to purchase hybrid seeds, based on claims that these varieties would increase the yield of food crops. Indeed, the yield was greater, but only under condi-

26. Recombinant DNA techniques introduce genes from an unrelated organism into the cells of a plant or introduces a plant cancer called agrobacterium to infect the plant. In either case, an antibiotic-resistant gene must be introduced as well to separate cells that received the new gene from others. Shiva, *Who Really Feeds*, 69.

27. See Shiva, *Who Really Feeds*, 67–83.

28. Hybrid seeds, created by crossing "parents" from two plant varieties to produce a more productive first generation of offspring, are unreliable beyond the first year, since they do not produce seed that is true to type. See Clare Hope Cummings, *Uncertain Peril: Genetic Engineering and the Future of Seeds* (Boston: Beacon Press, 2008), 7.

tions of intensive watering, chemical fertilizer, and a purchase of new seeds a year later, since hybrid seeds become unstable and unpredictable in the second generation.[29] Once in use, hybrid seeds quickly replaced the local varieties that had been saved and shared by farmers for countless generations, seeds that represented both a local diversity of foods, as well as the heritage of people's ancestors. Numerous varieties of edible plants were replaced by a few internationally sold strains, contributing to a massive loss of biodiversity, as well as the loss of collective memory of local communities. In Malawi, for example, indigenous strains of corn had evolved over centuries and had adapted to the climate and soil of the country. Known and valued as the "corn of our ancestors," the seeds from these local strains of corn have now been lost, replaced by a single, nonindigenous variety sold by corporate seed companies.

More recently, the genetic modification of seeds by large biotech corporations has raised alarm from biologists, ecologists, and consumers alike. Genetic modification of seeds has two aims: either to make the seed/plant impervious to massively sprayed herbicides (such as Monsanto's "Roundup") or to serve as an internal pesticide living within the seed/plant host that can kill attacking insects. The process by which a seed's genes are modified remains both primitive and violent. A gene from a different species of living being (plant, animal, or human) is shot with a gene gun into the receiving seed and, through the use of a virus, inserts itself into the genetic structure of the seed.[30] These altered seeds are then patented as intellectual property belonging to the agrochemical company who performed the modification, and royalties are charged of farmers who use them.

29. Ibid.

30. Vandana Shiva, "The Rights of Mother Earth" (lecture, Berkeley, CA, October 20, 2014). See also Jeffrey M. Smith, *Seeds of Deception: Exposing Industry and Government Lies about the Safety of Genetically Engineered Foods You're Eating* (Fairfield, IA: Yes! Books, 2003); Jeffrey M. Smith, *Genetic Roulette* (Fairfield, IA: Yes! Books, 2007).

Creation Betrayed

Critics of this system state that while the engineering of seeds might appear to be a technological success story, it is more rightly an act of "creation betrayed."[31] Craig Holdrege and Steve Talbott suggest that the long-standing resistance of plants to what seems like minor genetic variation ought to give us pause. "Can we claim to be acting responsibly when we overpower the plant, coercing a performance from it before we understand the reasons for its natural reticence? . . . Organisms are not mechanisms that can be altered in a clear-cut, determinate manner. The fact is that we simply don't know what we're doing when we manipulate them as if they were such mechanisms."[32] Norman Wirzba adds that such modification is a "refusal to attend to and respect what is there."[33] The seed and the food it produces are no longer received as gifts to be respected and cared for but are instead manipulated for an alien aim, and "the integrity, even sanctity, of the other"—in this case the seed—is denied.[34]

An even more disturbing use of genetic engineering and patenting is the creation of terminator seeds: altered seeds that will not reproduce in the next generation but kill their own offspring.[35] Plants that spring from such seeds grow normally until the crop is almost mature; then a lethal toxin is produced within the new seed embryo that destroys it by making it sterile.[36] Hence, farmers are unable to

---

31. Norman Wirzba, *Food and Faith* (New York: Cambridge University Press, 2011), 176.

32. Craig Holdrege and Steve Talbott, *Beyond Biotechnology: The Barren Promise of Genetic Engineering*, (Lexington: University Press of Kentucky, 2008), 25.

33. Wirzba, *Food and Faith*, 176.

34. Ibid.

35. See Shiva, *Who Really Feeds*, 69.

36. Martha L. Crouch, "How the Terminator Terminates: An Explanation for the Non-Scientific of Remarkable Patent for Killing Second Generation Seeds of Crop Plants," Edmonds Institute Occasional Paper, May 20, 2009, 1–2. See also Shiva, *Who Really Feeds*, 69. Shiva notes that the chemical company Monsanto owns the patent on terminator technology, together with the US Department of Agriculture.

save and share seeds each year but must purchase new ones from corporate "producers" over and again. More profound, the life cycle has been severely broken, interrupted by those whose motives seem only for profit, prestige, and control.[37]

How did these innovations come about, and how can the implications for the health and integrity of human and planetary life be assessed? Like industrial agriculture itself, the genetic modification of seeds and their plant offspring began with a small group of people who came to have uncommon influence on the current evolution of food and nutrition. Gathered in Pacific Grove, California, in the early 1970s, a cadre of scientists met to discuss safety concerns about emerging recombinant DNA technology. Their plan was to develop voluntary controls that would ensure that scientists, rather than government or the public, would maintain the oversight of its development.[38] By 1975, "serious safety issues were emerging, including the possibility of uncontrolled experiments, mutant viruses, new pathogens, and threats to human health."[39] A slightly larger group of engaged scientists met to wrestle with these possibilities. Public safety was not their primary concern, notes Claire Hope Cummings; rather, they were determined to prevent what could be an acrimonious public debate over the risks of genetic engineering.[40] Reasoning that they could devise a technological fix for any problems that might emerge, they unanimously determined to self-regulate future research, preserving for "themselves the exclusive right to define,

---

37. The biotech industry's engagement in these practices is essentially unregulated. For more information on genetic modification of seeds, see Hauter, *Foodopoly*, 227–76; Vandana Shiva, *Seeds of Suicide* (New Delhi: Navdanya, 2006), 118–22, and Shiva, *Who Really Feeds*, 67–83.

38. See Cummings, *Uncertain Peril,* xii–xiv. Material in this paragraph is taken primarily from this source.

39. Ibid.

40. Ibid., xiii. Cummings relies here on the work of science historian Susan Wright, *Molecular Politics: Developing American and British Regulatory Policy for Genetic Engineering, 1972–1982* (Chicago: University of Chicago Press, 1994).

regulate and benefit from genetic engineering."[41] Since that time, the US government has simply acceded to this policy, and, much to the detriment of our democratic process, there has "never been a public debate about the risks and benefits of this revolutionary technology."[42]

Genetic engineering was not a scientific discovery but a strategy introduced to manipulate life for the benefit of a few. It provided those who adopted it a previously unimagined mastery over both society and nature.[43] Yet to establish genetically modified organisms (GMOs) in the marketplace, the agrochemical industry had to dismantle US regulatory requirements that might stand in the way. In 1992, with George H. W. Bush as president, a long-standing interaction between the Monsanto Company and government leaders in Washington bore fruit in a policy of complete deregulation of GMO foods. Announced by Vice President Dan Quale, the policy would "speed up and simplify the process of bringing better agricultural products, developed through biotech, to consumers, food processors and farmers" without being hampered by unnecessary regulation.[44] The basis of such a policy was the claim, first made by the biotechnology industry itself and with no scientific basis, that GMO products are "substantially equivalent" to their corresponding natural foods; therefore, they needed no regulation, safety testing, or special labels. Thus, by simply declaring that GMO foods were the same as their natural counterparts, the biotechnology industry, with the approval of the US government, created a blanket exemption for all GMO products from all biochemical or toxicological testing and created a barrier to any further research into possible risks of eating

41. Cummings, *Uncertain Peril*, xiii.

42. Ibid.

43. Ibid., 8–9.

44. Smith, *Seeds of Deception*, 130. Subsequent to this announcement, the US Department of Agriculture (USDA), the Environmental Protection Agency (EPA), and the Food and Drug Administration (FDA) simply followed suit.

genetically altered food.[45] It is important to note that the concept of substantial equivalence was established in 1993, well before many of the most alarming risk concerns about GMO products had come to light. Today some 90 percent of Americans want labels on genetically engineered foods, yet Monsanto has spent millions of dollars to defeat state initiatives for such labeling laws.[46]

This lack of regulation means that corporations, whose goal is to make money and not moral decisions, are determining how potentially dangerous technologies are used.[47] To date, no significant testing of foods produced by transgenic seeds has occurred, despite the fact the 80 percent of processed foods available in US grocery markets contain GMOs.

Can Life Forms Be Patented?

Claiming intellectual property rights for transgenic seeds is likewise a betrayal of traditional understandings of copyright laws. Before 1995, countries had systems not only of rewarding inventiveness and creativity but also for deciding "the limits of rewarding creativity—what was the common property of the people and what could, for a short time, be treated as an exclusive right. At no point before 1995 did intellectual property cover the very life forms of this planet."[48] Yet from that date to the present, the Agreement on Trade-Related Aspects of Intellectual Property Rights (TRIPS),

---

45. Eric Millstone, "Beyond 'Substantial Equivalence,'" *Nature* (October 7, 1999).

46. Statistic taken from "Consumers Want Mandatory Labeling for GMO Foods," *Consumer Reports*, (December 2, 2015), accessed June 21, 2019, http://www.consumerreports.org/food-safety/consumers-want-mandatory-labeling-for-gmo-foods/.

47. Cummings, *Uncertain Peril*, 19.

48. Vandana Shiva, *Earth Democracy: Justice, Sustainability, and Peace* (Berkeley, CA: New Atlantic Books, 2015), 36. See this source for extensive information on intellectual property rights, their redefinition in global trade, and the impact on human and other forms of biological life.

established by the WTO, has enabled "cells, genes, plants, sheep, and cows to be owned as intellectual property."[49] Consequently, "our relationship with the rest of the living world is no longer that of partner, but one of consumer."[50] Corporations that manipulate a single gene in the complex structure of an Earth-yielded seed are now deemed creators, with a right to patent this "new creation."[51]

In India, aromatic basmati rice has been cultivated by farmers for centuries who, through observation, experimentation, and selection, have developed some twenty-seven documented varieties that are adapted to "meet various ecological conditions, cooking needs, and tastes."[52] India now grows 650,000 tons of basmati annually. Yet in 1997, a Texas-based company, RiceTec, was "granted patent #56663484 on basmati rice lines and grains," based on twenty claims regarding this "invention" that covered the "genetic lines of basmati and includes genes from varieties developed by farmers."[53] This enabled RiceTec to collect royalties from farmers who were growing varieties that they themselves and their forefathers had developed! Four years later, a major campaign overturned most of the company's patent claims to basmati.

In the United States, numerous cases are pending in which the pollen of GMO crops being grown by large agribusiness farms has been transmitted via wind into the fields of organic farmers. Subsequently, the corporations who own the patents on these transgenic crops have sued the organic farmers for "intellectual property theft," even though they are in no way responsible for growing the contaminated crop. From the farmers' perspective, their crops have been polluted by the company's pollen.[54]

49. Shiva refers here to article 27.3 (b) of the WTO's intellectual property agreement.

50. Shiva, *Earth Democracy*, 36.

51. Ibid.

52. Ibid., 131. Material in this paragraph from this source.

53. Ibid.

54. Ibid., 84. See also Hauter, *Foodopoly*, 227–55.

Beginning in the 1980s, agrochemical companies introduced another control and income-producing strategy: buying up small seed companies, which at their height had numbered nearly seven thousand.[55] These new acquisitions were a source of both power and profit: power, in that control of seeds is a control of life and the edible resources to sustain life; and profit, because transgenic seeds, with their unique traits such as herbicide tolerance, could boost sagging sales for herbicides like Monsanto's Roundup, creating a seed-chemical "platform" with increasing profitability. Today, Monsanto owns one-fifth of the $20 million global seed market, and three corporations—Monsanto, DuPont, and Syngenta—control 44 percent of the market, with Monsanto claiming 90 percent of transgenic seeds sold worldwide.[56]

One final comment is in order. Despite claims by food corporations that transgenic seeds and GMO crops are necessary to alleviate hunger across the globe—indeed to "feed the world"—no such outcome is actually envisioned.[57] In fact, current genetically modified seeds are not intended to increase crop yield or improve food quality but only to deal with insects and invasive plants, problems brought on by the very industrial agricultural system that the corporations have produced. Hunger, on the other hand, is a "complex social, political, economic, and ecological problem that requires social, political, economic and ecological solutions, none of which can be genetically engineered."[58] Moreover, the industry's aggressive techniques overlook the needs of the developing world completely, where poverty is extensive. Forecasts that the gene revolution will

55. Paul Roberts, *The End of Food* (Boston: Houghton, Mifflin, Harcourt, 2008), 258–60. Most of these seed companies were small, family owned, and committed to supporting the variety of seeds needed for local agriculture.

56. Ibid., 260.

57. See Andrew Kimbrell, *The Fatal Harvest Reader: The Tragedy of Industrial Agriculture* (San Francisco: Foundation for Deep Ecology, 2002), 32–36.

58. Roberts, *End of Food*, 263. What follows in this paragraph is taken from this source.

bring food security to places like Africa and southern Asia are simply using problems like hunger to gain political support for transgenic technologies the industry cannot afford to offer to the hungry.

Seeds are as critical to our survival as air, soil, and water and are essential to the regenerative capacity of the planet.[59] We need their natural resilience and adaptability today, especially as temperatures rise and climate chaos becomes the reality of planetary life. "Seeds have always been our silent partners in maintaining the Earth."[60] Today, we need to reaffirm that interdependence and to reembrace the covenant between ourselves and the seeded Earth. Genetic engineering is based on the assumption that we need to "reformulate nature according to our own designs. Even if it works, this is a dead-end strategy that forces us to live within the extremely limited confines of the human imagination."[61] Rather, every seed is a promise, a hope, an invitation to move together into an emerging future of mutual respect, reciprocated care, and abundant life. The call is to become seed-savers and seed-lovers once again.

Making Connections with Eucharist

Shortly before Jesus entered into his great paschal mystery of death and resurrection, he captured what was about to take place in these words: "Unless a grain of wheat falls into the earth and dies, it remains just a single grain; but if it dies, it bears much fruit" (John 12:24). The mystery of Jesus giving life through death is celebrated each time communities gather for Eucharist. The tiny seed of wheat tells the story. Buried in Earth's darkness, the seed follows "the way" of the whole of creation: that there can be no life without death and that whatever dies enters directly into the life of the living.[62] The eucha-

---

59. Cummings, *Uncertain Peril*, xvi. Inspiration for this paragraph drawn from this source, xvi, 202–5.

60. Ibid.

61. Ibid., 202.

62. See Margaret Denton-Daly, *John: An Earth Bible Commentary* (London: T & T Clarke, 2017), 162–63.

ristic loaf we share in Jesus' name is dependent on that wheat seed for its existence. In sharing the broken loaf, we are invited to participate in the great paschal mystery by which our lives are transformed as well, to become food for others.

Soils: A Matter of Life or Death

Upon this handful of soil our survival depends.
Husband it and it will grow our food, our fuel, and our shelter
and surround us with beauty.
Abuse it and the soil will collapse and die, taking humanity with it.[63]

The thin layer of topsoil that covers the Earth's land surface was
formed over long stretches
of geological time. . . . [But] sometime within the last century, soil
erosion began to exceed new soil formation! Now, nearly a third of the
world's cropland is losing topsoil faster than new soil is forming. . . .
Soil that was formed on a geological time scale is being lost on a
human time scale.[64]

These two descriptions of soil, written seven thousand years apart, underscore one foundational truth: soil is essential to human and other forms of life on planet Earth. While seeds are required to regenerate life, soil is the medium that enables seed to become the flourishing plants we need to survive. Today, this matrix of existence, formed over vast geological eras, is in jeopardy, threatened by erosion, degradation, contamination, and desertification, primarily from the strategies of industrial agriculture. We disregard this alarming reality to our peril. Fortunately, the human community has at its disposal an ever-increasing knowledge of the dynamics of healthy, living, and fruitful soil that can assist in its restoration.

---

63. The Vedas, Sanskrit Scripture, 1500 BCE.
64. Lester B. Brown, *Full Planet, Empty Plates: A New Geopolitics of Food Security* (New York: W.W. Norton and Co., 2012), 4.

Biology of Soil

Soil biologists tell us that healthy soils[65] are one of the most diverse habitats on Earth, providing home for over one-fourth of all living species.[66] The millions of organisms found in living soils weave an intricate food web capable of maintaining soil fertility.[67] Surprisingly, more microbes live in a teaspoon of Earth's soil than people live on the planet. "Soil is literally alive with a networked complexity greater than human brain tissue."[68] These networked creatures are dynamically at work all the time, "fixing" nitrogen to make it available to plants, maintaining soil structure, protecting plant roots, nourishing each other and restoring the soil's fecundity. In the words of soil biologist Kate Scow, this dynamic interaction among organisms is "like Times Square on New Year's Eve—all the time!"[69]

Throughout the history of life on Earth, microbes have deconstructed every bit of organic matter on the planet—leaves, bones, branches—fashioning new life from the dead.[70] Today's soil fertility

65. Peter Warshall, "Tilth and Technology: The Industrial Redesign of Our Nation's Soils," in *The Fatal Harvest Reader*, 169. Numerous types of soils exist, each designed through "thousands of years of sorting silt, clay, and sand granules, of balancing chemistry, water, and life forms," states Peter Warshall. "Of the 20,000 soil types in the United States, fewer than 1,000 remain virginal."

66. *Terra Vita: Our Soil, our Commons, Our Future* (Navdanya International, 2015), 43. www.navdanyainternational.it. Accessed June 1, 2019.

67. Shiva, *Who Really Feeds*, 215–25. This section draws on this source.

68. Warshall, "Tilth and Technology," 168. Warshall states that one teaspoon of rich grassland soil might contain five billion bacteria, twenty million fungi, and one million microscopic, single-cell protists that fertilize the soil and live in symbiotic relationship with plant roots. In addition to microbes, a single meter of topsoil might also contain 1,000 each of ants, spiders, wood lice, beetles, fly and beetle larvae; 2,000 each of earthworms and large myriapods; 8000 snails and slugs; 20,000 pot worms; 40,000 springtails; 120,000 mites; and 12 million nematodes.

69. Kate Scow, professor of soil science and microbial ecology, University of California, Davis, in *Symphony of the Soil*, directed by Deborah Koons (2012), film.

70. David R. Montgomery and Anne Biklé, *The Hidden Half of Nature: The Microbial Roots of Life and Health* (New York: W.W. Norton and Co., 2016), 5. What follows is taken from this source.

has its origin in the lives of organisms that have lived and died in the soil over time. From this matter, microbes have created a matrix of decomposed organic matter known as humus, a rich, dark, and crumbly soil that is extremely porous.[71] Fifty percent of humus is solid, and fifty percent is comprised of empty space. Within these empty pockets, humus can absorb and retain air and water and can store nutrients for use by plants. Moreover, humus functions as a sponge that can retain up to 90 percent of its weight in water, whereas soil that is lacking humus is left vulnerable to drought, erosion, and nutrient deficiency.[72] Humus provides habitat and nourishment for microbes and soil creatures, which create symbiotic relationships with plant roots, mobilizing moisture and making nutrients available for their nourishment. Bacteria living in humus can break down organic matter to create a glue that binds soil particles into aggregates. When soil does not bind in this way, it becomes dust that is easily blown away by wind or washed away by water.[73]

    In one of the most astounding soil processes, bacteria engage with plant roots to create a form of nitrogen readily available for plant use. Nitrogen is essential to living plants; it is the "green" of green plants. Although nitrogen exists in the atmosphere, 70 percent of its atmospheric form cannot be absorbed by plants.[74] To remedy this situation, soil bacteria collude with plant roots. They first draw nitrogen from the air, then transfer it to plant roots, which in turn enclose the nitrogen in small nodules where, in an oxygen-free atmosphere, the nitrogen is transformed, "fixed" into a form on which plant roots can feast. In exchange, plant roots feed the bacteria with "exudates"— sugars, proteins, and carbohydrates—produced specifically to nourish them. Traditional farming methods such as intercropping and

71. Jason McKenney, "Artificial Fertility: The Environmental Cost of Industrial Fertilizers," in *The Fatal Harvest Reader*, 122.

72. Shiva, *Who Really Feeds*, 18. What follows is taken from this source.

73. Ibid., 19.

74. Ignatio Chapela, microbial biologist, University of California, Berkeley, speaking in *Symphony of Soil*, directed by Deborah Koons (2012), film.

using cover crops fostered this form of organic nitrogen production, thus obviating the need for its synthetic counterpart.

Soil not only provides 99 percent of the food humans consume but also provides numerous ecosystem services.[75] Soil is Earth's primary cleansing and recycling medium, a "living filter" through which pathogens and toxins that could foul the environment are made harmless and transformed into nutrients.[76] Soil enables the purification of all the fresh water on and in the surface of the planet. It provides resilience against floods and drought and offers habitat and nourishment for a broad range of Earth's genetic biodiversity. Soil is rightly described as the "planetary tissue of Mother Earth"; it is "the heart of the biosphere, lithosphere, atmosphere, and hydrosphere of the planet."[77]

Yet over millennia, many human communities have lost, forgotten, or suppressed their sense of reverence for soil as a living matrix of life. Soil has been redefined as dead matter and assumed to need human technological input for its fertility and resilience. It has been reduced to dirt, inert and lifeless, an empty container, only to hold externally introduced chemicals.[78] To many contemporary farmers engaged in industrial agriculture, soil is a utilitarian medium in which one can grow profitable crops, a substrate that can be improved and reengineered through chemical inputs, and a financial asset in a larger economic arrangement. Any manipulation of the soil that improves its yield and lowers the cost of growing food is considered good, despite its long-term effects on the soil's health. Yet history has demonstrated that the fate of societies and civiliza-

---

75. See, for example, "The Role of Soils in Ecosystem Processes," in *Status of the World's Soil Resources* (United Nations Food and Agriculture Organization, December 2015), 13.

76. Daniel J. Hillel, *Out of the Earth: Civilization and the Life of the Soil* (New York: The Free Press, 1991), 23–34.

77. Warshall, "Tilth and Technology," 168.

78. *Terra Vita*, 43.

tions is closely connected to how their populations treat the soil. Civilizations that ignored the health and well-being of their soil, that exploited rather than renewed its fertility, have disappeared along with the soil.[79]

Soil and Agriculture

With the triumph of the Industrial Revolution in the mid-nineteenth century came a massive migration of people from farms to cities and the inherent challenge of finding a way to grow more food with less land and labor—a process that would take on new momentum with the strategies of corporate agriculture a century later.[80] "Soil specialists" were engaged to assist in this intensification of agriculture. Assuming that soil is an inert substance needing supplementation, they worked in labs and factories to create synthetic replacements for the nitrogen, potassium, and phosphorous essential to soil fertility but jeopardized by destructive strategies of industrial farming.[81] Hence the birth of synthetic fertilizers, deemed able to maintain the soil fecundity indefinitely and to restore depleted and degraded soils.[82] Early experiments with these chemical fertilizers were considered a success, judged only by the increase in food production

79. Ibid.

80. What follows is based on Tom Philpott, "Reviving a Much-Cited, Little-read Sustainable-ag Masterpiece," *Grist* (March 2, 2007), http://grist.org/article/soil/, accessed June 25, 2019.

81. Shiva, *Who Really Feeds*, 19–20. Nitrogen is "fixed" from the atmosphere in a process that converts it to ammonium. In organic farming, crops like pulses and legumes fix nitrogen naturally from the air and contribute it to the soil. Synthetic nitrogen is produced through a chemical process that uses large amounts of fossil fuels and energy.

82. See Shiva, *Who Really Feeds*, 21.What was unaccounted for was that natural soil fertility requires not three but thirty-three elements that work in synergy to maintain soil's health and that supplementing a few elements creates an imbalance of nutrients.

they enabled without an assessment of the long-term impact on the soil itself.

Learning how to create synthetic nitrogen was lauded as a double triumph; it was a war weapon as well as a soil redeemer. Synthetic nitrogen, it was discovered, provided ammonia, an ingredient necessary for the production of highly effective explosives. During the two world wars in the twentieth century, fertilizer-making techniques were pressed into service for mass-produced explosives. But as World War II came to an end, the huge factories that had produced these weapons of war went in search of another market for their products, specifically chemical agriculture.

Synthetic fertilizer became a keystone of industrial agriculture's primary strategies of increasing crop yield and building soil fertility. When an initial increase in crop productivity did not materialize, more fertilizer was applied to stimulate growth. Synthetic fertilizers were especially necessary in maintaining large fields of monocultures such as corn and soybeans that now mark the farmlands of the Midwestern United States. Lacking the natural soil fertility created by traditional farm methods such as intercropping, growing cover crops, and allowing soil to lay fallow, these massive fields could not sustain the incessant cultivation of single crops without the help of synthetic fertilizer.

The price of this process has been twofold: the loss of living soils and large-scale pollution. Synthetic fertilizer kills many of the microbes and bacteria that are essential to soil's natural fertility.[83] Moreover, some two-thirds of the nitrogen fertilizer applied to crops is not taken up by the plants themselves; instead, it contaminates ground and surface waters with nitrate pollution. These toxic waters then wash downstream to create large dead zones in coastal waterways.[84] Gases

---

83. Tom Philpott, "New Research: Synthetic Nitrogen Destroys Soil Carbon, Undermines Soil Health," *Grist* (February 24, 2010), http://grist.org/article/2010-02-23-new-research-synthetic-nitrogen-destroys-soil-carbon-undermines/, accessed June 25, 2019. Research is further corroborated by organic farmer McKenney, "Artificial Fertility," 121–29.

84. Shiva, *Who Really Feeds*, 21.

from nitrogen fertilizer also "escape into the air as nitrous oxide, which has an atmospheric life of 166 years and is three hundred times more damaging to the atmosphere than carbon dioxide."[85] Adding to these destructive outcomes, other strategies of industrial agriculture damage soils: excessive chemical herbicides and pesticides sprayed on plants that toxify the soil and the use of heavy farm machinery that compacts the soil. In the face of these onslaughts, even the most vibrant soil is sorely compromised, if not made lifeless.

Soils for Future Generations

Soil degradation is at the center of today's planetary crises, threatening food security and exacerbating climate chaos. One-third of the world's arable land has already been lost to soil erosion.[86] An estimated thirty soccer fields of soil are lost every minute, mostly due to intensive farming.[87] At this rate, Earth's topsoil, which in the best of places is only six inches deep, could be gone in sixty years.[88] "As countries lose their topsoil, they eventually lose the capacity to feed themselves," states Lester Brown of the Earth Policy Institute. Countries such as Mongolia, Lesotho, North Korea, and Haiti already face this situation, and all of them are heavily dependent on food imports.[89] Dust storms, created by nutrient-depleted soils, are forming with increasing frequency in

85. Ibid.

86. Maria-Helena Semedo, FAO deputy director-general, at forum marking World Soil Day, 2015. See "Top Soil Could be Gone in 60 Years if Degradation Continues": https://www.huffpost.com/entry/soil-degradation-un_n_6276508 Also www.fao.org/global-soil-partnership/resources/news/details/en/c/209642.

87. Volkert Engelsman, International Federation of Organic Agriculture Movements, FAO conference in Rome, 2015. See http://www.un.org/apps/news/story .asp?NewsID=48342#.WNmWLm_yyIU. Accessed October 25, 2016.

88. Stated by a senior UN official to the *Huffington Post* (February 14, 2015), http://www.huffingtonpost.com/2014/12/505/soil-degradation-un_n_6276508 .html, accessed October 25, 2016.

89. Brown, *Full Planet*, 55–56. He notes that in Lesotho, half the children under five are stunted physically, many too weak to walk for lack of nutrients. The county's collapsing agriculture is due to loss of soil fertility.

many parts of the world. Two giant new dust bowls have recently formed, one in the Asian heartland of Northwestern China and western Mongolia and the other in the African Sahel that stretches the continent from Senegal in the west to Somalia in the east.[90] Both are massive in scale; both threaten the health of human communities and mark the last step in a complete desertification of the soil.

Perhaps the worst fallout of the massive loss of soil's natural fertility is the inability of depleted soil to sequester carbon. As climate chaos threatens the future of biological life, soil could be our best ally in mitigating its impact on the planetary community. Yet industrial agriculture, already responsible for some 40 percent of Earth's greenhouse gases, has diminished soil's ability to sequester carbon from the atmosphere.[91] With proper management and care of soil, the situation could be reversed. Soil remains the largest potential "sink" for carbon, able to contain worldwide some four thousand billion tons of carbon, twice as much as the capacity of Earth's atmosphere.[92]

Bringing soil to the "center of our consciousness and our planning is vital for the future of our society."[93] The United Nations declared 2015 the "International Year of the Soils" in order to spread awareness of the "crucial role soil plays in food security, climate change adaptation and mitigation, essential ecosystem services, poverty alleviation and sustainable development."[94] Change in the current agricultural practices will come about only through a rebirth of soil-consciousness and a recommitment to local and national policies that regenerate and protect Earth's troubled soils.

90. Ibid., 48. See Brown's extensive coverage of new dust storms worldwide.

91. Shiva, *Who Really Feeds*, 24.

92. Institute for Advanced Sustainability Studies, "Fertile Soils: Crucial in the Fight to Hunger and Climate Change" (2012), 1. Also, "First Global Soil Week Will Urge Stakeholders to Take Action for Soils: They Are Crucial for Life!" http://sdg.iisd.org/commentary/guest-articles/first-global-soil-week-will-urge-stakeholders-to-take-actions-for-soils-they-are-crucial-for-life/, accessed July 1, 2019.

93. *Terra Viva*, 42.

94. Ibid., 16.

"What we do to soil, we do to ourselves," states Vanda Shiva. "It is no accident that 'humus' and 'humans' have the same etymological root."[95] The fate of our civilization, as in the past, is bound up with how we treat the soil.

Making Connections with Eucharist

What, then, does soil have to do with eucharistic eating? Everything. Without soil, there are no shared meals, no divine-human fellowship in the breaking of bread that begins in the *humus* of the Earth and flourishes in the mutuality of a common loaf and cup.

But the mystery of soil is even deeper. Soil—teeming with relationship and pregnant with new life—is itself an image of divine fecundity, a holy presence of the Spirit of God who "fills the whole world" (Wis 1:7). *Laudato Sí* describes soil as "a caress of God," a "divine manifestation," an essential part of the "sacredness of the world" (LS 84–85). In addition, soil summons us to "hear a message," "a teaching which God wishes to hand on to us," and invites us to "see ourselves in relation to other creatures" (LS 84–85). Persons of faith who connect with the potency and beauty of soil, writes Fred Bashon, come to "view soil as a sacrament, a physical manifestation of God's presence, a channel of Divine grace."[96]

Today, more than ever, as Earth's soils become degraded to a point beyond repair and food shortages loom for communities around the globe, the call is urgent: eucharistic communities must reconnect with Earth as our mother and sister and with her soils as the matrix of all health and nourishment. Eucharistic eating invites us to rediscover Earth as God's garden, as God's table, set for all living creatures to share, and as "a merciful Presence brooding over the bent world. The answer to our hunger for more than just bread."[97]

---

95. Shiva, *Who Really Feeds*, 22–23.

96. Fred Bahnson, *Soil and Sacrament: A Spiritual Memoir of Food and Faith* (New York: Simon and Schuster, 2013), 13.

97. Ibid.

Questions for Reflection

1) Plant a seed and watch it grow. What can you learn from this process? What reflections do you have as the first tiny shoot grows bigger and develops into a green plant? How does it speak of Jesus' life given for the life of the world?

2) What can you do to protect the integrity of seeds and soils today? Are there seed banks you can explore, farmers whose rights to save seeds you can advocate for, or GMO labeling initiatives you can support? Is there a community garden where you can interact with soil and nourish its potential to give life?

3) How is your life becoming fruitful for others? Like seeds growing in soil, and like Jesus himself, how are you offering your talents and time, your knowledge and creativity, so that others may experience new life?

4) When did you last hold living soil in your hands? Plant a garden vegetable? Walk reverently on Earth's soil, as if on a magnificent carpet of love? Which of these will you do soon?

5) World Soil Day is celebrated on December 5 each year.[98] Can you celebrate this day by learning more about Earth's many soils and their contributions to ecosystems and biodiversity, as well as to animal, plant, and human life? Invite friends to celebrate with you.

---

98. See https://observances.global/world-soil-day/ or https://www.un.org/en/events/soilday/ for more information.

chapter six

Industrial Agriculture Today
The Human Cost

Food is the most basic need of humans, the very stuff of life and well-being. As we have seen in chapter 5, the strategies of corporate agriculture jeopardize this basic human and humanizing gift, essential to people's right to life and a healthful existence. Not only are soil and seeds under attack, but the manner in which food is grown, manufactured, and marketed today seriously threatens human health. Described by Vandana Shiva as a "stolen harvest,"[1] the fruitfulness of Earth and her natural proclivity to set a common table for all peoples is being hijacked by a food system focused on excessive profits for a few with little regard for the human suffering that results.

Global food dynamics have resulted in two contradictory but related problems: overconsumption and underconsumption. In affluent areas like the United States, the expanded plentitude of available foods in recent decades has shifted from being a sign of

---

1. Vandana Shiva, *Stolen Harvest: The Hijacking of the Global Food Supply* (Cambridge, MA: South End Press, 2000).

economic progress to posing a major health risk.[2] By making foods cheaper and easier to obtain and to consume, the marketing strategies of corporate agriculture have removed two of the natural restraints on overconsumption. Moreover, scientifically bred produce is less nourishing and provides fewer micronutrients to consumers. Processed foods contain excessive quantities of habit-forming fat, salt, and sweeteners, along with chemical additives that can directly affect human health. Obesity is common, serious, and costly: 93 million American adults were obese in 2015 and 2016, and the annual medical cost for treatment was $147 billion.[3] Obesity and its related conditions, including heart disease, stroke, type 2 diabetes, and certain types of cancer are among today's leading causes of preventable premature deaths.

On the other hand, underconsumption, scarcity, and hunger create an ironic parallel to the problems of overconsumption and obesity-related disease.[4] The current industrial food system continues to increase the number of hungry and malnourished people around the globe by forcing many small farmers whose land has been appropriated by corporate enterprises to migrate to other countries in search of work. Numerous Mexican farmers who have lost their livelihoods and their right to own and cultivate their land with dignity have swollen the numbers of migrants seeking entry at US borders. In the poorly paid labor they find in US fields and slaugh-

---

2. Paul Roberts, "Tipping the Scales," in *The End of Food* (Boston: Houghton, Mifflin, Harcourt, 2008), 83–92. Information that follows from that source unless otherwise noted.

3. Statistics taken from the Centers for Disease Control and Prevention, https://www.cdc.gov/obesity/data/adult.html, accessed July 1, 2019. Obesity is a complex problem, dependent on more than quantity of food consumed; genetics, physical activity, and many other factors likewise contribute.

4. We note that obesity has no single cause but is a complex health problem that has "political, medical and financial ramification." It's counterpoint, the dieting industry, is today a multibillion dollar venture. Norman Wirzba, *Food and Faith* (New York: Cambridge University Press, 2011), 105–6.

terhouses, they are further robbed of security, health, and a prosperous life for themselves and their families. Indeed, the human cost of the industrial food system—hunger, obesity, landlessness, and exploitation—is high.

In what follows, we take a deeper look at the tragedy of human hunger and the injustice that surrounds the essential labor of farmworkers. Each concludes with a short reflection on its relationship to Eucharist.

Hunger: A Human Tragedy

Until every one of us has food for life,
we cannot consider ourselves fully human.[5]

In a world dominated by corporate agriculture, hunger abounds.[6] In the United States, one child in six suffers from inadequate nutrition. India, home to two hundred million hungry people, has the largest cohort of malnourished children in the world: one million die annually for lack of food.[7] In sub-Saharan Africa, more than ten million deaths occur each year from malnutrition. Globally, over nine hundred million people (one-seventh of the world's population) are hungry and malnourished, and another billion suffer chronic and destructive deficiencies in micronutrients. It is estimated that over 21,600 persons die of starvation every day.[8] Given that food is cheaper and easier to obtain now than at any time in

---

5. Frances Moore Lappé, source unknown.

6. Unless otherwise noted, statistics in this paragraph are taken from Roberts, *End of Food*, 113–43. Statistics vary somewhat among sources, but these are corroborated by the Food and Agriculture Organization of the United Nations.

7. Vandana Shiva and Kunwar Jalees, *Why Is Every Fourth Indian Hungry? The Causes and Cures of Food Insecurity* (New Delhi: Navdanya, 2009), 2.

8. Andrew Francis, *What in God's Name Are You Eating?* (Eugene, OR: Cascade Books, 2014), 20. At this rate, 6.5 million people die of hunger each year.

human history, we have here dramatic proof that our modern food economy is failing catastrophically.[9]

"Paradoxically," writes Vandana Shiva, "half the hungry people of the world are growers of food." Globalization has "enabled massive landgrabs, displaced farmers, and added millions to the ranks of the landless."[10] In 2010, the UN Special Rapporteur on the Right to Food reported that over five hundred million people that depend on small-scale agriculture are hungry because they cannot "compete" in global markets. Their small plots of land are arid, hilly, and without irrigation, while more fertile lands have been bought up by agribusiness.[11]

India, with its 214 million hungry and malnourished people, is today the hunger capital of the world.[12] Yet there is "no reason why India should face hunger," claims Shiva. "India is blessed with the most fertile soils in the world," and its climate "is so generous that we can, in places, grow four crops a year. . . . We have the richest biodiversity of the world [and] our farmers are among the most hardworking productive people in the world."[13] The tragedy is that small farmers, "who hold the potential to provide healthy food for all, are themselves dying because of agricultural and trade policies which put corporate profits above the rights and well-being of small farmers."[14]

---

9. Ibid., 21. Since 1960, global food production has increased over 135 percent; although, since the financial crisis of 2007–2008, yields have dropped worldwide.

10. Vandana Shiva, *Who Really Feeds the World? The Failures of Agribusiness and the Promise of Agroecology* (Berkeley, CA: New Atlantic Books, 2016), 100–101.

11. Olivier De Schutter, Report Submitted by the Special Rapporteur on the Right to Food (United Nations, December 17, 2010), 3, http://www2.ohchr.org/english/issues/food/docs/A-HRC-16-49.pdf, accessed June 22, 2019.

12. Shiva, *Who Really Feeds*, 101.

13. Vandana Shiva, "There Is No Reason Why India Should Face Hunger and Farmers Should Commit Suicide," Eco Watch (August 14, 2015), https://www.ecowatch.com/vandana-shiva-there-is-no-reason-why-india-should-face-hunger-and-farm-1882083425.html, accessed June 22, 2019.

14. Ibid.

A Broken Social Contract

Hunger on this massive scale represents broken relationships within the basic social contract that exists among peoples. The right to food is a foundational human right, recognized under international law, which ensures that all people have access to adequate food and the resources necessary to enjoy food security.[15] Spelling out the implications of all people's right to food, the UN High Commissioner for Human Rights underscored its threefold criteria: availability, accessibility, and adequacy.[16] Accessibility entails both economic and physical access to affordable food, "without compromising any other basic needs" such as schooling, shelter, or medicine, and its availability to persons who are physically vulnerable or living in remote places. Adequacy requires that food must not only satisfy the dietary and nutritional needs of persons of various ages and circumstances, enabling them "to live a healthy and active life," but also be "safe for human consumption and free from adverse substances," including "contaminants from industrial or agricultural processes, such as pesticides." Moreover, food must be culturally acceptable and consistent with the eating habits of those who will consume it.

Yet the economic strategies of corporate agriculture have no such aims. Rather than providing for human needs, industrial agriculture creates poverty, debt, and landlessness, the primary causes of hunger.[17] The industrial system forces small farmers off their land and

---

15. This right was recognized in the 1948 Universal Declaration of Human Rights and enshrined in the 1966 International Covenant on Economic, Social, and Cultural Rights. See United Nations Office of the High Commissioner for Human Rights, "The Right to Adequate Food," Fact Sheet #34 (Geneva: United Nations, 2010), 1–5.

16. United Nations Office of the High Commissioner for Human Rights, "The Right to Adequate Food," 2–3. What follows is taken from this source.

17. See Andrew Kimbrell, *The Fatal Harvest Reader: The Tragedy of Industrial Agriculture* (San Francisco: Foundation for Deep Ecology, 2002), 5–9. What follows

replaces the diverse crops, by which they have fed local populations, with export crops grown by agribusiness.[18] Landless farmers around the world have swelled the numbers of urban poor, whose low-paying jobs consign them to long-term hunger, even starvation. Unable to grow their own food, their only access to nourishment is now by purchase. Yet many lack the money to provide nourishment for themselves or their families.[19] According to a 2016 estimate, 896 million of the world's poorest people live on $1.90 a day or less. Yet, as hunger and poverty expand, corporate wealth abounds, providing enormous financial rewards to the very few who control industrial agriculture. Poverty, hunger, and social inequality are simply collateral damage resulting from their increasing corporate wealth.[20]

While poverty is indeed the primary cause of hunger, several other factors exacerbate the current situation, especially in developing countries. Climate change is increasingly recognized as a major contributor to present and future hunger around the globe. The first comprehensive study of the human impact of global warming states that climate change will have its most severe impact on water supplies, with water shortages threating food production, reducing sanitation, hindering economic development, and damaging eco-

is taken from that source. According to Andrew Francis, *What in God's Name*, 23, one out of seven of the world's population is living on less than $1 a day. Bread for the World notes that wages for the bottom 60 percent of US workers have fallen by 4 to 6 percent since 2009. Accessed June 1, 2019, https://bread.org.

18. Shiva points out that thousands of Indian small farmers have committed suicide due to the psychological and financial stress placed on them by such tactics as corporate land takeover. See Vandana Shiva, *Seeds of Suicide* (New Delhi: Navdanya, 2006), 64–110.

19. As Kimbrell in *Fatal Harvest Reader*, 8, points out, industrial agriculture causes mass starvation "not only among the urban poor but also in the world's farming communities," who struggle with the increased costs of chemical and technological inputs that are now necessary and, at the same time, with the lower prices paid to farmers because of high middlemen costs.

20. See Raj Patel, *Stuffed and Starved: The Hidden Battle for the World's Food System* (Brooklyn, NY: Melville House Publications, 2012).

systems.[21] Violent swings between floods and droughts will leave hundreds of millions of people water-stressed by 2030, causing food shortages that will only swell the ranks of Earth's starving people. Armed conflict is likewise a contributing factor. The head of the UN food agency, David Beasley, stated recently that the only way to end global hunger is to end conflicts, thus freeing up millions of dollars to build roads and infrastructure and promote economic growth in developing countries.[22] In 2017, nineteen countries were in situations of protracted conflict, and 80 percent of the World Food Programme's funds are being channeled to these conflict regions.

For more than a decade, the numbers of hungry people in the world had been steadily declining, spurred on at least in part by the resolve of the UN Millennium Development Goals to halve extreme poverty and hunger rates by the end of 2015. The numbers suddenly took an uptick in 2016, increasing from 777 million to 815 million in just a year's time. A report from the Food and Agriculture Organization of the UN points to three factors for this increase: climate change, increased violent conflict in various parts of the world, and an economic downturn in countries heavily dependent on commodity exports.[23] These factors are indeed interlocked. As climate change adversely affects agriculture, it often triggers conflict and war in areas where natural resources are scarce. The report warns that "the coincidence of conflict and climate-related natural disasters is likely to increase with growing climate chaos, which is threatening food security and exacerbating incidences of malnutrition and starvation."[24]

21. John Vidal, "Global Warming Causes 300,000 Deaths a Year, Says Kofi Annan Thinktank," *The Guardian* (May 20, 2009), https://www.theguardian.com /environment/2009/may/29/1, accessed June 22, 2019.

22. Edith M. Lederer, "Rising Hunger Tied to Endless Global Warfare," *San Francisco Chronicle* (November 12, 2017), 15.

23. James Dearie, "World Hunger Escalates, Says UN Report," *National Catholic Reporter* (September 28, 2017), https://www.ncronline.org/news/world/world -hunger-escalates-says-un-report, accessed June 22, 2019.

24. Ibid.

The diversion of food crops to create biofuels and to feed livestock is an additional cause of escalating hunger around the globe. Today, 98 percent of the corn and 90 percent of the soy grown in the United States are not feeding anyone.[25] Critics and advocates for the hungry have questioned the conversion of 47 percent of US-grown corn and 45 percent of soy into biofuels, stating that there is no social justification for conversion of food into fuel for cars when hybrid and electric vehicles are available.[26] Between 2005 and 2011, the grain used to produce fuel for cars climbed from 41 million to 127 million tons, causing food prices to soar and creating some of the most severe food inflation in history. By 2012, world wheat, corn, and soybean prices were roughly double their historical levels, exacerbating already high levels of hungry people, creating social unrest, and evoking food riots in many countries.[27] At the same time, international food assistance programs, like the UN World Food Programme, had to cut shipments to needy countries, since it too was affected by the rising grain prices.

Earth's Growing Capacity: Culprit or Solution?

One of the prevalent assumptions about hunger is that it results from Earth's inability to provide for growing populations. Arguments in support of genetically modified food are often built on this premise, stating that GMO crops are essential to feeding a hungry world. Yet

---

25. Biofuels are a false solution, states Vandana Shiva, that worsen the food crisis by taking land and food from people to feed the insatiable appetite for fossil fuel infrastructures and the limitless consumption it requires. See Vandana Shiva, *Soil Not Oil* (Cambridge, MA: South End Press, 2008), 5. See also Lester Brown, *Full Planet, Empty Plates: The New Geopolitics of Food Security* (New York: W.W. Norton, 2012), 116.

26. See Alison Hope Alkon and Julian Agyeman, *Cultivating Food Justice: Race, Class and Sustainability* (Cambridge, MA: MIT Press, 2011), for an excellent overview of issues of food justice.

27. Patel, *Stuffed and Starved*, 37, 40–41.

as study after study has shown, most of the world's hunger is caused by human interference with Earth's natural proclivity to feed and nourish its own. Foods that have been sprayed with pesticides and fertilized with toxic chemicals are creating an epidemic of diseases: diabetes, cancer, hypertension, infertility, and cardiovascular diseases.[28] As monocultures of limited food species replace the nutritious biodiverse crops that are locally cultivated, malnutrition is the predictable outcome. And, as exportable crops replace locally grown food intended to feed local communities, hunger is the inevitable result. Escalating food prices, driven by the volatile market that has characterized the global food economy for the past decade, have been devastating for the poorest in the global economy. Low-income families in many parts of the world are already spending 50 to 70 percent of their wages on food. As a result, many live on one meal a day in times of stress; families may even chose a day a week when they consume no food.[29]

In 2007 to 2008, a massive spike in food prices sent shock waves through the entire food system. Food riots and demonstrations erupted around the globe, and the numbers of hungry persons worldwide expanded precipitously.[30] Some analysts have reckoned that the rise in the cost of food was due to the confluence of specific, identifiable factors, such as extensive crop failures in many countries, the looming end to petroleum-based energy, a financial crisis in the US housing market that drove investors to more secure investments

28. Shiva, "There Is No Reason." She speaks of this epidemic as it affects India.

29. See Brown, *Full Planet, Empty Plates*, 114. Brown notes that world food prices have doubled in the past decade.

30. Here and in what follows, I draw on Christopher Rosin, Paul Stock, and Hugh Campbell, eds., "Introduction: Shocking the Global Food System," in *Food Systems Failure: The Global Food Crisis and the Future of Agriculture* (New York: Earthscan, 2012), 1–14; and Hugh Campbell, "Let Us Eat Cake? Historically Reframing the Problem of World Hunger and Its Purported Solutions," in *Food Systems Failure*, 30–45.

in grain futures, inequality of access to food resources, and mounting shifts in global climate.[31] But other critics conclude that these factors, while operative, were symptomatic of deep-seated failures in the system itself. To treat the food crisis as a single event or an episodic problem, they argue, is to undermine our ability to address the profound social inequality and environmental instability that is endemic to the corporate food system.

Feeling the Human Cost

Hunger remains a profound human tragedy. The impact of hunger on the human body and spirit is severe. Statistics can never tell the human story of children, women, and men caught in its grip. Indeed, they can numb us to the reality. Physically, hunger is a gnawing pain in the stomach and the stunted growth of a child who will never reach his or her potential development, either physically or intellectually. It is the bodily depletion of those who chronically suffer undernutrition, or the listless stare of a dying child being held in the arms of a weeping mother.[32] Emotionally, hunger creates some of the most profound human feelings: anguish (over choices to feed one's children or pay the rent), grief (over the unnecessary death of a loved one), humiliation (at being blamed for one's plight), self-blame (over perceived failure to provide), and fear (over how one will survive into the future). Socially, persons who are chronically hungry withdraw from relationships, consumed with their excessive need and totally depleted of their energy. "Hunger," writes Frances Moore Lappé, "is the ultimate symbol of powerlessness."[33] Spiritu-

---

31. Rosin, Stock, and Campbell, "Introduction," 5. These and other factors are often referred to as "the perfect storm," indicating that we know exactly what factors are at work. But this actually keeps us from the necessary restructuring of the system.

32. Ibid., 2.

33. Frances Moore Lappé, *World Hunger: Twelve Myths* (New York: Grove Press, 1999), 3.

ally, hunger leaves its victims disempowered, marginalized, denied a place in a society of shared goods, and ultimately denied God's precious gift of nourishment.[34]

In contrast, the "Zero Hunger" initiative launched in Brazil in 2002, a joint endeavor between dozens of religious denominations and then-president Luiz Ignácio Lula, stated that "hunger results from injustice and represents an offence against the Creator."[35] Together they committed themselves to ensuring that those currently hungry have access not only to food but also to social inclusion, to an education that avoids patronizing and that guarantees the benefits of dignity and citizenship, and to a way of life in which people can pursue Transcendence and nurture their spiritual hungers. "We believe," they stated, "that to share bread is to share God."

Making Connections with Eucharist

Monica Hellwig, in her classic *Eucharist and the Hungers of the World*, asks whether Eucharist and the Christian Gospel have anything to say to the social questions of our day that arise out of urgent and widespread human suffering.[36] Answering in the affirmative, she invites us to understand the rich symbolism of Eucharist by remembering hunger, our own and that of others. Experiencing hunger in our own bodies invites us to compassion for those who experience

34. See Monica K. Hellwig, *The Eucharist and the Hunger of the World* (Kansas City: Sheed and Ward, 1992), 1–14, for a rich description of the experience of hunger. See also Angel F. Méndes Montoya, *Theology of Food: Eating and the Eucharist* (Chichester, United Kingdom: Wiley-Blackwell, 2009), 40. Montoya and others stress that hunger is an ethical-political reality deeply related to issues of ethnicity, gender, sexuality, and social class.

35. Frei Betto, "Zero Hunger: An Ethical-Political Project," in *Hunger, Bread and Eucharist*, Christophe Boureaux, Janet Martin Soskice, and Luiz Carlos Susin, eds., Concilium, 2005/2 (London: SCM Press, 2005), 11–13. Remainder of paragraph from this source.

36. Reflections here taken from Hellwig, *Eucharist and the Hunger*, chaps. 1, 2, 7, 8. What follows is from this source.

the painful, brutalizing experience of chronic hunger and instills an urgency to respond. Moreover, hunger provides a basic experience of dependence, contingency, a need for others, an awareness that we are creatures, receiving our existence as gift, dependent on the bounty of nature and the providence of the transcendent creator. It opens us to understand Eucharist as a "celebration of the hospitality of God, shared by guests who commit themselves to become fellow hosts with God," to a mission of responding to the hungers of the world, for bread, yes, but also for dignity, freedom, empowerment, and peace. Jesus came to reveal this divine hospitality as both redemption and healing grace. The sharing of food in Eucharist signals that in God's world there is room for all.

Farmworkers: A Matter of Justice

Our exploration of global hunger, which has highlighted the loss of human dignity and glaring inequality, sets the stage for a consideration of one of the most essential parts of the corporate food industry: farmworkers. While the situation of workers has global dimensions, our focus here is on the United States, the richest country of the world, where the plight of farmworkers reveals the stark face of injustice, exploitation, and disregard.[37] Food injustice experienced by farmworkers is central to "the highly unequal, uneven dynamics of global agricultural production, trade, [and] consumption."[38] The vulnerability and exploitation experienced by agricultural workers

---

37. Sources for this section: Wenonah Hauter, *Foodopoly* (New York: The New Press, 2012); Sandy Brown and Cindy Getz, "Farmworker Food Insecurity and the Production of Hunger in California," in *Cultivating Food Justice: Race, Class, and Sustainability*, ed. Alison Hope Alkon and Julian Agyeman (Cambridge, MA: The MIT Press, 2011), 121–46; Thomas Fuller, "In a California Valley, Healthy Food Everywhere but on the Table," *New York Times* (November 23, 2016), https://www.nytimes.com/2016/11/23/us/in-a-california-valley-healthy-food-everywhere-but-on-the-table.html, accessed March 20, 2017; *Food Chains*, directed by Sanjay Rawal (2014), documentary film.

38. Brown and Getz, "Farmworker Food Insecurity," 121.

in the United States is systemically constructed within a corporate economy that interweaves the accumulation of capital with immigration politics and neoliberal trade policy.[39]

Of the three million farmworkers in the United States today, some 90 percent are foreign-born. A substantial majority are illegal, undocumented workers from rural Mexico, part of the 200 million people worldwide who live outside their countries of birth. This tremendous flow of workers from poorer to richer countries provides the essential cheap labor that fuels the economies of industrial countries. Residing in the United States illegally, they lack the protection of the law and are therefore unlikely to challenge the unfair conditions under which they labor. Indeed, their struggle is not primarily about immigration but about human rights.

Ironically, the catalyst for Mexicans leaving their homes and farms is, in most cases, the same neoliberal trade policy and its agrifood regime that relegates them to the bottom of the food supply chain in the United States. With the signing of the North American Free Trade Agreement (NAFTA) in 1994,[40] trade restrictions were lifted between the United States and Mexico, and farm prices in Mexico plummeted, forcing untold numbers of farmers off their land and into urban slums. Many chose instead to risk migration to become underpaid laborers in the United States.[41] Between 1994 and 2008, the population of Mexican-born persons in the United States tripled, an involuntary migration born of trade policies that have forced people to find work at a great distance from their homes and

---

39. Ibid.

40. Although NAFTA was revised in 2018, there are no significant data on how the changes are affecting Mexican communities at home. For a study of the original NAFTA agreement and its impact on the foodways and health of Mexicans, see Alicia Gálvez, *Eating NAFTA: Trade, Food Policies, and the Destruction of Mexico* (Oakland: University of California Press, 2018).

41. Hauter, *Foodopoly*, 93. American companies such as Green Giant that moved their operations from California to Mexico paid workers there $4.30 *per day* rather than the $7.60 *hourly* wage paid in Watsonville.

immigration policies that deny them legal status and make their
labor cheap.[42]

Farmworkers are at the bottom of massive supply chains that encompass the entire food industry. Fruit and vegetables, meat and dairy goods come to American tables through these chains. All decisions flow from the top down. Large corporate food retailers decide what prices consumers will pay, what fruits and vegetables will look like, and how much to pay the lower links in the chain, including farmers and farmworkers. In 1988, Walmart entered the grocery business. With its enormous economic clout, it shifted the priorities of the industry by purchasing food in massive quantities, demanding lower prices from farmers, and offering "cheap food" to customers. As a gargantuan buyer with the power to drive down prices, Walmart's policies forced a consolidation of hundreds of small supermarket chains and the emergence of a few corporate giants—Kroger, Safeway, Costco, Target, and Publix—which together generate well over half a trillion dollars a year in gross revenue. Yet these same corporations, which are totally dependent on their supply chains and ultimately on the farmworkers who tend and harvest crops, go out of their way to ensure that customers are not reminded of where their food comes from, by whom it is harvested, and what injustice takes place in the fields.[43]

Farmworkers in the United States today are part of a long history of exploitation of the agricultural labor force.[44] Working in unsafe and debilitating conditions, often for long hours in excessive heat and at a frenetic pace to keep up with the demands of their employers, farmworkers may pick some four thousand pounds of produce a day. Language barriers, lack of education, and fear of deportation make it unlikely that they will challenge conditions. Despite their essential part in providing fresh food for other tables, most cannot

42. *Food Chains*, David Bacon, investigative reporter, speaking.
43. *Food Chains*.
44. *Food Chains*, Eric Schlosser speaking.

afford to serve this same produce to their own children. Many are hungry and food insecure. As noted by César Chávez, cofounder of the United Farm Workers, "The food that overflows our market shelves and fills our tables is harvested by men, women and children who often cannot satisfy their own hunger."[45] Exposure to pesticides, inadequate sanitation, and poor nutrition coalesce in compromised health and obesity, yet workers have no access to health insurance.[46] Harassment and abuse in the fields are common; an estimated 80 percent of women farmworkers have experienced sexual harassment from employers and fellow workers.[47] Racial discrimination and lack of affordable housing leave many homeless, sleeping in fields or small encampments or crammed into small trailers with other workers. The majority of farmworkers live below the poverty line. Paid by the piece and during seasons when employment is available, those who do well are paid some $300 to $400 per week. Yearly income might reach $10,500 to $13,000, but the decade between 1991 and 2001 saw a 32 percent decline in their inflation-adjusted wages.[48] Perhaps the most debilitating aspect of farmworker existence is the lack of human dignity they experience. Forgotten and invisible, the hidden link at the bottom of the food chain, farmworkers soon learn "how little you mean to the people

45. Brown and Getz, "Farmworker Food Insecurity," 122.

46. Farmworkers' obesity is estimated to be at 85 percent because of the starchy food that is available and affordable. Jill F. Kilanowski, "Patterns and Correlates of Nutrition Among Migrant Farm-Worker Children," www.ncbi.nlm.nih.gov/pmc/articles/PMC3587771/.

47. *Food Chains.*

48. The US Department of Labor National Agricultural Workers' Survey claims that the average total family income in the United States is $17,500 to $19,999. *Food Chains.* See also Jessica Wright, "Biting the Hands Who Feed Us: Farmworker Abuse in the United States," *Foodtank*, June 2015, https://foodtank.com/news/2015/06/biting-the-hands-who-feed-us-farmworker-abuse-in-the-us/, accessed June 13, 2019.

for whom you are working."[49] Essential to the system, they are none-theless maligned for their poverty and undocumented status. California, with its "fertile valleys, warm climate and river water that make it a produce superstar," is a case in point.[50] More fruits and vegetables are grown there than anywhere else in the country, but large industrial growers benefit from "low-paid, seasonal harvest workers that live in grinding poverty."[51] Without their labor, the industry could not exist. Indeed, California's valleys reveal a tale of trouble. In the Salinas Valley, which is situated one hour south of the famous Silicon Valley and is known as the country's "salad bowl," many workers live in tents, encampments, abandoned buildings, or even a chicken coop.[52] Such poverty and neglect among farmwork-ers there is by no means new. John Steinbeck, native son of this valley, portrayed the exploitation of farmworkers in the 1930s in his famous novel *The Grapes of Wrath*, puzzling about the "curious atti-tude toward a group that makes our agriculture successful."[53] Simi-larly, those who live and work in California's great Central Valley, home to some of the nation's richest agricultural resources, face elevated levels of air and water pollution because the agricultural practices of this basin create a pool of pollution, exacerbated by emissions from large diesel trucks hauling produce.[54] Children in this valley have a 35 percent higher chance of suffering from asthma than in other parts of the state.[55] Finally, the incredibly beautiful Napa Valley, home to one of the most famous wine producing re-gions of the world, disguises a demeaning poverty. An inflated real estate market leaves no affordable housing for workers who harvest the fields. While part of a multimillion-dollar wine industry, many

49. *Food Chains*, comment of a California farmworker.
50. Hauter, *Foodopoly*, 82.
51. Ibid., 84.
52. Fuller, "In a California Valley."
53. Ibid.
54. Hauter, *Foodopoly*, 84.
55. Ibid.

workers are left homeless or must find housing as many as sixty miles away.[56] As author and investigative journalist Eric Schlosser points out, the cost of labor that produces a bottle of wine that sells for $40, or $100, or $200 is about twenty-five cents.[57]

In the mid-1960s, farmworkers César Chávez and Dolores Huerta cofounded the United Farm Workers, the first union of its kind in the United States. Peaking at 100,000 members, the UFW had a significant impact on improving the working conditions of farmworkers in California. A national boycott of nonunion grapes brought wide attention to the inadequate wages and adverse labor conditions faced by farmworkers. In 1975, California passed the California Agricultural Labor Relations Act, the nation's first collective bargaining act for farmworkers. The purpose of the law was to guarantee justice for all agricultural workers and stability in labor relations. In 1983, however, the newly elected Republican Governor George Deukmejian "sharply cut the budget of the Agricultural Labor Relations Board which enforced the act."[58] This action, coupled with other hostilities against the union, significantly crippled the future actions of the UFW.

A second farmworkers' initiative, the Coalition of Immokalee Workers (CIW), was organized in 1993 in Immokalee, Florida, an agricultural area made famous by Edward R. Murrow's 1960 CBS documentary *Harvest of Shame*.[59] Detailing the plight of migrant workers in post-Depression American prosperity, Murrow gave millions of Americans a closer look at what it means to live in dire

56. Significant efforts by some Napa Valley growers to ensure better conditions for workers have been spearheaded by Pat Garvey of Flora Springs Winery. Today there are three centers for workers in the Napa Valley, providing them with resources and assistance of various kinds.

57. *Food Chains.*

58. Robert Lindsey, "Cesar Chavez Tries New Directions for United Farm Workers," *New York Times* (September 9, 1982).

59. See https://billmoyers.com/2013/07/19/watch-edward-r-murrows-harvest-of-shame/, accessed July 10, 2019.

poverty and suffer the injustice of the farm fields. Three decades later, tomato workers in Immokalee organized to address similar concerns. Today, CIW sustains three major programs: (1) the Fair Food Program, a worker-driven initiative that creates partnerships between farmworkers, growers, and participating retail buyers; (2) the Anti-Slavery Program, uncovering "numerous multi-state farm slavery operations across the Southeastern U.S."; and (3) the Campaign for Fair Food, educating "consumers on the issue of farm labor exploitation . . . and [forging] alliances between farmworkers and consumers."[60] While CIW has won the participation of several grocery and fast-food chains in their Fair Food Program—Taco Bell, McDonald's, Chipotle, Trader Joe's, and Whole Foods—the coalition continues a several-year attempt to negotiate with the Publix food chain to pay one cent more per pound for tomatoes purchased from Florida growers. That single cent per pound, if given directly to farmworkers, would double their salary! To date, despite hunger strikes and continued protests, the corporate leaders of Publix—a chain that claims to be "your friendly neighborhood grocery store"— have refused to talk with CIW leadership.[61]

Schlosser has stated that of all the problems facing the United States today, a change in our care for farmworkers would be one of the easiest to address. If agricultural corporations and food retailers decided to eliminate poverty and massive food exploitation among farmworkers, it could happen very quickly, simply by charging consumers pennies more on purchases of fruit and vegetables. If Publix paid the one cent more per pound of tomatoes that CIW is requesting, their cost would be around $1 million per year from the company's $27 billion annual profit. If the extra penny cost was passed on to the public, each family of four would pay only 44 cents a year more than it pays for produce now.[62]

60. See Coalition of Immokalee Workers, http://www.ciw-online.org/about/, accessed June 23, 2019. See also *Food Chains*.

61. *Food Chains*.

62. Ibid.

This glaring injustice of continued farmworker exploitation has garnered the interest of a small group of US senators over the last decade, notably Senator Bernie Sanders, who brought national attention to the negotiations of the Immokalee workers with various food corporations. To date, however, no new national legislation has emerged.

Making Connections with Eucharist

That all be fed and cared for was a preoccupation of the earliest Christian communities gathered for eucharistic table fellowship. For them, solidarity and justice were played out in a daily sharing of food described in Acts as the "daily distribution" (6:1). The goal was that there would be no needy persons because "possessions were shared and meals were eaten in common" (Acts 4:34).[63]

Bread and justice are at the heart of the struggle for farmworkers' right to food security that we witness today. When César Chávez and Dolores Huerta founded the United Farm Workers in the mid-1960s, they described their efforts as a revolution, "a revolution of the poor seeking bread and justice."[64] But bread and justice are still denied those who provide an essential link between agricultural fields and the tables of most Americans and beyond. The system by which food is produced is itself producing hunger and food insecurity.

Bread and justice are at the heart of eucharistic eating. A recent joint Methodist-Catholic statement on Eucharist and ecology calls attention to the reality that eucharistic foods may come from oppressive agricultural practices, and it urges communities to ensure that the wheat and grapes used for their eucharistic elements are produced in safe and suitable work environments where just wages are paid to laborers.[65] These issues "are at the heart of the church's

63. See Reta Haldeman Finger, *Of Widows and Meals: Communal Meals in the Book of Acts* (Grand Rapids, MI: Eerdmans, 2007), 251–57.

64. Brown and Getz, "Farmworker Food Insecurity," 140.

65. " 'Heaven and Earth Are Full of Your Glory.' A United Methodist and Roman Catholic Statement on the Eucharist and Ecology" (2012), http://www.usccb

social justice concerns as derived from our Eucharistic practice," the document states, and are essential to "vigorous Eucharistic theology and practice."[66]

Questions for Reflection

1) Frances Moore Lappé states that "the way people think about hunger is the greatest obstacle to ending it."[67] How are your understandings of hunger changing? What do you know about hungry people in your local area?

2) How do you assess the plight of farmworkers in your region? Have you had a conversation with someone who harvests crops that will come to tables near you, and, if so, what did you learn? What action might support their protection and foster more compassionate immigration policies?

3) How are bread and justice related to your experience of Eucharist? How might an awareness of this interplay between food and right relationships open new ways of thinking about this sacramental ritual?

4) How do you feel called to extend God's eucharistic hospitality to a world where so many suffer the debilitating effects of hunger, malnutrition, exploitation, and abuse?

.org/beliefs-and-teachings/ecumenical-and-interreligious/ecumenical/methodist /upload/Heaven-and-Earth-are-Full-of-Your-Glory-Methodist-Catholic-Dialogue -Agreed-Statement-Round-Seven.pdf, accessed June 15, 2019.

66. Ibid.

67. Lappé, *World Hunger*, 7.

chapter seven

A Way Forward

The Reemergence of Regenerative Agriculture

The current industrial food system has left us with profoundly broken relationships. While bringing profits to a few who were already privileged, it has wreaked havoc on the natural world and has jeopardized the lives and livelihoods of countless people around the globe. An ideology that justifies exploitation of Earth's peoples and resources sustains it,[1] and its promise to feed the world has proven false. Although Earth currently produces sufficient calories per person to feed twelve to fourteen billion people, close to one billion people suffer from chronic starvation and another two billion are malnourished, poorly fed, or obese.[2] Chemically intensive industrial agriculture is highly unsustainable and has so degraded the

---

1. Christopher Rosin, Paul Stock, and Paul Campbell, eds., *Food Systems Failure: The Global Food Crisis and the Future of Agriculture* (New York: Earthscan, 2012), 9.

2. Pramod Parajuli, "Searching for Annapurna; or Cultivating Earthbound Regenerative Abundance in the Anthropocene," in *Religions and Sustainable Agriculture: World Spiritual Traditions and Food Ethics*, ed. Todd LeVasseur, Pramod Parajuli, and Norman Wirzba (Lexington: University Press of Kentucky, 2016), 343.

productive capacity of our natural systems—the soil, the water, and the air—that it remains unclear how we will feed the nearly ten billion people expected to share life on this planet by midcentury.

Today the call for change in the entire food system comes from numerous sources, from the top agencies of international leadership to communities of peasant farmers joined in solidarity for food justice and food sovereignty. A mounting consensus that a massive paradigm shift is needed in agriculture and food is evident even in current reports from the World Bank and the United Nations Conference in Trade and Development (UNCTAD), both of which previously promoted large-scale industrial food production and consumption.[3] A recent UNCTAD report calls for a major transition from a Green Revolution to an "ecological intensification" approach, that is, a shift "toward a mosaic of sustainable, regenerative production systems" that can improve the productivity of small-scale farmers.[4] These findings echo an earlier report from the United Nations Environmental Programme that, based on nine hundred participants from 110 countries, cited the "urgent need to build local and national capacity for biodiverse, ecologically resilient farming to cope with increasing environmental stresses, including the rise in global temperatures."[5] We are at a crossroads, a point of no return—or a point of creative possibilities for a resilient, if challenging, future. How we choose will make all the difference.

What would such a mosaic of resilient and abundant food systems look like? How can they heal the ravaged Earth and feed its people

3. Ibid., 350.

4. United Nations Conference on Trade and Development, *Wake Up before It Is Too Late* (New York: United Nations, 2013), as quoted in Parajuli, "Searching," 351.

5. United Nations Environmental Programme, *International Assessment of Agricultural Knowledge, Science and Technology for Development* (2009), http://documents.worldbank.org/curated/en/636821468316165959/International-assessment-of-agricultural-knowledge-science-and-technology-for-development, accessed October 15, 2017.

both nutritionally and spiritually? Could this healing of the food web address other pressing issues, such as the excess of greenhouse gases in Earth's thin atmosphere? Imagining such a vital and plentiful food system begins by reembracing a truth that is at the heart of this volume: that food is not a thing but a relationship. Vital and essential, food is a basic human right at the heart of the interconnected relationships of human communities—with Earth, with her numerous species, with the human family, and foundationally with the One who is the source of Earth's bounty. Hence, any imagining of alternative food systems that are more resilient, fair, and bounteous begins with reembedding food in its social, ecological, and spiritual relationships. Food itself must also be revalued, from a commodity viewed as a capital investment that can be traded and sold to a precious gift, an essential part of the common good and vital to the survival and heath of all God's living creatures.

This chapter weaves a vision of what an alternative food economy might look like, a mosaic of local systems that can better acknowledge the moral imperatives of accessible, healthy, and culturally appropriate food for all peoples.[6] While requiring radical change, this vision is already emerging in the concrete lives of groups around the world. In the face of a failing food system, lived evidence of the viability and effectiveness of this vision can lure communities and governments into dialogue and a refocusing of strategies for a new food system.

From these many initiatives and the insights of numerous authors, I draw five foundational characteristics that mark an alternative food economy that can be sustainable into the future: (1) small in scale, (2) locally based, (3) organically sustained, (4) regenerative of Earth's resources, and (5) rooted in justice. Taken together, this new paradigm has the power to reconnect farms, food, and communities and to reweave social, nutritional, and spiritual relationships that have been torn asunder by the industrial food system.

---

6. Rosin, Stock and Campbell, *Food Systems Failure*, 221.

Small in Scale

Food systems that can sustain Earth's peoples into the future will first of all be small in scale. Given the global hegemony of large agribusiness and its underlying myth that "big is better," it is surprising to learn that 70 percent of the world's food is still being grown by small farmers and gardeners, most of whom are women.[7] The need for industrial agriculture has been predicated on the assumption that small-scale farming is far less productive than large industrial farms, yet statistics paint quite a different picture. Small-scale farmers in Ukraine, for example, produce 55 percent of the agricultural output of the country on only 16 percent of the land.[8] Peasant farmers in Russia account for more than half of the country's agriculture while occupying only a quarter of the agricultural lands. In the United States, the USDA confirms that smaller farms produce considerably more food per acre, whether measured in tons, calories, or dollars.[9]

Researchers today confirm what small-scale farmers have known for a long time: that abundant quantities of food can be produced in relatively small spaces with little or no synthetic fertilizer or chemicals.[10] One key to this success is flexibility. Bill McKibben recounts walking through a field of tall corn in Beijing, only to find green beans hidden between the rows, an impossibility if a large

7. Vandana Shiva, *Who Really Feeds the World? The Failures of Agribusiness and the Promise of Agroecology* (Berkeley, CA: North Atlantic Books, 2016), 56. "Big is better" has rippled into the entire Western food system: serving sizes have increased, the size of refrigerators has increased, and even the size of the average dinner plate has increased!

8. Ibid., 61.

9. Bill McKibben, *Eaarth: Making a Life on a Tough New Planet* (New York: St. Martin's Griffin, 2011), 168.

10. Peter Rosset, "Small Is Beautiful," *Ecologist* 29, no. 8 (December 1999): 63, quoted in McKibben, *Eaarth*, 168. Researchers studying data from the past several decades conclude that small farms are more productive in Africa, Asia, and Latin America.

tractor would need to drive these paths.[11] In Honduras, velvet beans grown between the rows of corn not only add nitrogen to the soil but when cut and left in place act as "green manure" to create a new layer of soil that can triple or quadruple the yield the following year.[12] Jules Pretty describes how small farmers in Indonesia grow fish between the rows of rice in their rice paddies. Fish eat pests, circulate nutrients, and provide several hundred kilograms of fish protein per hectare annually to eat or sell.[13]

In each of the cases just cited, small farmers and gardeners not only make use of every inch of available space but, by intercropping various species, also create natural pest control, support plant synergy, and increase biodiversity. In contrast to the large-scale monocropping of industrial agriculture that reduces Earth's natural biodiversity to single crop species, small biodiverse farms and gardens are providing the variety of crops needed for good nutrition, protection against disease, and resilience in the face of climate impacts.[14] Vandana Shiva notes that in Java, some 607 species of food are cultivated in home gardens, a diversity comparable to that of a deciduous tropical forest. In Papua New Guinea, as many as five thousand varieties of sweet potatoes are grown, with as many as twenty of these often appearing in a single garden.

Small farmers and gardeners have proven to be not only more efficient, more flexible, and more sensitive to biodiversity in their growing practices but also better caretakers of soil, water, and the whole web of Earth's resources. Small-scale agriculture thrives on attention to natural food webs and the symbiotic relationships that mark the interaction of plants and the natural resources they depend on. In contrast to massive irrigation systems of industrial agriculture,

---

11. McKibben, *Eaarth*, 168.

12. Ibid., 169.

13. Jules Pretty, *Agri-Culture: Reconnecting People, Land and Nature* (London: Earthscan, 2002), 90.

14. Shiva, *Who Really Feeds*, 128.

small farmers can use water more judiciously, preserve it from contamination and often recycle it using the natural cleansing systems of rocks and pools. Soil is likewise protected and rejuvenated through crop rotation and the use of nitrogen-fixing cover crops, techniques that have marked small-scale agriculture for centuries. Moreover, the cultivation of biodiversity increases the presence of beneficial insects, pollinators, and soil bacteria, all of which are essential for the production of healthy and nourishing crops.

As we imagine a new proliferation of small-scale farms and gardens, one thing is clear. Such a resurgence will depend on engaging more people in the actual cultivation process. In Vermont's main city, Burlington, Intervale Farms supplies some 8 percent of the city's produce using just 120 acres of land, but it employs some fifty people to cultivate these acres.[15] Big agriculture has sought to minimize the role of human labor by substituting massive, fossil-fuel-driven machinery on the assumption that this will not only increase productivity but also liberate humans from the drudgery of work.[16] Time has proven that quite the contrary is true: replacing human energy with the burning of fossil fuels has left many small farmers around the world stripped of their land and at the same time deprived of the dignity of their work.

Increasing the number of persons involved in small-scale operations has much to offer a world plagued by poverty, unemployment, and the disposability of people. Bringing people back into the food economy and redefining human work as dignified rather than debilitating has the potential of rebuilding communities while at the same time enabling a far more sustainable food system. Human energy is the largest renewable energy source we have, offering not only physical vigor but also spiritual, cultural, emotional, and intel-

---

15. McKibben, *Eaarth*, 175.

16. Shiva, *Who Really Feeds*, 128; McKibben, *Eaarth*, 175. McKibben notes that substituting oil for human energy is why we have more prisoners than farmers in the United States.

lectual strength and creativity to the cultivation of Earth's productivity.[17] When the intelligence of Mother Earth and her potential for creating abundance is coupled with hardworking people, who have a right to their land, their seed, their knowledge, and their creative work, diverse resilient systems of growing the food necessary to sustain human communities and Earth herself can be restored.

Locally Based

A second aspect of the turn toward more sustainable agricultural practices is the relocalization of food, a trend essential for restoring our human connection with food in all its complexity. Key to the industrial food system is distancing the biological and social aspects of growing food from the persons who will consume it. Food that reaches most tables in the United States has traveled some 1,500 miles. This production-at-a-distance not only isolates communities from the miraculous processes of food growth but also costs more, pollutes more, and creates more waste. Emissions from long-distance transportation contribute significantly to increased climate change. Seventy-five cents of every dollar spent on supermarket food covers the cost of transportation, packaging, storage, and advertising.[18] Spoilage along the way means that one out of every four vegetables and fruits never makes it to our tables.[19] Local foods, in contrast, taste better and are more nutritious because they can be harvested and enjoyed at the peak of ripeness.

Distancing food production likewise disempowers consumers. Much of the hegemony of corporate agriculture is its ability to keep consumers from knowing what is actually happening to their food— where it is grown and under what conditions—therefore making them less likely to act on behalf of the safety and reliability of the

17. Vandana Shiva, *Soil Not Oil* (Berkeley: North Atlantic Books, 2015), 139.
18. McKibben, *Eaarth*, 176.
19. Ibid.

food they purchase.[20] Relocalization, on the other hand, rebuilds trust and co-responsibility among those who grow food and local consumers, reweaving trusting relationships among people and the land they inhabit while reinvigorating familial, community, and civic culture.[21] The emergence of Community Supported Agriculture (CSA)—partnerships that mutually benefit farmers and consumers—establish economic exchanges based on friendship, affection, loyalty, justice, and reciprocity, in addition to factors of cost (not price) and quality.[22]

One evocative metaphor for the relocalization of food is that of "foodsheds."[23] Just as local communities have watersheds that give a sense of place and connection to Earth's resources, foodsheds are shaped by natural and social geography, both the ecosystems that make up the local landscape—the plant communities, soil types, and climate conditions—and the ethnicities, cultural traditions, and culinary patterns of the communities who inhabit these places. The discovery and cultivation of their foodshed by local communities can instill a sense of self-reliance, commitment to social and environmental sustainability, care for the welfare of co-citizens, and a renewed sense of interdependence among people and their land. Moreover, being aware of one's foodshed underscores that human life and nourishment are embedded in the natural capacities and resources of a particular place and must be respected, cultivated, and learned from as communities develop more intimate relationships with the land they inhabit.

---

20. Jack Kloppenburg Jr., John Hendrickson, and G. W. Stevensen, "Coming in to the Foodshed," *Agriculture and Human Values* 13, no. 3 (Summer): 36.

21. Ibid.

22. Ibid. CSAs are enabled by local people who contribute financially to the workings of a farm and who are rewarded with regular installments of the food produced by those who farm.

23. See ibid., 38–40, for the information that follows.

Urban agriculture will be key to the development of foodsheds that can feed communities into the future. Given the massive shift in population from rural to urban centers over the last several decades, a relocalization of food cultivation will necessarily invade urban and suburban spaces: vacant lots, backyards, porches, and reclaimed parking lots.[24]

Growing food in urban centers is nothing new. During World War II, Britain managed to increase its food production 91 percent through small gardens and "allotments" that sprang up everywhere. Bill McKibben recounts that the "wife of the keeper of coins and medals at the British Museum planted rows of beans, peas, onions, and lettuces at the museum's entrance."[25] Today, Los Angeles has a waiting list for the ten-by-thirty-foot plots the city offers to local citizens. On the other side of the Pacific, the city of Shanghai employs 270,000 people in its urban farming industry. Community and rooftop gardens dot urban areas in many parts of the world and across the United States. A recent study of sixty-three inner-city community gardens in New York found that they supply far more than produce. With the development of a common garden, the attitudes of local residents toward their neighborhood have changed; care for properties has improved, littering has been reduced, pride in neighborhoods is on the rise, and people are working cooperatively on a range of local needs.[26]

New alliances between city and surrounding countryside are also critical to the relocalization of food. Farmers' markets are now the fastest growing part of the US food economy, with sales up by 10 to

---

24. See David Holmgren's recent book, *Retrofitting Suburbia: The Downshifters Guide to a Resilient Future* (Hepburn Springs: Melliodora Publishing, 2018) for ideas about transforming suburbia into a garden.

25. McKibben, *Eaarth*, 166. What follows is from same source, 178–79.

26. Donna Armstrong, "A Survey of Community Gardens in Upstate New York: Implications for Health Promotion and Community Development," *Health and Place* 6, no. 4 (2000): 319–27.

15 percent a year. The number of farmers' markets has doubled and then doubled again in the last decade.[27] Buying directly from local farmers creates alliances of mutual support, trust, and reciprocity between urbanites and small farmers and enables people to know where and by whom their food is grown. In Western Massachusetts, when a small bakery was looking unsuccessfully for local varieties of wheat, they persuaded hundreds of neighbors to plant small patches of wheat in their yards.[28] Jules Pretty has documented the growth of community foodsheds and rural partnerships around the world, a trend that is developing more vibrant local communities while creating a massive increase in agricultural productivity using locally adapted and sustainable technologies.

Growing crops locally can involve many challenges, especially weather and climate, yet innovative new technologies are emerging every day. Pete Johnson has been pioneering year-round farming in snowy Vermont through the use of solar greenhouses that he first designed as a senior project at Middlebury College.[29] Today, Johnson has devised an even more productive system: by moving his greenhouses from place to place on tracks, he grows greens eleven months out of the year without extra heat. Solar greenhouses hold great potential to enable northern communities to grow at least some of their food year-round.

"Think globally, act neighborly," reads a bumper sticker. Local agriculture is more than a supply chain of products. It is a network of relationships. As the wise agrarian Wendell Berry writes, "Everything needed locally cannot be produced locally. But a viable neighborhood is a community, and a viable community is made up of neighbors who cherish and protect what they have in common. . . . It does not import products that it can produce for itself. And it does

27. McKibben, *Eaarth*, 177.
28. Ibid., 179.
29. Ibid., 161–62.

not export local products until local needs have been met."[30] Relocalization cultivates not just food but community. It creates deeper connections between food producers and eaters, supports local farmers, and rejuvenates local economies.[31] Local means diversity, freshness, safety, and taste and a revitalization of Earth's food web.[32]

Organically Sustained

Called the "delicious revolution" by chef Alice Waters, a wave of organic agriculture is expanding across the United States and around the globe.[33] In contrast to the aggressive techniques of industrial agriculture, organic modes of farming and gardening are based in friendship with the Earth and a belief that her natural processes are the wisest approach to growing nutritious food for the world's tables. Organic agriculture conceives of a farm or garden "as an organism, in which the component parts—the soil, minerals, organic matter, micro-organisms, insects, plants, animals, and humans—interact to create a coherent and stable whole."[34] Food is grown in harmony with nature, recognizing that "soil, seed, water, farmers and our bodies are intelligent beings, not dead matter or machines."[35] Seed and soil are understood to be "living, self-organizing, self-renewing systems that can give us food without the use of chemicals and poisons."[36]

---

30. Wendell Berry, "The Idea of a Local Economy," http://home2.btconnect.com/tipiglen/localecon.html, accessed June 30, 2019.

31. McKibben, *Eaarth*, 75. Much more might be said here about local economies. As McKibben points out, in developed countries only 15 percent of the price of a loaf of bread goes to the farmer.

32. Shiva, *Who Really Feeds*, 131.

33. Clare Hope Cummings, *Uncertain Peril: Genetic Engineering and the Future of Seeds* (Boston: Beacon Press, 2008), 152.

34. Nic Lampkin, Welsh Institute for Rural Studies, as quoted in Pretty, *Agri-Culture*, 114.

35. Shiva, *Who Really Feeds*, 127.

36. Ibid., xxii.

Organic does not describe a thing or a product, contends Vandana Shiva, but a philosophy, a way of thought, of knowledge, and of living, based on an awareness that everything is connected and in relationship with everything else.[37] Organic practices reach back millennia, cultivated by native agrarians in settings across the globe who considered Earth an educator, a healer, and a technologist.[38] Human technologies aimed to cooperate with Earth's proclivities, with natural forces, and with local resources enable the growth and health of Earth's edible abundance.[39]

Corporate industrial agriculturalists have long claimed that large-scale, chemically dependent farming was the only road to high yields. Yet today, organic family farms are producing two to six times more per acre than industrial farms. A major study by the University of Michigan documented that, in developing countries, organic agriculture is outproducing the yields of its industrial counterpart by 180 percent.[40] In 2008, the United Nations Environment Programme reported that yields across Africa "doubled or more than doubled where organic or near-organic practices had been used. In East Africa, harvests jumped 128 percent. Not only were harvests better, but the organic soils were retaining water and resisting drought."[41] Jules Pretty notes that in one review of Kenyan organic farming practices in twenty-six communities, "three-quarters of participating households were now free from hunger during the year," and the proportion of people having to buy vegetables had fallen from 85 to 11 percent.[42]

37. Ibid., 133.

38. See Thomas Berry, *The Dream of the Earth* (San Francisco: Sierra Club, 1988), 35.

39. Ibid., 64–65.

40. Eric Holt-Gimenez and Raj Patel, *Food Rebellions! Crises and the Hunger for Justice* (Food First Books, 2009), 107.

41. McKibben, *Eaarth*, 171.

42. Pretty, *Agri-Culture*, 90.

Organic agriculture has a direct relationship with the emerging scientific paradigm of agroecology, combining the wisdom of traditional, sustainable farming systems with knowledge from new sciences such as epigenetics, quantum theory, evolutionary biology, and ecology.[43] Agroecological knowledge challenges many assumptions of industrial agriculture: that humans are separate from Earth, that nature is composed of dead matter, that exploitation and violence are appropriate ways to press Earth into submission and make up for what it lacks, and that human survival is possible only in opposition to the genetic coding of the natural world.[44] In contrast, these new sciences demonstrate that Earth is a living, self-organizing system at every level, that inseparability is the defining characteristic of a quantum universe, and that everything that exists is integral to the web of life.[45]

In 1997, the USDA released a set of standards for organically produced foods, meant to ensure the integrity of foods claimed to be organic.[46] Ironically, agribusiness corporations saw in these standards a way to reach a profitable niche market, making large profits by creating organic products without adopting the overall ethic of organic agriculture. Aided by industrial food lobbyists in Washington, they used their financial and political clout to weaken these standards in whatever way possible.[47] For example, the current guidelines allow organic ingredients to be "sourced from around the world, wherever they are cheapest," a clear violation of the basic philosophy of organic growing. Today, the organic market in the

43. Shiva, *Who Really Feeds*, 3, 12.

44. See Berry, *Dream*, 39–46, 213.

45. Shiva, *Who Really Feeds*, 5.

46. Winonah Hauter, *Foodopoly: The Battle over the Future of Food and Farming in America* (New York: The New Press, 2012) 199. What follows is taken from this source, 98–103.

47. Katherine Paul, "Organic Farming Explained," Organic Consumers Association (May 21, 2019), https://www.organicconsumers.org/blog/organic-farming -explained, accessed June 29, 2019.

United States is an almost $50 billion business dominated by the largest food corporations. For example, Odwalla juice is owned by Coca-Cola, and Celestial Seasonings tea is owned by Hain, whose investors include Phillip Morris, Monsanto, and Exxon Mobil.[48] Being labeled organic does not necessarily mean a company or product is contributing to the emerging food revolution we are exploring here. To truly be organic, it must be integrally related to the four other aspects vital to sustainable food cultivation for future generations—small in scale, locally based, regenerative of Earth's resources, and oriented toward justice.

Regenerative of Earth's Resources

The word "regeneration" is on the lips of many today who see it as a pathway to healing ecosystems that are stressed, damaged, and depleted by current agricultural methods. Regenerative food cultivation leaves the Earth in better condition than when the growing started. It revitalizes tired soil and builds new topsoil, increases biodiversity, improves water cycles, enhances ecosystem services, builds communities' resilience against climate fluctuation, and increases the well-being of the larger human-biotic community that depends on the produce of the land. No wonder analysts are looking to regenerative processes as critical strategies for enabling communities to grow food into the future.[49] But it also requires planning, intentional-

48. Vandana Shiva, *Earth Democracy* (Cambridge, MA: South End Press, 2005), 37, for notes on Odwalla and Celestial Seasonings. See Hauter, *Foodopoly*, 98–115, for a more complete exploration of the paradox of corporately owned organic food. Hauter mentions that fourteen of the twenty largest processers of food sell organic brands that rarely make use of their corporate names.

49. Regenerative Agriculture Institute and The Carbon Underground, "What Is Regenerative Agriculture," https://regenerationinternational.org/2017/02/24/what-is-regenerative-agriculture/, accessed June 29, 2019. See also "Regenerative Agriculture," https://en/wikipedia.org/iki/Regenerative.agriculture. While practices of livestock grazing and the integration of animal and plant cultivation are

ity, the culling of wisdom from many sources, experimentation, and ultimately commitment to the future of a planet that is in crisis. On a planet prone to drought, flooding, heat waves, and unstable weather patterns, new pathways to resilience are essential.

Regenerative growing systems encompass several approaches to farming and gardening: permaculture, biodynamic and biointensive agriculture, agroforestry, carbon farming, keyline systems, and regenerative design.[50] These methods share a common principle articulated by Sir Albert Howard in the 1940s, namely, the "law of return." According to this principle, nutrients are regularly given back to the soil so as to sustain and increase its fertility. Howard, who is considered the father of modern sustainable farming, maintained that "the foundation of all good cultivation is not so much in the plant as in the soil."[51] He demonstrated that feeding the soil with organic matter and green manure contributes to a 200 to 300 percent increase in crop yield. Contrast this to what Vandana Shiva calls the "law of exploitation," by which industrial agriculture takes from the soil without giving back, leaving it on the verge of collapse and threatening the food supplies of future generations. The law of return has enabled societies throughout history to maintain living soil. Civilizations that neglected their soil eventually collapsed.[52]

Permaculture, a highly regenerative system of growing food, is rooted in a threefold ethic: Earth care, people care, and fair share.[53] As this ethic suggests, permaculture seeks to work with nature rather

---

often part of regenerative agriculture, I focus here primarily on plant cultivation in relation to ecosystem and bioregional vitality.

50. Shiva, *Who Really Feeds*, 1–14. Also, numerous resources on agroecology and its many approaches can be found on the web.

51. Albert Howard, *The Soil and Health: A Study of Organic Agriculture* (Oxford: Benediction Classics, 2011), xxv.

52. See David R. Montgomery, *Dirt: The Erosion of Civilizations* (Berkeley: University of California Press, 2007).

53. See David Holmgren, *Permaculture: Principles and Pathways beyond Sustainability* (Hepburn, Victoria, Australia: Holmgren Design Services, 2002).

than against it; to design ways of growing crops that enable people, land, and animals to thrive together; and to maintain an awareness of the needs of the greater community. The dual starting points for permaculture farming/gardening are observation and design, two strategies that amplify cooperation with Earth's natural giftedness.[54] Observation identifies the natural factors already at work in a place to be cultivated—the sources of water, patterns of shade and sunlight, soil type and quality. These are the basis for an intentional garden design that can enhance what is already at work by nature's grace while fostering a dynamic interaction between people and the crops they cultivate. Herbs and foods used often are grown closest to the gardener's home. Garden beds are designed to be enjoyed for beauty and harmony, and flowers and vegetables are integrated so as to attract pollinating bees and other beneficial insects.

Permaculture, along with other forms of regenerative agriculture, recommends "no-till" or "minimum-till" soil cultivation. No-till practices replace techniques of deep plowing so integral to industrial farming, which break down natural soil aggregation and disrupt the integrity of microbial, fungal communities in the soil. Tillage greatly increases soil erosion and a release of soil carbon into the atmosphere because it introduces increased oxygen into the soil. Coupled with intercropping of a wide range of plant species, composting with green and animal manure, and the planting of nitrogen-fixing cover crops during nongrowing seasons, no-till gardening mirrors the restorative patterns of Mother Earth herself by which ecosystems rejuvenate and restore themselves.

The health of local waters, as well as soil's ability to retain water, are likewise greatly increased by these regenerative practices. Degraded soils are less able to hold the water essential for crop growth. In contrast, restorative techniques enable water to penetrate through and be retained in the soil, decreasing the need for external irrigation

54. Ibid., 13–24.

systems and avoiding the use of ground and surface waters that have been contaminated by pesticides and chemical fertilizers. Catching water and snowmelt in rain barrels, wells, or small on-site reservoirs not only stores it for garden use but, when water is left open to natural elements, it is naturally purified by an infusion of wind-supplied oxygen, keeping it fresh, living, pure, and resilient. As water is retained and its health restored, whole ecosystems are transformed from brown barren terrain to lush green growing places.

In addition to all these advantages, regenerative agriculture has the remarkable potential to cool an overheated planet! Over the last decade, the potential of soil to sequester large quantities of carbon from the atmosphere has held out great promise for the mitigation and even the reversal of global climate change. A white paper released from the Rodale Institute in 2014 claimed that "we could sequester more than 100% of current annual CO_2 emissions with a switch to widely available and inexpensive organic management practices, which we term 'regenerative organic agriculture.' "[55] The paper states that "taken together, the wealth of scientific support for regenerative agriculture has demonstrated that these practices can comfortably feed the growing human population while repairing our damaged ecosystem." The paper also makes astounding claims about how much of our polluted atmosphere can be cleansed through restorative land practices.[56] First, if management of all current cropland shifted to regenerative agriculture, more than 40 percent of annual emissions could potentially be sequestered. Second, if all global pastureland was managed using a regenerative model, an additional 71 percent could be sequestered. Even when the most modest assumptions are made, regenerative agriculture can easily

55. The Rodale Institute, "Regenerative Organic Agriculture and Climate Change." The paper can be found at https://rodaleinstitute.org/wp-content /uploads/rodale-white-paper.pdf, accessed September 21, 2017.

56. Ibid. What follows is from this source.

keep annual emissions within a desirable range.[57] These claims hold
out enormous promise for the contribution of agriculture to a sustainable future.

Finally, regenerative practices are intended to rebuild communities
along with Earth's biosystems, supporting attitudes and social skills
that enable communities to work together for a resilient future. Edible
schoolyards are unlocking this potential.[58] Beginning with the youngest generations, school gardens engage students in growing, preparing, serving, and sharing food, awakening them to the transformative
values of care for community and stewardship of the land. Begun in
a vacant lot in Berkeley, California, by chef Alice Waters, edible
schoolyards are now found around the globe integrating organic and
regenerative ways of growing food into the whole educational cur-
riculum and into the multigenerational lives of Earth's youngest citizens. In addition to fostering their knowledge of food systems and
how to prepare healthy meals, edible schoolyards bring students
together in educative and fruitful ways in a common effort to transform the Earth for a future that is abundant for all.

Rooted in Justice

No food revolution can lead the planetary community into a sustainable future unless it is rooted in principles of justice, human dignity,
fair share, and the protection of Earth's precious resources. Food
justice, Earth justice, and the common good are key to the future of
food and the right of all people to participate in Earth's abundance.
Although numerous strategies are emerging to bring about a more
just and equitable food system, I will focus briefly on five: food
democracy, food justice, food sovereignty, the right to food, and a
restoration of the global commons. While distinctive in their focus,

57. Ibid.
58. For more information on edible schoolyards, see https://edibleschoolyard
.org/berkeley and https://edibleschoolyard.org/network.

these movements coalesce in a profound concern for the well-being of the Earth and especially her most vulnerable creatures. While these strategies do not spring directly from religious sources, they resonate deeply with ethical principles for a just and peaceful world that mark the world's various religious traditions.

Food democracy, a strategy described by Vandana Shiva, is "the right of all citizens to have access to healthy, nutritious, safe, affordable, culturally appropriate, and sustainably produced food."[59] Moreover, these same citizens have the right to know what is in their food. In Shiva's portrayal, food democracy includes seed freedom and food freedom: "the right of farmers to save and share seed; . . . to practice poison-free agroecology," and "to grow and share diversity through diversified and fair markets." Shiva contends that such an ecological and just alternative has become an imperative in the face of an industrial food system that has "brought us to a triple crisis: a dying planet, diseased citizens, and debt-ridden farmers."[60] Industrial agriculture has unleashed untold violence against Earth's fragile web of life and her most vulnerable peoples.[61]

Food justice, while related to notions of food democracy, responds specifically to the "ways that race and class are enmeshed in the food system."[62] Described by Alison Hope Alkon and Julian Agyeman, food justice is a movement that responds to how communities of color and poor communities have been systematically "denied access to the means of food production," and how people in these communities, "due to both price and store location, often cannot access" a

---

59. Shiva, *Who Really Feeds*, 138. What follows is from that source.

60. Ibid., 138–39.

61. Ibid., 3.

62. Alison Hope Alkon and Julian Agyeman, "Introduction," in *Cultivating Food Justice: Race, Class, and Sustainability*, ed. Alison Hope Alkon and Julian Agyeman (Cambridge, MA: The MIT Press, 2011), 4–5. What follows is taken from this source. This volume focuses primarily on communities of color and low-income communities in the United States.

healthy diet. Time and again, the authors claim, communities of color have been subject to laws and policies that deny their "ability to own and manage land for food production," while members of these communities continue to be exploited as farm laborers. In response, food justice is activated by communities to create local food systems that protect their right to grow, sell, and eat food that is "fresh, nutritious, culturally appropriate, and grown locally with care for the well-being of the land, workers, and animals."[63]

A burgeoning of food justice organizations have grown up in West and North Oakland, California, over the last decade; People's Grocery, City Slicker Farms, Village Bottom Farms, Phat Beets Produce, and Planting Justice have taken over vacant lots and underutilized park land to grow fresh produce for local residents. In neighboring East Oakland, Food Connection teaches urban gardening and offers cooking classes to children, while "PUEBLO's Youth Harvest program works with at-risk teenagers to harvest fruit for distribution at senior centers."[64] Coupled with school gardens, these initiatives are restoring lives and neighborhoods through an emancipatory vision of food justice and community solidarity.

Food sovereignty has emerged as the rallying cry of the largest grassroots movement on the planet, *La Via Campesina*, a coalition of small farmers, native peoples, and landless workers who together are redefining their rights vis-à-vis food: their right to live in the countryside, to produce their own food, and to secure a dignified life.[65] Moved by the urgent need for global political action to ensure these rights, representatives of three smaller movements merged in 1993 to create the World Movement of Peasants' Organizations, or *La Via Campesina*, which today includes 180 million small farmers

---

63. Ibid., 5, as quoted from the veteran food organization Just Food (2010).

64. Nathan McClintock, "From Industrial Garden to Food Desert: Demarcated Devaluation in the Flatlands of Oakland," in *Cultivating Food Justice*, 112.

65. Gustavo Duch Guillot and Fernando Fernández Such, *Agro-Industry under Suspicion* (Barcelona: Christianisme I Justicia Booklets, 2011), 24–28.

from around the globe. The food sovereignty for which they work echoes concerns already mentioned: the "right of peoples to healthy and culturally appropriate food produced through ecologically sound and sustainable methods."[66] But it also underscores their right to design, determine, and define their own food and agricultural systems.Hence, it places the needs and vision of those who grow and consume food at the heart of the food system, superseding the demands of markets and corporations.

The struggle for food sovereignty, as led by *La Via Campesina*, demands that national governments guarantee their people an adequate food supply and access to natural resources, as well as protect the rights of agricultural workers and native peoples.[67] It looks to the Food and Agricultural Organization of the United Nations to determine international policies relating to food supplies and to evaluate agricultural strategies to ensure they are not destroying natural resources. It speaks out against the WTO's international norms for agricultural commerce that seriously undermine the food security of small farmers in developing nations and advocates for government policies in developed countries that enable small-scale, local agriculture.

The right to food that underscores the three strategies just explored is inscribed in the Universal Declaration of Human Rights and the Internal Covenant on Economic, Social and Cultural Rights.[68] While described in great detail in these documents, the right to food is "above all the right to be able to feed oneself in dignity." It is much less about dependency on governments or charity to feed people than about the empowerment of individuals and communities

66. Defined by the Declaration of Nyéléni, the first global forum on food sovereignty, Mali, 2007.

67. Duch Guillot and Fernandez Such, "Agro-Industry," 24–28. What follows is from this source.

68. Clare Mahon, "The Right to Food: A Right for Everyone," in Rosin, Stock and Campbell, *Food Systems Failure*, 83. See pages 83–95 for what follows.

to provide themselves with adequate, culturally appropriate food through systems of food production of their own choosing. Based on such a human rights approach, Clare Mahon identifies seven principles for reframing agricultural policies: participation (especially of small-scale farmers), greater accountability, nondiscrimination, empowerment, transparency, the rule of law, and, most especially, a safeguarding of human dignity.[69] Mahon proposes four strategies that are imperative for the systemic change necessary to ensure justice and empowerment: (1) "prioritizing the protection of the most vulnerable," recognizing that poor rural families represent 75 percent of the people currently suffering from hunger; (2) replacing policies/practices of food aid (often simply a dumping of surplus farm goods from developed nations in developing countries) with an obligatory commitment to international cooperation, including a sharing of markets, materials, finance, and expertise; (3) a reframing of polices regarding biofuel production to protect the human right to food and Earth's right to healthy ecosystems; and (4) a closer regulation of agricultural commodities trading that disciplines excessive market speculation and ensures the availability of staple foods at stable prices.

According to Vandana Shiva, the final component of a just food system for the future involves a reclaiming of Earth commons— those spaces and resources that are understood to belong to all and not to a few, namely, water, land, seeds, and intellectual knowledge.[70] A commons implies that resources are owned, managed, and used by a community. A commons embodies social relations based on interdependence and cooperation and on clear rules, principles, and systems of decision making. Moreover, a commons represents ethical boundaries that have been created over the centuries by faiths, cultures, and societies who declared certain things are not

---

69. Ibid., 91–92. What follows is taken from this source.

70. See Shiva, *Earth Democracy*, 2–4, 18–19. What follows is taken from this source.

part of commerce but are governed by values other than commodity values. Today, corporate globalization, a key strategy of the industrial food system, is enclosing the commons, turning them into privatized entities under the control of a few. Enclosing the commons entails both exclusion and violence—an exclusion of people from access to resources that were once considered common property, and the turning of Earth's abundance, able to provide numerous services to meet many needs, into raw materials for the market. The result is the creation of private property from what formerly belonged to all and of disposable people, disowned economically, politically, and culturally. Shiva contends that reclaiming these commons as places "where justice and sustainability converge" and "where ecology and equity meet" is essential for the future of food.

Questions for Reflection

1) What aspect of a revitalized mosaic of food systems described in this chapter most engages your imagination? Where do you see it taking root, in what setting, and by what initiatives?

2) How do images like regeneration, justice, and food sovereignty spark your hopes for a revitalized human/planetary community?

3) What links do you see between new forms of food production and new ways of building up communities of faith, their spirituality, and their liturgical practice?

part three

Eucharist

The Meal That Reconnects

The joy and hope, the grief and anguish of the people of our time, especially of those who are poor or afflicted in any way, are the joy and hope, the grief and anguish of the followers of Christ as well. Nothing that is genuinely human fails to find an echo in their hearts. For theirs is a community composed of people who, united in Christ and guided by the Holy Spirit, press onwards towards the kingdom of God and are bearers of a message intended for all people. (GS 1)[1]

At all times, the church carries the responsibility of reading the signs of the times and of interpreting them in the light of the Gospel. (GS 4)

1. Vatican II, *Gaudium et Spes* 1, 4, in *Vatican Council II: The Conciliar and Post Conciliar Documents*, ed. Austin Flannery (Collegeville, MN: Liturgical Press, 2014).

These stirring words, articulated in *Gaudium et Spes* at the climax of the Second Vatican Council, invite us to reflect on what has unfolded in the first two sections of this volume and prompt us to ask: How is the current food crisis that is creating manifold forms of human suffering around the globe and violating the productive capacity of the Earth a glaring "sign of the times" calling Christians to pay attention? How is it finding an echo within the hearts of those who claim to be the body of Christ in the world and moving them to act in solidarity with those who suffer? How might Christians embrace more fully their vocation as bearers of good news as they press onward toward the kingdom? How might they express that message in their ethical, liturgical, and spiritual lives? And, how might the celebration of Christian Eucharist be key to the healing of broken human and planetary relationships, shaping new patterns of living marked by compassion, respect, and equity?

The two chapters that follow address these questions. Chapter 8 invites a reclaiming of the foundational meal character of eucharistic celebration, engaging a hermeneutic of liturgical symbols and actions[2] to explore its significance in forming communities for prophetic action in a world of broken relationships. Chapter 9 probes the embeddedness of Eucharist in ecological, social, and economic forces that shape today's global society and asks how Christian table fellowship can become a moral force for goodness, justice, and planetary healing.

---

2. See David N. Power, "Eucharistic Justice," *Theological Studies* 67 (2006): 857.

chapter eight

Reclaiming the Foundational Meal Character of Eucharistic Celebration

Laudato Sí, promulgated by Pope Francis in 2015, is a clarion call, a strong and heartfelt plea to people around the globe to wake up, recognize the global emergency that surrounds us, and come head-to-head with the crisis that politicians skirt and corporate beneficiaries deny and falsify. The whole Earth cries out, claims Pope Francis. Earth, our mother and sister, is being destroyed, and, as we have seen in earlier chapters of this volume, the corporate agricultural system is making money off its destruction. While corporate executives become wealthier, the poor of the Earth, devoid of power, suffer the ravages of a world made inhospitable to and unsupportive of their life projects.

Where else can these truths be proclaimed, if not in the community of the living church, who claim to be disciples of Jesus and to live his gospel message of justice and compassion? And where better than at the symbolic meal that is at the heart of Christian practice, a meal celebrated in memory of Jesus, whose table fellowship was a continuous response to human need, estrangement, suffering, and exclusion?

Pope Francis's appeal adds urgency to reading the signs of the times concerning a broken food system, and it offers insight into how we might respond as persons of faith. Furthermore, if Christian Eucharist is to be a "meal that reconnects," that reweaves broken relationships and forms communities for prophetic action, communities must reclaim and revitalize the foundational character of Eucharist as a meal. This means change, as Pope Francis indicates so strongly (LS 202), change in the attitudes and strategies that have served eucharistic communities over many years and a new openness to the transformative action of the Holy Spirit who, the Scriptures tell us, is always doing something new!

Why this emphasis on the Eucharist as a meal? Invoking the earliest chapters of this volume, we recall that in Jesus' ministry table fellowship was a primary place for the in-breaking of God's reign and a sign of God's new creation. Meal gatherings were places of rebuilding human unity, of responding to real human needs, of restoring relationships of mutuality, acceptance, reconciliation, and equality.[1] Jesus turned not to the religious institutions of his day but to the practice of simple meals where a new, inclusive fellowship was formed, rooted in service, love, and friendship. Gathered at table, Jesus formed his disciples for a prophetic ministry of peace and reconciliation in a world where oppression, poverty, and stratification reigned. And it was at table that he breathed on them the awaited and transformative Holy Spirit who would guide them into the future (John 19:23).

Likewise, the earliest Christians, in birthing a eucharistic tradition, came together for the sharing of food and drink, telling and retelling stories of Jesus and experiencing his presence among them. Their table gatherings were filled with challenge: whether and how to eat together across boundaries of food restrictions, and how, in

---

1. See Ched Myers, *Binding the Strongman: A Political Reading of Mark's Story of Jesus* (Maryknoll, NY: Orbis Books, 1988), 440–41.

coming together, to discern the true body of Christ and to live the inclusion and mutual care this invited (1 Cor 11:29). In meals that embodied values of service, mutual support, friendship, generosity, and hospitality, they offered thanks and shared food in ways that resisted imperial power, claiming a Lord whose name is above all other names (Phil 2:9) while they responded to the daily needs of all in their midst.

Today, both the broken food system and the urgency of *Laudato Sí* call Christians to reembrace a vital meal fellowship as integral to eucharistic practice.[2] First, sharing real food and drink at the heart of a eucharistic gathering invites a deeper recognition of our kinship with the Earth, our dependence on its gifts of nourishment, and the costly love entailed in providing a community with precious sustenance. Sharing simple gifts of food and drink can reveal our interconnected existence as creatures of God, dependent on one another and created to form a "sublime communion" (LS 89). The wholeness and integrity of these nourishing foods speak not only of the beauty of creation but of its brokenness, of those whose tables are not graced with food and drink and whose suffering is deeply related to Earth's suffering.

Second, Pope Francis is clear: individual responses, or a "united effort bred in an individualistic way," even when rooted in a real spirit of conversion, are simply not adequate to the enormity of the challenges we face. Rather, a "union of skills and a unity of achievement" that grow out of a "deep communal conversion" are essential (LS 219). A true meal fellowship, where bonds of friendship and networks of service are nurtured, can inspire and build this community response.

Third, encountering the risen Christ in the setting of table fellowship where the Gospel is preached and ministries of service, one to another, are actualized, can deepen communities' awareness of Jesus'

---

2. David Grumett muses that "it is extraordinary that the Eucharist, in which . . . food items are central, is so infrequently related to agriculture and food supply." *Material Eucharist* (Oxford: Oxford University Press, 2016), 69.

abiding and sustaining presence. Jesus calls Christians to embody his provocative ways of inclusion, justice, and hospitality; his identification with the poor and suffering; and his self-sacrificing dedication to the work of God in the world. Moreover, Jesus' attentiveness to those not present—those missing, discouraged, scandalized, disillusioned, angered, or simply disabled—calls communities to seek out those who have been estranged, especially the young, whose creativity and insight are especially needed for a vital response to complex needs. Widening the horizon of our tables and expanding the complexity of our communities is essential to restoring a broken food system.

Fourth, the ecological conversion by which communities become true disciples and active agents of God's transformative love in the world is best sustained by the shared inspiration, bold creativity, wild imagination, and acts of care and tenderness experienced in the community's meal sharing, all enabled through the workings of the Holy Spirit whose transformative presence is at the heart of Eucharist.

With these invitations in mind, we now focus on five aspects of the eucharistic celebration that are critical for a revitalization of its meal character. We assume throughout that Eucharist is a relational and embodied event, with power to shape affections and imaginations and to evoke lived experience in its ambiguity and complexity. What is tasted, touched, heard, seen, and felt as movements in space and vibrations in one's body awaken imagination and shape a community's sense of call to come to the eucharistic table so as to be God's healing and transforming presence in a hurting world.

An Assembling Community

Assembling as a community of disciples is a foundational action; coming together, acting together, living into the community's identity and mission as Christ's body in the world are crucial to all that takes place in eucharistic celebration. But how is this action uniquely shaped today by the challenges of a planet experiencing deep suffering and an imbalanced human community where many are deprived of basic human necessities?

Assembling is a powerful act in today's world, illegal under some repressive governments, yet cropping up in every part of the planet. The freedom to come together, to express shared values, to agitate for change, and to press for renewal is a potent force. In marches, demonstrations, and rallies, women march for justice and equality, children unite their voices for climate action, and farmworkers press for a revolution of bread and justice. Each group engaging together, gaining strength from the felt union of purpose, expresses a common passion for values that only bodies assembled can adequately capture. Assembling in each case is both a political and a social act, shaping minds and hearts of those who assemble as much as the social and political forces that surround them.

Assembling as a eucharistic community, expressing its identity and mission visibly and together, and allowing the church to be "manifest" in the world[3] recognizes the powerful presence of Christ and the Spirit acting in the community in the face of political and social forces. Like the meal practice of the earliest Christians, whose gatherings around a table became a countersign to the imperial hegemony at work in their context, so the embodied action of assemblies today situates each Christian community vis-à-vis the political and social arena in which they live.

In light of the calls of *Laudato Sí*, assembling communities cannot be neutral about the destructive forces that are ravaging Mother Earth. A strong sense of interconnectedness with and responsibility for the Earth must be nurtured and expressed in words and concrete actions within the event of eucharistic worship and beyond. Recognizing,

---

3. Vatican II, *Sacrosanctum Concilium* 2. I use the term "assembling" rather than "assembled" because the action of coming together in self-offering and common thanksgiving must happen repeatedly throughout the eucharistic celebration for a true "active participation" to unfold.

feeling within one's body and spirit, that we are part of nature, an inter-related part of a fragile planetary community (LS 139), as Pope Francis writes, takes on salience over time and deepens slowly. With this realization that we are part of Earth and her vital forces comes the call for repentance—not a personal beating of the breast, but a crying out about the devastation that is happening, an acknowledgment that we are complicit. As part of the problem, we must change our lives. Repentance as a quick acknowledgment of personal sin is simply not enough. What is taking place in the global food system is serious social sin and it must be named and repented of. Truth telling and change go hand in hand.

Christian assemblies have deep roots. Beginning with the ancient Hebrew people, God's action of calling and gathering a people has been experienced by generation after generation.[4] The Hebrew people, called out of Egypt and liberated from slavery, were given a new identity and invited to embrace Torah as a way of life. Assembled at Sinai, they were named "God's people"—the "*Qahal Yahweh*" or "Assembly of Yahweh"[5]—with an active mission in the world (Exod 19–24). But first they had to endure a desert experience, a sojourn that taught them the essentials of the life to which they were called: to trust God for nourishment and to embrace a "manna economy" in which accumulation, hoarding of more than one's daily needs, became counterproductive, since stored manna became corrupt and soured (Exod 16). Still on the move, they were taught to travel lightly. Displaced and without a home themselves, they learned to remember their neighbor and be kind to the alien stranger in the land.

Christian assembling is likewise a response to being called to a new identity and mission in the world, one that is always evolving and must be embraced anew in light of the world's changing needs.

---

4. See A. G. Mortimort, *The Church at Prayer: Principles of the Liturgy* (Collegeville, MN: Liturgical Press, 1987), 92–98.

5. Ibid., 92.

Called to be the living body of Christ, to embrace his gospel of justice and mercy, to act in solidarity and service, and to express values in prophetic action, assembling communities are likewise both "settled" and "on the move." As pilgrims who follow Christ, who "goes before them into Galilee" and who is always on the road ahead of them (Mark 16:7),[6] Christian communities are missioned as both "servants of God and servants to the world,"[7] caring for "the least of these" as incarnations of Jesus in their midst (Matt 25:31-45). Like Christ, they are called to seek greater unity and solidarity with all persons of faith, especially those united by a common Christian baptism,[8] inviting them to share the same eucharistic table, as Pope Francis encouraged recently, and embracing eucharistic eating as "a unifying sacrament" that enables Christians to "work together in service of the poor, the sick, and the marginalized."[9]

It is essential that the justice sought in the world beyond the eucharistic gathering be operative within the assembling community, that the voices who speak out in solidarity with the suffering Earth be heard within the liturgical gathering, and that all members of the community feel empowered to witness to the Good News of Christ. Gathering in such a way that all present feel close to the action,

6. Myers, *Binding the Strong Man*, 443. The phenomenon of being "settled," in contrast to being in migration or on the move, is explored in Thomas Tweed's *Crossing and Dwelling: A Theory of Religion* (Boston: Harvard University Press, 2016).

7. Image taken from National Conference of Catholic Bishops, Committee on the Liturgy, *Environment and Art in Catholic Worship* (Washington, DC: USCC Publication Office, 1978), nos. 37–38.

8. The opening sentence of *Sacrosanctum Concilium* of Vatican II states that fostering "whatever can promote union among all who believe in Christ" was a primary aim of the council. *SC* no. 1.

9. Thomas Reese, " 'Let's Not Wait for the Theologians,' Says Pope Francis about Sharing the Eucharist," *National Catholic Reporter* (June 6, 2019), https://www .ncronline.org/print/news/vatican/signs-times/lets-not-wait-theologians-says -pope-francis-about-sharing-eucharist, accessed July 5, 2019.

invited to engage in its "living words and gestures,"[10] and enabled to speak their heart's truth, where differences do not divide but enrich the whole community, and where all members are actively welcomed and engaged—these shape the community for witness and liberating action beyond the gathering.

Assembling at the threshold of a eucharistic celebration today, communities need to see, hear, and experience the reality of a suffering Earth and her struggling people in such a way that it awakens their desire to rebuild broken relationships. Two communities offer food for thought. A community in western Canada has transformed a vacant lot beside the church into a permaculture garden where members toil to raise fruits and vegetables for local food pantries. Passing through this colorful and fragrant expression of God's creation on Sunday morning—and occasionally gathering there for opening rites—members are often met by neighbors who contribute daily to the work of the garden and who wish to join them for Sunday worship. Indeed, they are always welcome.

St. Boniface Parish in San Francisco's Tenderloin district provides sacred space and sanctuary within its church for people who otherwise would sleep on the streets. Offering compassionate respite during the day and blessed sleep at night,[11] St. Boniface has become a welcoming force within an asphalt jungle where life on the streets is raw and dangerous. As members of the parish arrive for morning Eucharist, houseless guests are often resting in the pews nearest the main entry and at times gather with the assembling community.[12]

10. NCCB, *Environment and Art*, no. 29.

11. For more information, see the website of St. Boniface Catholic Church, http://stbonifacesf.org/, and specifically "The Gubbio Project," https://www.thegubbioproject.org/.

12. See Heather Knight, "Project Gubbio at St. Boniface: Sanctuary of Sleep," *San Francisco Chronicle*, Sunday, January 26, 2014, https://www.sfgate.com/bayarea/article/Project-Gubbio-at-St-Boniface-sanctuary-of-sleep-3407103.php, accessed July 11, 2019.

Many of these guests will find their daily meals at St. Anthony's Dining Room a few blocks away, meals at which some of the parishioners will serve.

In both cases, what communities encounter at the threshold of their eucharistic gathering speaks of mission, justice, and God's transformative love, poured out and pulsing in this very place.

A Common Table

Throughout Christian history, the church has oscillated between understandings of altar and table. In early church communities, altar and table were often the same, as the community shared food both for the body and for the soul. On the other hand, the great cathedrals of Europe, with their towers spiraling toward the heavens, required more than a simple table to celebrate the "holy mysteries."[13] In today's world, with its brutal inequalities between who eats and who does not, a Christian sense of justice invites a full focus on the table—a common table—as the evocative center of an assembling community.[14] A simple table can speak eloquently of food and feeding and of Christ's call to find him precisely in the hungry peoples of the Earth.

The table used for eucharistic eating should be modest in size and quality, becoming part of the "serving environment" within which the liturgy takes place.[15] "Less is more," states Pope Francis, describing the qualities of the new lifestyle that can counter the extreme consumerism of today's market economy that so easily becomes the

13. Recent liturgical documents from Catholic sources, such as the General Instruction on the Roman Missal, use both terms, although "altar" predominates.

14. The General Instruction on the Roman Missal 8 speaks of the "two tables" of Word and Eucharist that together form the heart of eucharistic liturgy. What is proposed here in no way denies the importance of the "table of God's Word" but simply invites reflection on the nature of the eucharistic table.

15. NCCB, *Environment and Art*, no. 24.

"seedbed for collective selfishness" (LS 204). In using these images, Pope Francis proposes that we must reduce our environmental footprint, rather than enlarge it, and deepen our sense of social responsibility (LS 203, 206). A table for eucharistic eating might likewise speak of the community's Earth consciousness and social relatedness. *Laudato Sí* speaks of "the awakening of a new reverence for life, the firm resolve to achieve sustainability, the quickening of the struggle for justice and peace, and the joyful celebration of life" (LS 207).[16] These too speak to the table's quality: beautiful yet unassuming, made of local materials by a local artist, and evocative of the daily nourishment, the bread we beseech of God in the Lord's Prayer.

Focusing on the table raises questions about relationships within the assembling community: who serves at table, who has access, who ministers to whom and when. Too easily the table becomes a source of distinctions, of establishing prestige, of marking hierarchies, and of keeping the community divided into those with power and those without. Yet the call to all communities is to become a serving church in the world, ministering in the name of Jesus so that God's kingdom may arrive. Such a shared calling of the people of God challenges power distinctions, which, when practiced in liturgy, shape daily lives. How do communities become united in the gospel calling to ministry that flows from their common baptism? How does eucharistic eating form the whole community as active participants in the mission of the church?

Today, the common table needs to link the community who gathers around it to the common good.[17] Images of the common good

16. Pope Francis is here quoting from the closing sentence of *Earth Charter* (The Hague: June 29, 2000), https://earthcharter.org/discover/the-earth-charter/, accessed July 7, 2019.

17. Several explanations of the common good exist in Catholic Social Teaching. *Gaudem et Spes* of Vatican II, for example, states: " 'God intended the earth with everything contained in it for the use of all human beings and peoples. Thus, under the leadership of justice and in the company of charity, created goods should be

shape the whole social doctrine of Christian churches and bring a moral imperative to those who gather for Eucharist. The community's table is linked to tables around the world—in poor villages, refugee camps, and urban dwellings—where the planetary community negotiates who has access to nourishment and who does not. In a poignant image from *Laudato Sí*, Pope Francis speaks about the vast amounts of food that are wasted today: "whenever food is thrown out, it is as if it were stolen from the table of the poor" (LS 50). What responsibility does each assembling community have for those who lack basic necessities? Is a community's access to good food simply a mark of privilege, or can the eucharistic meal awaken it to the needs of the tables of others? There is indeed a strong connection between what communities put on this holy common table and what they share so that others may live.

The shape, size and placement of the common table speak of the common life of the community. Like other furnishings in the worship space, the table should be beautiful in its simplicity, should "invite and need the assembly to complete it," and should bring it closer together, enabling participants to feel connected, become involved, and "see and hear the entire liturgical action."[18] For disciples who followed Jesus in his day, "the primary personal and social virtue sought by members of this newly emergent . . . community was to be *diakonia*, service at table."[19]

---

in abundance for all in like manner.' It added that 'the universal destination of earthy goods' supersedes even legitimate, societal forms of property. This amounts to a radical statement of distributive justice: 'everything contained in' the earth is intended by God 'for the use of all human beings and peoples . . . for all in like manner.' " See *Gaudium et Spes*, 1965, no. 69. As noted in Christiana Zenner, *Just Water: Theology, Ethics, and Fresh Water Crisis*, rev. ed. (Maryknoll, NY: Orbis Books, 2018), 75–76.

18. NCCB, *Environment and Art*, no. 24.

19. Nathan Mitchell, *Eucharist as Sacrament of Initiation* (Chicago: Liturgy Training Publications, 1994), 100.

Reflecting on the eucharistic table's size and shape, Peter Phan critiques the powerful influence Leonardo da Vinci's portrayal of Jesus' Last Supper has had on the imagination of Western theologians and worshiping communities.[20] Jesus is here portrayed as seated at a long, rectangular table with twelve male disciples on either side of him. The scene suggests "a private banquet of an elite male-only club," notes Phan.[21] Where are the faithful women? Where are the children whom Jesus blessed? Where are the outcasts, the sick, and the poor with whom Jesus sat at table? Moreover, the long, rectangular table, with its sharp edges and corners, leaves some diners out of reach of Jesus, creating an implicit hierarchy among them. Phan concludes that a Vietnamese artist would undoubtedly have portrayed the table as round, as found in most Asian families, accommodating as many people as necessary, offering easy access to food and conversation to all and enabling women, men, children, guests, and host to be equal, since the circle begins with anyone and ends with everyone. Phan notes that metaphysically, this inclusiveness is expressed "in Asian experience by the symbols of *yin* and *yang* forming a circle where opposites are united to achieve cosmic harmony."[22]

Phan's comments invite communities to reflect interculturally and interdenominationally regarding their eucharistic table. What can we learn from each other? How can we energize our common mission in a hurting world? Welcoming others to our tables can release a new vigor into our shared striving for justice, a goal that was articulated in the first paragraph of the first document of Vatican II: "This Sacred Council . . . desires to impart an ever increasing vigor to the Christian life of the faithful [and] to foster whatever can

20. Peter Phan, *Being Religious Interreligiously* (Maryknoll, NY: Orbis Books, 2004), 254. What follows is from this source.

21. Ibid.

22. See Agnes M. Brazal's exploration of "Church as Sacrament of Yin-Yang Harmony: Toward a More Incisive Participation of Laity and Women in the Church," *Theological Studies* 80, no. 2 (2019): 414–35.

promote union among all who believe in Christ."[23] How fitting that the eucharistic table should draw us together! As Pope Francis said recently, "Ecumenism is not getting to the end of discussions, it's done walking together."[24]

Always, vessels for food and drink are placed on the common table. The quality and beauty of these vessels speak of the community's reverence. But standards of what bespeaks quality may differ, especially in the context of the glaring inequalities of the Earth community today. Precious metals, often held up as essential for the holy mystery they will facilitate, may instead convey privilege, wealth, and power. Patristic theologian, John Chrysostom, offered this norm to his community: "Do you wish to honor the body of Christ? Do you ignore him when he is naked? Do not pay homage in the temple clad in silk, only then to neglect him outside where he suffers cold and nakedness. He who said, 'This is my body,' is the same One who said: 'You saw me hungry and gave me no food,' and 'Whatever you did to the least of my brothers you did also to me.' . . . What good is it if the eucharistic table is overloaded with golden chalices, when he is dying of hunger? Start by satisfying his hunger, and then, with what is left, you may adorn the altar as well."[25]

A Common Loaf and Cup

Earthy gifts of food and drink, placed on the common table, can speak of the interconnectedness communities have with each other, with Christ, with soil, sun, and pollinators, and with human and other creatures who depend on the Earth for nourishment. How

---

23. *Sacrosanctum Concilium* 1.

24. Reese, "Let's Not Wait."

25. John Chrysostom, *Homilies on the Gospel of Matthew* 50.3–4. J.-P. Migne, *Petrologiae cursus completes: Series Graeca.* As quoted by John Paul II in *Dies Domini* 71, in *The Liturgy Documents*, vol. 2 (Chicago: Liturgy Training Publications, 1999), 39.

this interdependence is evoked and realized is critical to revitalizing eucharistic eating today. In a world where millions suffer hunger and malnutrition, the ability of eucharistic food and drink to bespeak earthly sustenance and care, to express divine hospitality and human ingenuity, and to be experienced as real nourishment is pivotal for the fullness of the eucharistic action.

Foods shared at the eucharistic tables of the earliest communities spoke of this interdependence. What was most distinctive about the early communities, writes O'Loughlin, was not so much the contents of the food itself but the emphasis they placed on the "one loaf," broken and shared by all.[26] St. Paul, writing to the Corinthian community, remarks that "the singularity of the loaf is a realization of the unity of the new people: 'Because there is one loaf, we who are many are one body, for we partake of the one loaf' (1 Cor 10:17)."[27] To eat of the common loaf is to share life, bonded in a common faith in Jesus. The *Didache* further nuances Paul's understanding, stressing that the unity of the loaf depends on multiple grains, drawn from their separateness and transformed into a single whole through the action of Christ.[28] The image is dynamic and evocative: Christ actively forming and transforming the gathered community into his body in the world.

The symbolic power of the one loaf, though, does not end with the coming together of grains of wheat to form a single loaf but rather in its being taken, blessed, broken, and shared. These actions speak of discipleship and mission, of Christ's self-sacrificial offering and kenotic love poured out in his paschal mystery, and of his call to his disciples to "Follow me." For the one loaf to image the world's feeding through the ministry of Christ's followers, it must undergo the rupture of being broken, split apart, and transformed into nourishment, so that those who partake of the loaf may become leaven for the world. Hence, a clear, evocative action of breaking the common

26. O'Loughlin, *Eucharist*, 159–66. What follows draws on his perspective.
27. Ibid., 160.
28. Ibid., 151.

loaf in eucharistic gatherings today is critical to reconnecting eucharistic eating with service to a world of human suffering.

Likewise the cup: early focus was not on the contents of the cup but on Jesus' invitation to drink from a common vessel, drinking from the same cup rather than drinking the same wine. Sharing a common cup was a boundary ritual, a bonding in a collective commitment to costly discipleship. In Mark's gospel, Jesus' response to James and John, when asked if they could sit beside him in glory, was a query: "Can you drink the cup of which I drink?" (Mark 10:38). Indeed, they would drink the cup of his suffering. For disciples then and now, drinking from a common cup affirms the community's embrace of the dangerous memory of Jesus' life and ministry and their own shared discipleship. Moreover, it invites them to overcome boundaries of race, sex, social status, ethnicity, and religion that would otherwise divide them (Gal 3:26-28) and to love one another as a community of friends, partners in the radical call to discipleship (John 13:15).

In earliest practice, community members made the bread, a custom that offered a deep sense of engagement in the whole process of eucharistic offering. Milling grain, sifting flour, combining ingredients, shaping loaves, all the while cooperating with the processes of growth and transformation begun in the Earth itself, creates an intimacy with the feel of the dough and the compelling fragrance of baked bread, an intimacy that can only become more profound in the sharing of Christ's body.

The question of who makes the bread for eucharistic eating—who shapes the one loaf— is a significant one today. Since the shift to unleavened bread near the turn of the first millennium, touching and shaping the bread has been relegated to a progressively smaller and more elite set of persons: clerics, monks, and men and women religious.[29] Today, the token wafers that have replaced nourishing

---

29. See, for example, Mary Collins's exposé of "The Bread Sign: Layer upon Layer of Meaning," in "Critical Questions for Liturgical Theology," in *Worship: Renewal to Practice* (Washington, DC: The Pastoral Press, 1987), 119–23.

bread for many communities are the product of mechanized processes by huge industrial machinery, losing all connection with the
ministry of the assembled community. Moreover, wafers lack the
evocative quality essential to revitalizing eucharistic eating: the
image of the one loaf, composed of many grains and broken for
world's healing. In contrast, recovering the communal ministry of
baking eucharistic bread at a time when food crises encircle the
globe is a potent way to inspire and impel communities to engage
in feeding the world. Moreover, reconnecting with Earth's transformative processes of growing and ripening the grain and oil needed
for making bread can awaken a deeper sense of the hidden sacra-
mentality of all natural elements.[30]

An additional concern regarding the nature of the loaf and cup
marks many of our churches across the globe. How do these elements become images of shared discipleship with Christ in settings
where wheat bread and grape wine are imported elements, with little
or no association with the "fruits of the Earth" grown locally? Could
not the loaf broken and cup shared in a community's eucharistic
eating be drawn from foods that nourish them daily?[31] How does a
community's Eucharist suffer when these foundational symbols of
God's nourishment do not honor the produce of their own lands?

---

30. David Grumett comments that "eucharistic matter is more like other matter,
not less like it, than might be supposed. The recognition of this fact opens the
exciting possibility of viewing Christ's eucharistic body in continuity with other
material bodies in the world." See *Material Eucharist*, 8.

31. David Power, "Eucharistic Justice," *Theological Studies* 67 (2006): 867. See
also David Power, "The Eucharistic Table: In Communion with the Hungry,"
Worship 83, no. 5 (September 2009): 386–98. For timely proposals, see Elochukwu
E. Uzukwu, "Food and Drink in Africa and the Christian Eucharist," *African Ecclesial Review* 22, no. 6 (1980): 370–85; and Stephen Victor M. Ofo-ob, "The Appropriateness of Rice Wine in the Celebration of the Holy Eucharist in the
Episcopal Church in the Philippines" (Berkeley, CA: MTS thesis, Church Divinity School of the Pacific, 2017).

Should not the "loaf broken" and the "cup shared" reflect the gift of today's ecclesial diversity and affirm the plurality of the living body of Christ? And, as David Power suggests, is this not a matter of eucharistic justice? [32]

A Table of Abundance: Enough for All and to Spare

One of the myths of the industrial food system is that Earth is unable to provide enough for all to eat, that scarcity is the future, and that some will always be without the food they need.[33] Such a myth of Earth's incapacity gives license to manipulate, control, and force her into submission so that the superior intelligence of a corporate enterprise can make up for her deficiency. Yet research shows that, despite our abuse, there remains enough today for everyone's need, if shared equitably.[34] And, when the living Earth is freed from its servitude through organic and restorative nurture, its produce multiplies. Frances Moore Lappé concludes that hunger and famine "are not natural disasters but social disasters: the result of human arrangements, not acts of God. Blaming nature, we fail to see that *human institutions* determine who will have a claim on food; . . . who will be chronically vulnerable; . . . and who will use hunger against whom. Food is often used as a weapon of war," writes Lappé, "and hunger is always a product of it."[35]

32. See Power, "Eucharistic Justice," 867–69, for an excellent reflection on the integrity of the food.

33. Frances Moore Lappé, *World Hunger: Twelve Myths* (New York: Grove Press, 1998), 8–24.

34. See Christopher Uhl, *Developing Ecological Consciousness* (Lanham, MD: Roman and Littlefield, 2013), 194. Uhl notes that, "even in the face of our burgeoning population and our poor stewardship of Earth's soils, there is still the potential to adequately feed all human beings alive today."

35. Lappé, *World Hunger*, 23–24.

Many eucharistic communities today likewise ritualize scarcity.[36] Restrictions surround the bread and wine, the holy gifts that are at the heart of their eucharistic table fellowship. Ingredients in the bread may be limited (flour and water); only token wafers of bread may be used and in very small pieces; only a sip from the cup may be available, and drinking from the cup may be further restricted to only a few members of the assembly.[37] Often there are not enough altar breads consecrated for all participating in this service, so yesterday's portions must be retrieved from where they have been stored. Ministers who host the eucharistic gathering may eat before others are served, lest they not partake of the bread and wine consecrated at this celebration, and holy gifts of bread and wine may only be offered to some of those present whose lives are deemed worthy.[38] Finally, the eucharistic celebration itself is usually limited to situations where an ordained minister can take leadership.

The stories we tell and the myths we embody in liturgy shape the story we live in the world. [39] Ritualizing eucharistic scarcity impacts the vision we have of Earth's fruitfulness, our participation in it and the very generosity of God who sustains Earth and universe. Most especially, it flies in the face of Jesus' life and ministry: his eating with publicans and sinners and his promise that "no one who comes to me will ever be hungry" (John 6:35). The gospels overflow with generous feeding, boundless welcome, and ultimately Jesus' self-sacrificing death for the life of the world. How do these practices of "not enough" and "only some count" hold up in the scrutiny of the gospel?

---

36. My reflections here focus primarily on Roman Catholic communities, but they may resonate with practices in other congregations as well. On the other hand, communities that acknowledge the inappropriateness of eucharistic scarcity can be inspired by the practices of other assemblies across denominational lines.

37. I refer here to local jurisdictions restricting the reception of the eucharistic wine by most of the assembly.

38. I refer here to restrictions placed on persons divorced and remarried.

39. See Cynthia Moe Lobeda, *Resisting Structural Evil* (Minneapolis: Fortress Press, 2013), 262–63.

It is striking that in the iconography of the earliest centuries, Jesus' "Last Supper" is never pictured.[40] Rather, the frescos of the Roman catacombs are redundant with depictions of the multiplication of the loaves and fishes, with the baskets of leftovers surrounding each scene.[41] By far, images of this miraculous abundance of food provided by Jesus are the "earliest and always the favorite symbol of the Eucharist." And the frescos that depict these scenes of plentiful nourishment often appear in close architectural proximity to where an altar intended for Eucharist would have been located. In addition to portrayals of the great feeding, two other scenes appear as early icons of the Eucharist: the "banquet" of bread and fish, provided for the seven disciples on the shore of Tiberius shortly after Jesus' resurrection and in conjunction with a miraculous catch of fish; and the miracle of the wine at Cana in Galilee. Both incidents extend the themes of a generous bestowal of food and drink at Jesus' command. Both image the Eucharist as a prodigious banquet with enough food and drink to satisfy everyone's needs, with some to spare. How might these scenes of God's abundant hospitality shape the understandings of contemporary eucharistic communities? And how do they challenge the practice of eucharistic scarcity?

Accounts of the great feedings, recorded in all the gospels and twice in Mark, are instructive. In Mark's first account we are told that Jesus' heart went out to the crowd who followed him. Tired and hungry, they were like sheep without a shepherd (Mark 6:34-44). The disciples entreat him to send the crowd away to find bread for themselves. When pressed by Jesus to feed them from their own resources, the disciples can imagine only the scarcity of a market-based economy—two hundred denarii and still not enough to buy bread for all. Jesus challenges them to alternative ways of thinking:

---

40. Maurice Hassett, "Early Symbols of the Eucharist," *The Catholic Encyclopedia*, vol. 5 (New York: Robert Appleton Company, 1909), www.newadvent.org /cathen/05590a.htm, accessed July 5, 2019.

41. The contrast with the "Last Supper" as an image for Eucharist is notable: a small, male gathering, with only bread and wine.

the abundance of the kingdom arrives when their own limited resources, five barley loaves and a few fish, are put at the service of the
community, when cooperative sharing trumps individual posses-
siveness. Jesus takes, blesses, breaks, and gives the loaves and fish to
the disciples to distribute, a sign of God's boundless generosity
breaking through in simple acts of openhandedness and sharing that
were doubtlessly set in motion as food was offered. Mark tells us
that everyone ate, all were satisfied, and abundance overflowed.[42]

Pope Francis speaks of this alternative economy in terms of the
ecological conversion that he urges in *Laudato Sí*. Market economics
today, he points out, lead to extreme consumerism, to collective
selfishness, to greed, and to a loss of a sense of the common good
(LS 203–204). But God's "grace at work deep in our hearts," the
same grace that moved through the great feeding on the shore of
Tiberius, can bring about change: a new sense of social responsibility
that leads to self-limitation and simplicity and a deep concern for
the poorest in our midst (LS 205, 213). Earth's proclivity for abundance can only provide for all if individuals and communities are
willing to take only what is their fair share and shape their lifestyles
in light of global neighbors.

Abundant eucharistic tables are critical at this time of crises for
Earth and her peoples; they must be tables where real food and drink
are blessed and broken to nourish the generosity, service and self-
sacrificing love of all who surround them and where the overflow
of Jesus' self-offering becomes nourishment to sustain human and
planetary life. The plenitude of the eucharistic table will be recognized not by the excess of things placed on or around it but in the
simple beauty of human food and drink—enough for all and to
spare—and by the generous service of those who minister that food
one to another.

Early Christian communities, notes David Power, brought food
to their eucharistic gatherings from which they selected the loaf and

---

42. I follow the interpretation of Ched Myers in *Binding the Strongman*, 441–43.

wine used for the Breaking of the Bread.[43] What food remained was for the use of the community gathered and for all who were poor and in need. This practice of a threefold gathering of gifts might engage communities today. Moreover, offering food to all present, no matter what may be their affiliation with the baptized community, can speak of gospel generosity and Jesus' inclusive table. By drawing on the ancient practice of *eulogia*—bread that is blessed but unconsecrated—communities might offer bread to all.[44] *Eulogia* has extensive roots in Western Christian liturgy and remains normative in many Orthodox Christian traditions today. In Orthodox practice, *eulogia* is usually cut from a whole leavened loaf that is too large to consecrate. What is not consecrated is distributed at the end of the service.[45] Historically, *eulogia* was offered at the conclusion of the eucharistic liturgy to catechumens, to the poor and sick, and to all who wished to receive it. Blessings of *eulogia* acknowledge food as a gift of God and may invoke the divine fullness to abide in this earthly nourishment. Recovering the practice of *eulogia* through study, discernment, and pastoral sensitivity might enable communities to extend eating together at the Lord's table to include all who are present.

Thanksgiving for Earth and All Creation

Eucharist has been understood from the earliest centuries as an event of thanksgiving, an offering of praise that wells up in the created universe and in the hearts of the assembling community.[46] Only in union with creation can human praise and thanksgiving be complete.

---

43. Power, "Eucharistic Justice," 866.

44. I draw this information from Grumett, *Material Eucharist*, 258–63.

45. Often in Orthodox churches, the number of those who receive the consecrated bread and wine is limited.

46. See Justin Martyr, for example, *Apology* 65.1, 66.1, in R. C. D. Jasper and G. J. Cuming, *Prayers of the Eucharist*, 4th ed., ed. Paul F. Bradshaw and Maxwell E. Johnson (Collegeville, MN: Liturgical Press, 2019), 25–26.

Without intermingling with the stars and galaxies, the rivers and oceans, the singing birds and composting microbes, human praise would fall far short of the glory of the living God revealed in Christ.[47] *Laudato Sí* speaks of Eucharist as "the living center of the universe" that unites heaven and Earth. According to Pope Francis, "Joined to the incarnate Son, present in the Eucharist, the whole cosmos gives thanks to God" (LS 236).

Why, then, is creation so often missing from the consciousness of celebrating communities and from the prayers, hymns, homiletic imagery, and art by which they express their praise and thanksgiving? And when made explicit, do the creational images and narratives truly take hold of the assembling community, strongly evoking in their hearts an awareness of their integral bond with every other creature in God's living cosmos and their deep responsibility for the future viability of planet Earth? How might an assembly's thanksgiving, expressed throughout the Eucharist, awaken and motivate their ethical and ecological response to the crises facing our world—especially those crises that deprive Earth's peoples of food and adequate nutrition—and move them to new initiatives for the sake of future generations?

Although thanksgiving should permeate the eucharistic event, it becomes most explicit in the great table prayer, the *anaphora*, or eucharistic prayer, that gathers up the energies of the entire eucharistic action in one expression of thanksgiving, praise, and offering. Although a plentiful remembrance of creation is typical of the earliest *anaphoras* to which we have access,[48] and is played out fully in

---

47. See Terrance E. Fretheim, "Nature's Praise," in *God and World in the Old Testament: A Relational Theology of Creation* (Nashville: Abingdon, 2005), 249–66. Fretheim speaks of a human-creaturely "symbiosis of praise." See also LS 159.

48. See Denis Edwards, "Eucharist and Ecology: Keeping Memorial of Creation," in *The Natural World and God: Theological Explorations* (Adelaide: ATF Publications, 2017), 137–56. Edwards traces creation motifs in many of the *anaphoras* used throughout history.

many of the newest prayers written for use within various denominations, many eucharistic prayers still make little reference to creation, focusing primarily on the redemptive action of Christ toward the human community in his great paschal mystery.

But creation and redemption are two parts of one great mystery: God's life poured out on behalf of the universe (LS 73), and Christ's "holding all things together" and reconciling all things to God, "whether on earth or in heaven," through the blood of his cross (Col 1:17, 20). Christ is the "first-born of creation," claims Paul's letter to the Colossians, and all things were created through him (Col 1:15, 16). Moreover, as Pope Francis elucidates in *Laudato Sí*, "the ultimate destiny of the universe is in the fullness of God," and this destiny "has already been attained by the risen Christ" (LS 83). Hence, the ultimate purpose of the created world "is not to be found in us," Francis states. "Rather, all creatures are moving forward with us and through us towards a common point of arrival, which is God, in that transcendent fullness where the risen Christ embraces and illumines all things" (LS 83).

These images of the interweaving of creation and Jesus' redemptive paschal mystery invite a much fuller expression in all eucharistic prayers. Across ecumenical lines, the imagery of newly composed prayers is being shaped by contemporary theologies of both creation and redemption and by emerging understandings of evolutionary biology, cosmology, and ecological consciousness.[49] An excerpt from one such prayer follows:

> O God triune, how majestic is your name in all the earth.
> Over the eons your merciful might evolved our home, a fragile
> tree of life.

49. See the work of Robert Daly and Gail Ramshaw in creating ecologically sensitive eucharistic prayers. Robert Daly, "Eucharistic Euchology," *Worship* 89, no. 2 (2015): 166–72; Gail Ramshaw, *Pray, Praise and Give Thanks* (Minneapolis: Augsburg Fortress, 2017). Also Catherine Vincie, *Worship and the New Cosmology* (Collegeville, MN: Liturgical Press, 2014), 105–8.

Here in your wisdom are both life and death, growth and decay,
  the nest and the hunt, sunshine and storm.
Sustained by these wonders, we creatures of dust join in the
  ancient song:
The earth is full of your glory!
The earth is full of your glory!

O God triune, you took on our flesh in Jesus our healer.
In Christ you bring life from death: we remember his cross
  and laud his resurrection.
Broken like bread he enlivens our body.
Outpoured like wine, he fills the earth with goodness.
Receiving this mystery, we mortals sing our song:
The earth is full of your glory!
The earth is full of your glory![50]

While finding appropriate words and images for prayers of
thanksgiving is important, communities need to ask: how do these
prayers of thanksgiving become vital, living expressions of our gratitude to God for the living Earth, acknowledgment of her abundant
care for all, and a communal commitment, through the grace of the
Holy Spirit, to protect and foster creation's future? The manner in
which prayers are offered—rhythm, tempo, interplay of voices, dynamic movement—affects how the prayers take root in the hearts
of participants. Given the presidential nature of the prayer—voiced
by one in the name of the whole assembly—new patterns of call and
response, of rhythmic and musical exchange, that engage communities dynamically in the outpouring of praise, can heighten people's

---

50. Gail Ramshaw, excerpt from "An Earth Eucharistic Prayer," in *Pray, Praise,
and Give Thanks*, 76. Copyright © 2017 Augsburg Fortress. All rights reserved.
Reproduced by permission. Note how she balances images of Earth as beautiful
and fragile, engaged in both life and death.

awareness that the created universe, its present and future flourishing, are integral to eucharistic praying and eating.[51]

Beyond voiced prayers, thanksgiving for creation needs to permeate the whole meal event of Eucharist. We touch briefly here on several directions. First, there needs to be liturgical engagement directly with the Earth, such as outdoor opening rites, harvest rites of blessing gardens and crops, tree plantings as part of the closing rite, or baptismal rites or renewals in local rivers. Second, artistic expressions that are part of the event must expand their focus on creation: hymnody, stained-glass imagery, baptistery iconography, and architecture that makes the natural world visible. Third, scriptural interpretation in homilies and shared reflection needs to be sensitive to the presence of Earth and her creatures, such as that invited by the recent work on the Earth Bible.[52] Fourth, closing rites should be transformed into true missioning events by which communities are actively sent forth from the Eucharist to heal a suffering planet and live in solidarity with her troubled peoples.

All of this is holy work; this is lived Eucharist. Revitalizing the meal character of eucharistic celebration through discernment, study, and creativity allows assembling communities to respond to the complex challenges of a verdant, suffering, struggling, and too often maligned planet home while providing a source of moral energy to work for the healing and well-being of all who share its gifts.

51. See Richard Fragomini, "Liturgy at the Heart of Creation," in *The Ecological Challenge: Ethical, Liturgical, and Spiritual Responses*, ed. John T. Pawlikowski (Collegeville, MN: Liturgical Press, 1994), 67–81.

52. See Norman C. Habel, ed., *Readings from the Perspective of Earth*, The Earth Bible (Sheffield: Sheffield Academic Press, 2000), 1. See also subsequent volumes in this series on particular books of the Bible.

Questions for Reflection

1) What new insights into the nature of Eucharist and its vitality for contemporary communities have you gained from this exploration? What might your community implement?

2) What new connections are you making between Jesus' table-fellowship, Pope Francis' directives in *Laudato Sí*, and your community's eucharistic eating?

3) Are there other aspects of eucharistic celebration that might be revitalized in light of the global food crisis? If so, how might your community address them?

chapter nine

Revitalizing the Ecological, Social, and Economic Embeddedness of Eucharistic Eating

The eucharistic tables at which Christians gather are situated at the intersection of vast global forces and relationships too numerous to name. "At the table, everything that creates the world is present: economics, politics, power, the potential for rivalry and competition, bonds among friends, boundaries against enemies."[1] This was as true for Jesus' meal fellowship and that of his early followers as it is for Christians today. It was precisely at this intersection that Jesus' meals became a "strategy for rebuilding human community on principles radically different from those of his surrounding social and religious culture."[2]

In a world highly stratified into rich and poor, Jesus' meal fellowship embodied a radical egalitarianism based on the innate worth of

---

1. Nathan Mitchell, *Eucharist as Sacrament of Initiation* (Chicago: Liturgy Training Publications, 1994), 79.

2. Ibid., 79–89.

each person.[3] In the face of Roman oppression, and the hoarding of wealth for a few, Jesus preached that the reign of God belongs to the destitute, the undesirables. His table sharing was not almsgiving—power giving to need—since almsgiving reinforces social and economic divisions rather than making people equal. Instead of offering charity, Jesus' meals created a common table, a shared egalitarianism of spiritual and material resources, rooted in a deep respect for the land and a realization that its abundance belongs to all. Likewise, when St. Paul addresses the Corinthians, he invites them to "discern the body" when they gather for community meals (1 Cor 11:29). Discerning the body, Michael Northcott points out, meant recognizing that the Body of Christ "was an alternative political order to the imperial polity of Rome . . . one based on a way of common sharing in which the weak are respected alongside the strong, the rich eat and drink alongside the poor."[4] Discerning the body meant bringing to birth in the common meals of Christ's followers and the acts of ministry that flowed from them an alternative moral economy inaugurated by Christ in which the strong "give honor to the weak, and those with less respect in society are given voice."[5]

What would it mean today for Christian communities engaged in eucharistic eating to "discern the body"? How, in our contemporary world where industrial agriculture has raped the land, depriving uncountable poor ones of livelihood, health, and well-being and ensuring that wealth continues to accrue to wealth, can Christian table fellowship rebuild the human-biotic community on principles radically different from those of the surrounding corporate culture? At a time when climate change is exacerbating the already depleted agricultural lands needed to nourish an ever-expanding global population and when the integrity of seeds, crops, and animals are being violated by

3. Ibid.

4. Michael Northcott, "Faithful Feasting," in *A Moral Climate: The Ethics of Global Warming* (Maryknoll, NY: Orbis Books, 2007), 253. What follows is from this source.

5. Ibid.

methods of industrial farming and genetic engineering, how can eucharistic eating form communities for alternative Earth-honoring and justice-bestowing ways of living? What new vision of the world and of human moral responsibility needs to emerge within eucharistic communities so as to motivate them to become agents of change within the economic, social, and political spheres in which they live?

This chapter assumes that worship is morally formative, shaping attitudes, forming values, and providing motivation for communal action.[6] For this reason, the vision of the world, of a community's social responsibility, and of its relationship with God's good creation embodied in eucharistic celebration will impact the values and virtues by which community members live in their personal and communal lives. How does their practice of Eucharist align with the social principles, economic vision, and ecological ethics expressed publicly by our Christian churches? What new experiences, insights, and impulses of the Spirit need to awaken communities to an alternate vision of how the world might be transformed and healed through a community's discipleship?

Our focus in this chapter is on four pervasive attitudes and orientations that can find redundant expression in the prayers, intercessions, preaching, psalmody, hymnody, ways of eating and drinking, and gathering and sending of a community's Eucharist. These orientations include: (1) acknowledging that "the Earth is the Lord's"; (2) embracing a more radical *koinonia*; (3) reconnecting the fruit of the Earth and the work of human hands; and (4) realizing a eucharistic economy. These ritual attitudes are rooted in biblical and eco-theological perspectives; they draw on principles of Catholic

6. Louise Marie Chauvet, *The Sacraments: The Word of God at the Mercy of the Body* (Collegeville, MN: Liturgical Press, 2001), 65. Chauvet claims that there is a mutual relationship between sacraments and ethics: "The sacrament gives ethics the power to become a 'spiritual sacrifice' [while] it is ethics that gives the sacrament a means of 'veri-fying' its fruitfulness." See also Cynthia Moe-Lobeda, *Resisting Structural Evil: Love as Ecological-Economic Vocation* (Minneapolis: Fortress Press, 2013), 259, for discussion of the Eucharist's formative character.

Social Teaching, especially its most recent compendium, the encyclical *Laudato Sí*. Each has the potential to shape a community's vision of restored relationships—with the fruitful Earth, with the triune God, and within a human community that embraces greater justice for all. Each is an implicit call to a *metanoia* of heart, mind, and action that can enable a prophetic and faith-filled response to the challenges and crises that stem from the industrial food system. And each is dependent on the powerful action of the Creator Spirit at work in eucharistic celebration.[7]

In contrast to chapter 8, which focused on reimagining particular aspects of eucharistic eating, the four orientations explored here are meant to revitalize the connection between eucharistic eating and the social, economic, and ecological forces that shape our local-global society, creating a moral force for goodness, justice, and planetary well-being. Each orientation is meant to shape the narrative of the whole eucharistic action, informing the imagination and affections of community members and serving as a bridge to the ethical responses they embody in daily life. Pursuing the course laid out here is a profound act of faith, a belief that this is how God desires to reshape the world and that God's power is moving within each community, empowering them to be emissaries of God's emerging dream for the world.

Proclaiming That "the Earth Is the Lord's and All Who Dwell There" (Ps 24:1)

The first orientation—proclaiming that the Earth is the Lord's—situates eucharistic communities at the heart of a suffering world, God's beautiful creation brought to its knees by disrespect and life-threatening aggression. Earth "groans in travail" (Rom 8:22), her

---

7. The transforming work of the Holy Spirit is prayed for explicitly in most eucharistic prayers, calling on the Spirit to transform the community into the body of Christ in the world.

"sickness evident in the soil, in the water, in the air, and in all forms of life."[8] The crisis is not far from any community, calling out to them to speak and act on creation's behalf, to proclaim that Earth is a living sanctuary, a dwelling place of the Holy One, filled with God's presence and glory (Isa 6:3).[9] All diminishment of this holy place is an affront to the living God. Embracing a vision of Earth's value and wholeness in eucharistic celebration and welcoming Earth's creatures as partners in the assembly's praise are vital to how communities give witness at this critical intersection with ecological, social, and economic life.

The biblical claim that "God owns this planet and all its riches,"[10] stands in stark contrast to the attitudes of corporate agriculture. Rooted in a misperception of human ownership of Earth's resources and the right to destroy them at will, agricultural practices that poison land and water and genetically modify seeds and plants are accepted as collateral damage in service of productivity and profits. Christians are not alone in decrying these practices. "The Earth does not belong to man, man belongs to the Earth," claimed Chief Seattle of the Suquamish tribe in 1848. More recently, responses to corporate globalization have evoked cries of "Our world is not for sale! Our water is not for sale! Our seeds and biodiversity are not for sale!"[11] From Bangalore (1993) to Seattle (1999) to Cancun (2003),

8. Pope Francis, *Laudato Sí* 2. Subsequent references from *Laudato Sí* appear within the text as "LS."

9. Image of Earth as sanctuary is taken from Norman C. Habel, "Ninety-Five Eco Theses: A Call for the Churches to Care for Earth," in *Eco-Reformation: Grace and Hope for a Planet in Peril*, ed. Lisa E. Dahill and James B. Martin-Schramm (Eugene, OR: Cascade Books, 2016), 176.

10. International Commission on English in the Liturgy, translation of the opening verse of Psalm 24. See *Psalms for Morning and Evening Prayer* (Chicago: Liturgy Training Publications, 1995), 21.

11. See Vandana Shiva, *Earth Democracy: Justice, Sustainability and Peace* (Berkeley: North Atlantic Books, 2015), 1–5. Comments by Chief Seattle are from a speech attributed to him, as quoted in Shiva.

communities are speaking out: the planet is not private property but a commons; the Earth is a family.[12] Christian resources can make a unique contribution to this conversation.

Biblical theology underscores that creation in its manifold expressions is a divine gift, without which human existence would be impossible. The lives of those who gather for Eucharist depend on the generosity, creativity, and fertile genius of the triune God at work in the very tissue of the material world. The vast "universe speaks of God's love, his boundless affection for us. Soil, water, mountains, everything is . . . a caress of God" and a "constant source of wonder and awe" (LS 84). Earth has a purpose and a destiny. Loved into existence, Earth is already partnered with God, missioned to care and support life in all its forms (LS 77). Each creature has dignity and value, a right to its own existence, and by its very existence, it blesses and gives glory to God (LS 69).

From an ethical and biblical perspective, Earth is a common good, a fragile and infinitely precious endowment entrusted to the human community by God "to work and serve it" (Gen 2:15). This injunction from the book of Genesis, traditionally translated "to till and keep it," is better translated in terms of service.[13] "Adam comes to the garden as a protector, answerable for the well-being of the precious thing that he did not make; he is to be an observer, mindful of limits that are built into the created order."[14] For the human community to serve and honor creation's integrity, vitality, and purpose, it must abandon the anthropocentric misperception of humanity's mandate to "have dominion" (Gen 1:26), which has led to a conflictual relationship with Earth and an unbridled exploitation of

---

12. Ibid., 2. References relate to: Bangalore, when half a million Indian peasants pledged to resist the classification of seeds as private property; and Seattle and Cancun, when protesters stopped the WTO ministerial meetings.

13. See Ellen F. Davis, *Scripture, Culture, and Agriculture: An Agrarian Reading of the Bible* (Cambridge: Cambridge University Press, 2009).

14. Ibid., 30–31.

nature (LS 66–67). Instead, Christians must embrace the vocation of being "protectors of God's handiwork." This is essential to the life of virtue not optional or secondary (LS 217). Moreover, suggests Pope Francis, Eucharist should be a motivation to accept the challenge of becoming Earth's protectors (LS 236). How, then, is this vocation articulated and embodied in a community's eucharistic celebration? How does it shape their discipleship beyond the gathering: their use of resources, ownership of property, food choices, respect for Earth's laws and rhythms, and defense of the right of all creatures to life and growth?

Earth and her many dying species cry out in lament. Diminished today in their ability to support life, made fragile and vulnerable, the soil, atmosphere, water, animals, and crops—all of them close to the very heart of God—voice their suffering in cries that are reaching deaf ears and closed hearts. Do we listen for their voices, asks *Laudato Si*? Are we willing to "hear a message" from each and join them, not only in praise of God, but also in lament?

Communal lament, as part of Eucharist, can enable communities to express grief, alarm, frustration, and horror, all in the context of faith in the triune God. It can release the energies of compassion and conversion while invoking the power of the Holy Spirit, who can "bring good out of the evil we have done" and enable something new to emerge (LS 80).[15] Lament can bring people together in honest and empowering acknowledgment of the crises, as Joanna

---

15. Laments can be found in Gail Ramshaw, *Pray, Praise, and Thanksgiving* (Minneapolis: Augsburg Fortress, 2017), as well as Anne Rowthorn and Jeffery Rowthorn, *God's Good Earth: Praise and Prayer for Creation* (Collegeville, MN: Liturgical Press, 2018). Biblical laments are also suitable. See also Timothy Hessel-Robinson, "Requiem for the Baiji: Liturgical Lamentation and Species Extension," in *Spirit and Nature: The Study of Christian Spirituality in a Time of Ecological Urgency*, ed. Timothy Hessel-Robinson and Ray Maria McNamara (Eugene, OR: Pickwick Publications, 2011), 176–200.

Macy has so clearly shown,[16] and underscore the critical nature of the community's ministry of healing the Earth.

Jesus' paschal mystery, celebrated at the heart of Eucharist, is reflected today in Earth's processes of dying and rising, whether it be devastating droughts and floods, poisoned rivers and polluted oceans, or regeneration, reforestation, and revitalization. In his deep incarnation,[17] Christ united himself with all biological life: he became incarnate in the very tissue of Earth's existence, entering her processes of growth and decay, wedding himself to Earth's rhythms and cycles, made present bodily to a world made whole through him.[18] In his death, Jesus identified with all creatures of the flesh in their suffering of death and decay.[19] Do homilists speak of Christ's incarnation as solidarity with the suffering of all human and biological life? Do they explore how God, in Christ, is "bearing every creature and all creation forward with an unimaginable promise"?[20] Do they reflect on how union with the risen Christ, present in the Eucharist, offers a dynamic vision of hope for the suffering world that can energize the community's mission to heal its broken systems and threatened biodiversity?[21]

---

16. See Joanna Macy and Molly Brown, *Coming Back to Life* (Gabriola Is, BC: New Society Publishers, 2014). Eco-psychologist and activist Joanna Macy believes that fear leads people to silence about the crises—fear of the pain and guilt they feel or fear of the humiliation and shame they might experience if they speak out. She invites people to truly feel and express their pain as a way to deeper compassion and collective healing.

17. This image of deep incarnation is explored by several theologians, for example, Denis Edwards, *Deep Incarnation: God's Redemptive Suffering with Creatures* (Maryknoll, NY: Orbis Books, 2019); and Elizabeth Johnson, *Creation and the Cross: The Mercy of God for a Planet in Peril* (Maryknoll, NY: Orbis Books, 2018), 183–94.

18. See Edwards, *Deep Incarnation*; also Denis Edwards, *Ecology at the Heart of Faith* (Maryknoll, NY: Orbis Books, 2006), 58–60.

19. Johnson, *Creation and the Cross*, 188.

20. Ibid., 189.

21. Edwards, *Ecology at the Heart of Faith*, 106.

Over and again, Pope Francis calls his hearers to a sense of kinship with Earth's creatures, to feelings of closeness and intimacy, to affectionate and humble respect that can awaken them to the "sublime" and "universal communion" by which we are united with all living beings (LS 76, 89–92). Joined in intimate union with Christ in eucharistic eating, communities are, at the same time, joined in profound communion with all of Earth's creatures. Eucharistic intimacy and creaturely communion coexist. In Eucharist, Christ chooses to reach the most intimate human depths through a fragment of matter, an element of his creation (LS 236). Moreover, "in the bread of the Eucharist, creation is projected towards divinization, towards the holy wedding feast, towards unification with the Creator himself" (LS 236), a journey that communities make with all creatures into the heart of God (LS 83). But do the prayers that surround eucharistic communion speak of the community's oneness with the good Earth and all living things? Do they acknowledge their "sublime communion" with the Earth community as integral to their union with Christ? Does their missioning at the conclusion of Eucharist send them to live compassionately within the planetary community?

Finally, how does this first orientation, a proclamation that "the Earth is the Lord's and all who dwell there," address the socio-ecological-economic forces that embed the community's Eucharist and shape their responses to the food webs that surround it? Communities might well focus on their local foodsheds: on the soils, farming practices, food distribution, and agricultural impact of food production in their local places and the call to justice and care that they may evoke.[22] Foodsheds are commons, meant to be cherished as

---

22. The nature of foodsheds is discussed in chapter 7. The understanding I explore here regarding a community's engagement with its foodshed parallels in some ways Ched Myers's work on "watershed discipleship." See Ched Myers, "Prophetic Visions of Redemption as Rehydration: A Call to Watershed Discipleship," *Anglican Theological Review* 100, no. 1 (2018): 61–78.

a common good[23] that serve and support all and where every living organism is interdependent. They are a sacred trust, a sacramental sanctuary that speaks of God's generosity and the compassionate care of the divine Spirit.[24] As a commons, foodsheds depend on human engagement for their health and flourishing, and they thrive in the measure that communities commit themselves to sustainability for present and future generations.

Communities can "learn their foodshed" by exploring the flow of food that takes place: the cost of its production to Earth's systems; the fairness or unfairness of food distribution; who eats well, who doesn't, and who decides; the effectiveness of groups seeking food justice; and the positive initiatives to regenerate soils and water taking place. Developing a sense of discipleship here and engaging with other groups in advocacy and care for the Earth can in turn flow back into a community's eucharistic celebration. Naming in prayer its distinctive places, the biodiversity that marks its life and the edible produce that thrives in this foodshed can invite a community to inhabit this part of creation with intentionality, faith, and prophetic commitment. It might also invite communities to move worship outdoors: to pray, at least on occasion, in the very sanctuary that is their foodshed, mindful of the interdependent relationships that comprise it and on which they depend.

Embracing a More Radical *Koinonia*

Our second orientation springs from the vast inequalities of our contemporary global community that cry out to eucharistic communities to embrace a more radical *koinonia*. In the earliest Chris-

---

23. The notion of common good is a foundational principle of social teaching. See David J. O'Brien and Thomas A. Shannon, eds., *Catholic Social Thought*, 3rd rev. ed. (Maryknoll, NY: Orbis Books, 2016).

24. See John Hart, *Sacramental Commons* (New York: Rowman and Littlefield, 2006).

tian communities, *koinonia* was a primary mark of life together in Christ, one that was experienced in a unique way when they gathered for the breaking of bread. *Koinonia*, described in the New Testament, entails a willingness to show kindness and compassion to each other (Eph 4:32); to speak the truth in love (1 Pet 1:22); to honor and accept each other (Rom 15:7); to serve and live in harmony (Gal 5:13; Rom 12:16; 1 Pet 3:8); in a word, to devote themselves one to another (Rom 12:10). Hospitality and love were key to a Christ-centered life (1 Pet 4:9; 1 John 3:11). This mutuality draws its strength and vision from the community's deep rootedness in Christ, present to them in their gatherings, enabling the community to "walk in the light" and have fellowship with one another (1 John 1:6-7).

Today, the massive inequality experienced in the global community in which the majority of the planet's people are excluded from the benefits of Earth's resources cries out for new understandings of who is included in the *koinonia* of Christian table fellowship. As Pope Francis contends in *Laudato Sí*, a compromised environment degraded by industrial food production impacts the most defenseless of people: "The gravest effects of all attacks on the environment affect the most vulnerable people on the planet"; they are suffered by Earth's poorest (LS 48). Billions of people today, who comprise "the majority of the planet's population," experience hunger, agricultural exploitation, food insecurity, disease, and premature death. They are wounded by a staggering inequality that allows a minority of the human family to consume the majority of Earth's goods and produce. Yet too often the plight of the poor is considered tangential to political and economic discussions, and their suffering, if acknowledged at all, is "treated as collateral damage" (LS 49).

How does this vast suffering impact worshiping communities, especially those in the global north? What room is made at the eucharistic table for the experience and needs of the Earth's hungry and suffering peoples, especially those closest to home? How does worship form human communities for the work of love in a world where the "least of these" face the gravest suffering?

Part of the problem, notes *Laudato Sí*, is one of seeing and hearing (LS 49). Many communities, especially in affluent urban centers, are removed from the poor, have little direct contact with them, and live a standard of life well beyond the reach of a majority of the world's population. Lack of encounter can lead to a numbing of conscience, an inability to "hear both the cry of the Earth and the cry of the poor" (LS 49). But in truth, the poor are never far away—immigrant families hidden in the shadows of urban life, hungry women and men who line up at food pantries, laborers in agricultural fields or laid off from menial jobs.

These are the very people to whom Jesus continuously reached out, whom he gathered at table, welcomed to his teaching, sought out like a shepherd seeking lost sheep. Encountering Christ at the heart of eucharistic eating, communities must likewise encounter those with whom he most identified, embracing his preferential option for the poorest (LS 158).[25] He described his mission as bringing good news to Earth's poor, proclaiming liberty to captives, and letting the oppressed go free (Luke 4:18). Of all the settings in which Jesus revealed this good news, the table became the center.[26] Shared meals were for Jesus a place of reaching out to the hungry, to outcasts, and to those dismissed by society, allowing their real human need for food and inclusion to draw him to an evocative table fellowship, an incarnate expression of God's acts of justice, feeding, liberating, and empowering recorded in the Hebrew Scriptures.

Eucharistic assemblies today are challenged to a more radical *koinonia*, an orientation toward a more public and global vision of relatedness and responsibility for brothers and sisters who suffer the

25. This principle is a cornerstone of Catholic social teaching. See O'Brien and Shannon, *Catholic Social Thought*.

26. See Ched Myers's interpretation of Mark's gospel, *Binding the Strong Man: A Political Reading of Mark's Story of Jesus* (Maryknoll, NY: Orbis Books, 2008), 443.

wound of inequality. The event of the Eucharist can support that expanded vision. Gathering as an assembly should always evoke the questions of "Who is missing?" and "Whose voices have yet to be heard?" The Scriptures in turn, both Hebrew and Christian, proclaim a God who reaches out to the poorest and most vulnerable members of society. Psalm 146 asserts that God acts to secure justice for the oppressed, to give food to the hungry, to set prisoners free, to raise up those bowed down, and to protect with special care all who are strangers, orphans, and widows. Homilists interpreting the Scriptures in light of global inequality and injustice—or inviting someone, for whom the American dream is more like a nightmare, to speak to the community of the suffering and cost—can stir intercessions that call out from the heart and move the conscience of community members.

At the heart of Christian Eucharist is the memory of the cross of Christ, "a dangerous memory," writes Denis Edwards, that challenges "all complacency before the suffering of others."[27] The cross of Jesus is an abiding challenge to eucharistic communities because it "brings those who suffer to the very center of Christian faith"[28] and the radical *koinonia* that communities are called to embrace in light of Jesus' paschal mystery. The cross of Christ challenges any "ideological justifications of the misery of the poor and the victims of war, oppression and natural disasters."[29] As pictured by Niels Gregersen, Jesus' anguished death is an icon of divine solidarity, of God's redemptive co-suffering with all who suffer, as well as with the victims of social exclusion.[30] Having chosen to accompany them in his earthly ministry, Jesus remains in solidarity with them in his death

27. Edwards, *Ecology at the Heart*, 106. Image of dangerous memory from Johannes B. Metz.

28. Ibid.

29. Ibid.

30. Niels Henrik Gregersen, "The Cross of Christ in an Evolutionary World," *Dialogue: A Journal of Theology* 40 (2011): 205.

and resurrection. Their suffering is "forever imaged in the wounds of the risen Christ."[31]

Do communities ponder this mystery of God's co-suffering with the poor as they "proclaim the death of the Lord until he comes again"? Do homilists speak of Christ's solidarity with those made vulnerable by inequality? At the heart of Eucharist is the common table, which, as we noted earlier, should speak of the common good. This connection might be at the heart of the community's missioning, a point from which to discern how they can provide nourishing food to those whose access is severely limited, how the voices and stories of those deprived of basic necessities can enter the narratives of their worship, how the social and political issues involved in advocating for food justice can be addressed, and how these concerns affect a community's vision of what it means to share fellowship around the eucharistic table.

At the heart of a more radical *koinonia* is the importance of encounter: encounter with the members of Christ's body who are denied food, basic education, health care, access to social participation, and political voice—all of which enable a dignity of life that is theirs as children of God.[32] Encounter—taking time, coming to know, seeing and hearing reality through another's experience—can lead to change, to personal and political action, and to choices of alternative lifestyles. It may also be a call to other tables. In writing about Sunday as a day of solidarity, Pope John Paul II proposed that the whole of the Lord's Day should be a time of mercy, outreach, and intense sharing, especially with the very poor: "inviting to a meal people who are alone, . . . providing food for needy families, spending a few hours in voluntary work and acts of solidarity." These, he suggests, "would certainly be ways of bringing into people's lives

31. Edwards, *Ecology at the Heart*, 106. See also Johnson, *Creation and the Cross*, 183–94.

32. Patxi Álvarez, ed., "Justice and the Global Economy: Building Sustainable and Inclusive Communities," *Promotio Iustitiae* 121, no. 1 (2016): 121.

the love of Christ received at the eucharistic table . . . and prolonging in time the miracle of the multiplication of the loaves."[33]

Communities turn to the poor, not only to share their suffering, but to learn from their impassioned dreams for a new future. It is they, writes Leonardo Boff, who are bearers of new hope.[34] Deprived of an adequate past or present, they have only the future, and their dreams that things can be different spurs them on, engendering a courage that at times defies all odds as they search for greater life and liberation. By engaging with them, opening to their imaginative creativity, communities can envision a world different from the present, one in which all can participate together, a society—global and local—marked by solidarity, mercy, collective compassion, respect for diversity, shared goods, integration with nature, and human persons gathered into communion. To welcome those who suffer into the eucharistic community is to begin to build a new future based in equity and justice, participation and solidarity— indeed, a true *koinonia*.

Reconnecting the Fruit of the Earth and Work of Human Hands

Our third orientation—reconnecting the fruit of the Earth with the work of human hands—is imaged in an evocative prayer, voiced as gifts of bread and wine are brought to the eucharistic table. Modeled on the traditional Jewish prayers of blessing (*berakoth*), the invocation captures a profound truth: that the cooperative efforts of Earth's fruitfulness and human labor are foundational for human life and central to the act of Eucharist. Lifting up the fruits of creation affirms their dignity and beauty and calls communities who bless them to

---

33. Pope John Paul II, *Dies Domini* 69–73, in *The Liturgy Documents*, vol. 2 (Chicago: Liturgy Training Publications, 1999), 38–40.

34. See Leonardo Boff, *Ecology and Liberation* (Maryknoll, NY: Orbis Books, 1994), 104–6. What follows reflects that source.

respect their integrity, life processes, natural laws, structures, and patterns of growth. Moreover, what is brought to the common table are not simply wheat and grapes but a loaf and a cup, both of which require human cooperation with the life-giving Earth.

Bringing these gifts of human-Earth cooperation to the table situates the community at the intersection of their own self-offering and the paschal self-offering of Christ. It also locates them at four dynamic intersections that mark current global economic-social-ecological relationships: (1) between global economic forces and the integrity of creation's biosystems; (2) between human cultivation of the land and ethical responsibility for its protection and preservation; (3) between the dignity of human labor and the exigencies of poverty, migration, and exclusion; and (4) between the drive for profit, accumulation, and growth and the cost to both Earth and her peoples who suffer impoverishment and misery.

Each of these four intersections points to crises in today's global society and invites eucharistic communities to reflect on the ethical implications of their Eucharist. Can renewed attention to how the eucharistic bread is prepared—reconnecting Earth's organic fruitfulness with the labor of caring hands—lead to wise action regarding calls to heal a broken world and restore right relationships? Can such reflection bring insight regarding their eucharistic discipleship? And should the use of manufactured wafers be reconsidered for the sake of the integrity of both Eucharist and the whole of God's creation?

Throughout part 2 of this volume we see evidence of the critical intersections noted above. They unfold like headlines: Agribusiness's drive for profit forces poor populations to even greater breakdown. Soil, atmosphere, and climate in crisis, negatively impacted by industrial farming. Hunger and malnutrition hand-in-hand with corporate appropriation of the land of smallholders. Farm laborers robbed of dignity through oppressive work requirements and regular abuse. The "silent emergency" of poverty causing deaths of thirty-five thousand children a day from diseases preventable by adequate nutrition and health care. Ecological destructiveness implicit in agricultural methods embraced for efficiency. Comments by two leading economists sum these up. "Creative destruction is at the heart of the market process," states one; "it's not a market failure."[35] "A given amount of health-impairing pollution should be done in the country with the lowest cost," contends the second, "which will be the country with the lowest wages. I think the economic logic behind dumping a load of toxic waste on the lowest-wage country is impeccable and we should face up to that."[36]

Although Eucharist is often experienced as removed from these intersecting crises, the materiality of eucharistic symbolization places it quite close. "In the global economy," writes Timothy Gorringe, "the production of grain is part of the balance of payments and the relation between nations. The bread of the eucharist is the bread of the economy."[37] Rising global temperatures currently make it far more difficult to grow wheat than in the past, with hotter temperatures seriously diminishing the world's ability to feed herself. German agronomists have found that "wheat grown under the levels of carbon dioxide we expect by midcentury will contain markedly less protein and iron and 14 percent more lead."[38] Moreover, wheat production in the hands of industrialized agribusiness is precipitating gross inequality as soaring corporate profits exacerbate poverty and hunger. In the midst of the world food crisis in 2007, the Archer

---

35. Words of economist Brik Lindsey, quoted in Stephen A. Marglin, *The Dismal Science: How Thinking Like an Economist Undermines Community* (Cambridge: Harvard University Press, 2008), 233. Noted by Norman Wirzba, *Food and Faith* (New York: Cambridge University Press, 2011), 37.

36. Words of Lawrence Summers, one-time chief economist of the World Bank and president emeritus of Harvard University, from a memo leaked to *The Economist* (1992), claiming that the logics of economic efficiency and growth will require the destruction of places. Quoted in Marglin, *The Dismal Science*, 37.

37. Timothy Gorringe, *The Sign of Love: Reflections on the Eucharist* (London: SPCK, 1997), 36.

38. Bill McKibben, *Eaarth: Making a Life on a Tough New Planet* (New York: St. Martin's Griffin, 2010), 154.

Daniels Midland Company (ADM), one of two US companies who together own two-thirds of the world's grain market, increased its profits by 42 percent while small farmers' profits plunged.[39] It is not surprising that the rising price of bread in Egypt in 2010 to 2011 triggered demonstrations against the government that inaugurated a hoped-for "Arab Spring." Central to the revolutionary chants of the Egyptian marches was a demand for "bread, freedom, and social justice."[40]

All of these situations impact the integrity of wheat used for the common loaf, the processes by which it is formed into loaves, and the significance of its offering at the Lord's table. They underscore that a true cooperation between creation's integrity and the labor of human hands by which loaves are formed is both a prophetic and a provocative enterprise. A recent joint United Methodist and Roman Catholic statement on Eucharist and ecology explicates this challenge:

> Bread and wine are necessary for the Eucharist, but wheat and grapes may come from oppressive agricultural practices. Nevertheless, a vigorous Eucharistic theology and practice would require us to care about agricultural practices, and not only for wheat and grapes. . . . Issues of safe and suitable work environments and just wages are at the heart of the church's social justice concerns as derived from our Eucharistic practice. . . . Both Methodists and Catholics [need] to attend more carefully to the production of the sacramental bread and wine, both in itself and as a sign of the interconnection of worship, economy and nature. To participate in the

39. Eric Holt-Himéez, "Food Security, Food Justice, or Food Sovereignty," in *Cultivating Food Justice: Race, Class, and Sustainability*, ed. Alison Hope Alkon and Julian Agyeman (Cambridge, MA: The MIT Press, 2011), 312.

40. Thanassis Cambanis, "The Arab Spring Was a Revolution of the Hungry," *The Boston Globe*, August 23, 2015, https://www.bostonglobe.com/ideas/2015/08/22/the-arab-spring-was-revolution-hungry/K15S1kGeO5Y6gsJwAYHejI/story.html, accessed June 30, 2019. The three words of the chant rhyme in Arabic.

Eucharist without discerning these interconnections is the result of indolence and may lead to diminished communion with the Lord. . . . It is appropriate that the Church's worship include concern for the economic conditions and environmental impact of the production of the sacramental elements.[41]

The statement offers a serious call to communities to assess the production of the material elements of bread and wine used as eucharistic offerings and for communities who follow the longstanding custom of "token elements" manufactured at a far distance from the community to ask if these are an adequate and truthful symbolization of the "fruit of the earth and work of human hands."[42]

Today, 80 percent of the altar breads used by communities in the United States are manufactured by a single company, the Cavanagh Company in Rhode Island.[43] Given the size and scale of Cavanagh's

---

41. "Heaven and Earth Are Full of Your Glory," (April 2012), http://www.usccb .org/beliefs-and-teachings/ecumenical-and-interreligious/ecumenical/methodist /upload/Heaven-and-Earth-are-Full-of-Your-Glory-Methodist-Catholic-Dialogue -Agreed-Statement-Round-Seven.pdf, accessed June 15, 2015. Remainder of this paragraph from this source.

42. An often forgotten statement in the General Instruction of the Roman Missal (2011) regarding eucharistic bread claims that by "reason of the sign, it is required that the material for the Eucharistic celebration *truly have the appearance of food*" (321, italics added). The bread should be "recently made" (320) and the eucharistic bread "be fashioned in such a way that the priest . . . is able to break it into parts and distributed these to at least some of the faithful" (321). "Moreover, the gesture of the fraction or breaking of bread, which was quite simply the term by which the Euchrist was known in apostolic times, will bring out more clearly the force and importance of the sign of the unity of all in the one bread, and of the sign of charity by the fact that the one bread is distributed among the brothers and sisters" (321).

43. In the reporting that follows, I rely on Rowan Moore Gerety, "Buying the Body of Christ: How the Communion Wafer Arrived in the Capitalist Marketplace," Killing the Buddha, www.killingthebuddha.com/mag/dogma/buying-the -body-of-christ/, accessed May 3, 2019.

operation, the wheat used to produce the millions of patented hosts produced regularly can no longer be sourced locally, as in the early years of their operation. Today their wheat is supplied by one of the largest agribusiness corporations in the United States, the Archer Daniels Midland Company (ADM) mentioned above, which ships forty-two to forty-five thousand pounds of wheat to Cavanagh every three weeks. ADM, a Fortune 500 company, has been cited for numerous environmental and human rights violations, as well as a now infamous price-fixing conspiracy.[44]

Cavanagh's mechanized processes turn out rolls of 100 processed hosts per second.[45] Their products are shipped to Lutheran, Episcopal, Roman Catholic, and Southern Baptist communities around the globe—hosts of all sizes, textures, and thicknesses to fit communities' stipulations.[46] The elements arrive, processed, packaged, and with a two-year shelf life. Like much of the industrially produced food on the market today, the food that will nourish these communities spiritually and materially has no direct connection with them, nor do the communities have information about how the crops are grown or the farm laborers treated. In contrast to eucharistic bread that is "the work of human hands," the company proudly claims that these eucharistic breads are "untouched by human hands."[47]

44. Gerety notes that the most famous scandal associated with ADM was the lysine price-fixing conspiracy that became the basis of the nonfiction book *The Informant* by Kurt Eichenwald (New York: Broadway Books, 2000). Little is known about ADM's wheat growing processes and those who labor in their fields. Most likely they "dry" the harvested wheat by spraying Monsanto's Roundup on it to speed up the drying process generally used for commercially raised wheat in the United States.

45. Cavanagh Altar Bread, "About Us," https://www.cavanaghco.com/about-us, accessed July 9, 2019. Gone are the days when generations of women religious prepared "altar breads" for nearby communities, "accompanying production and packing with prayer." While Cavanagh far outproduces them, the only religious community that is still a major source of altar breads, the Benedictines of Clyde, Missouri, ships over two million hosts each week.

46. Ibid.

47. Ibid.

Commenting on the altar bread marketplace that has turned bread for the eucharistic celebration into "products" or "commodities," Rowan Moore Gerety muses that it is not surprising that communities remain unconcerned about the sourcing of their bread. Worship embeds communion wafers in sacramental language and a liturgical context that discourages "the realization among congregants that what is now the body of Christ was produced in a factory, bought and sold in a contentious, secular marketplace and traded hands repeatedly among truck operators and postal workers who had no idea what they were handling."[48] Moreover, "hosts" are considered customary and therefore authorized. But as normative practice, they are much in need of critique and prophetic change.

A different option for sourcing wheat is provided by Honoré Farm and Mill in Marin County, California.[49] Under the direction of Elizabeth DeRuff, agricultural chaplain for the Episcopal Diocese of California, Honoré grows heirloom varieties of wheat, farmed sustainably on a small scale without irrigation or pesticides, then stone milled with a specific concern for eucharistic use.[50] Honoré Growers Guild, a network of farmers, millers, bakers, and churches, grow, mill, bake, and serve communion bread with care for the environment and the healing of the Earth as the stated core of its mission. Honoré Mill—named for a seventh-century French saint who is the patron of bakers, eucharistic bread makers, and flour merchants—invites friends and supporters to participate in the harvesting and milling of their wheat each August.

For central eucharistic elements of loaf and cup to be truthful, evocative, and connected to the life and labor of the community, a new set of norms might be considered: (1) the common loaf should bear the imprint of the hands of community members, (2) who form the dough with love and care, (3) from grain that is locally grown,

48. Gerety, "Buying the Body of Christ."

49. https://honoremill.org/about-honore#our-story-continued, accessed May 25, 2019.

50. Honoré Farm and Mill, https://honoremill.org/, accessed May 15, 2019.

related to the community's everyday sustenance, (4) with methods that honor nature's wisdom, and (5) in fields where growers are given just wages and solicitous care.[51] For eucharistic bread and wine, transformed by the Holy Spirit to become the body of the living Christ, the Bread of Life, they must "evoke, by their heartiness, fragrance and flavor, nature's bountiful fertility—thereby symbolizing the nurturing, inexhaustible presence of the Risen One" in our midst.[52]

Transforming these elements is of critical importance to the whole meaning of eucharistic eating and invites communities to take up the bigger work of reconnecting creation's integrity with the creativity and dignity of human labor.[53] These efforts can be imaged in the eucharistic celebration in prayers, intercessions, and preaching and might move a community to embrace a Covenant with Creation.[54]

Beyond the Eucharist, the community's ethical response might be directly integrated into their local foodshed discipleship and outreach to those who are vulnerable and economically poor by exploring the labor practices involved in local food production, assessing the agricultural techniques used in growing farm produce and advocating for just practices that can enable those who cultivate Earth's produce to live healthy, safe, and secure lives.

All of this relates profoundly to Eucharist, writes Timothy Gorringe. "Eucharist is a challenge to construct a just, participatory and sustainable world order in which the poor are no longer fed with crumbs from the rich man's table."[55] "I do not come to eucharist," he continues, "to escape from sordid political reality and get in touch

---

51. These concerns are implicit in "Heaven and Earth Are Full of Your Glory," cited above.

52. Nathan Mitchell, *Eucharist as Sacrament of Initiation* (Chicago: Liturgy Training Publications, 1994), 142.

53. O'Brien and Shannon, *Catholic Social Thought*, 14–40. The dignity of human labor is a key aspect of social teaching. In fact, it was concern over labor practices that launched the first Catholic social teaching by Pope Leo XIII, *Rerum Novarum*.

54. One example is published in *Maryknoll* 87, no. 3 (March 1993): 1.

55. Gorringe, *Sign of Love*, 36–37, including what follows here.

with some quite different spiritual reality, but to find the one reality which frames my whole life interpreted, refracted, and made more hopeful. The eucharist itself teaches me that I can only come to Truth, ultimate reality, through material—political, social, economic—means. Of this the bread and wine are a sign." Christians gather as eucharistic communities in order to better perform their task in the world: to become the living sacrament of God's nourishing presence and power alive in the world.

Realizing a Eucharistic Economy

Christians live "at the intersection of two stories about the world: the Eucharist and the market," writes William Cavanaugh. "Both tell stories of hunger and consumption, of exchanges and gifts; the stories overlap and compete."[56] They speak of two different economies, two ways people order and structure their lives and identify the outcomes they expect from their choices. This last orientation—realizing a eucharistic economy—points to the work of Christ at the heart of eucharistic eating and its power to transform a community's activity, expectations, and priorities, reorienting their lives toward the values of God's kingdom and the arrival of God's shalom.

The market story holds that deep happiness, security, and purpose are achieved through the accumulation of money and abundant possessions. Behind these personal acquisitions is the market's drive for perpetual economic growth and increased productivity, no matter the cost to Earth or her creatures. Satisfaction and fulfillment of human desires are the goal of acquisition, and although material goods can never truly satisfy, no matter how many are amassed, the attraction to acquiring them still remains. The pleasures of consuming, be it food or other products, come not from possessing goods but from their pursuit. Hence, the search for true satisfaction is endless.

---

56. William T. Cavanaugh, *Being Consumed: Economics and Christian Desire* (Grand Rapids, MI: Eerdmans, 2008), 89.

Within this drive for consumption is the notion that some people will always be without.[57] Those with little means, who suffer crippling hunger or excessive deprivation, are simply unable to engage in these deceptive addictions of a consumer culture. Moreover, claims Cavanaugh, the desires aroused by a consumer society distract those who have economic wealth from seeing the needs of the poor and hungry, especially "those who experience hunger as life-threatening deprivation." The reason, he argues, is not simply that the pursuit of more and better goods becomes a preoccupation but that "the market story establishes a fundamentally individualistic view of the human person." Within that story, "goods are not held in common."[58] The consumption of goods is essentially a private experience, and money, as a means of acquiring things, becomes a way to that independence.[59] Paying for goods removes the receiver's obligation to the one from whom the goods are acquired. Hence, people can maintain their separateness, including their distance from those in severe want. Charitable giving to those in need is, of course, possible, but such giving is relegated to the "private realm of preference, not justice."[60] Ultimately, the market story claims that the needs of the hungry will be addressed through the "providential care of the market." Increased consumption will unleash the "miracle of the market"—and escalating consumption on the part of a few will help feed the others: "abundance is just around the corner."[61]

Consumer capitalism, based in the market story, is one of the most comprehensive systems the world has ever known,[62] and the corpo-

57. Ibid., 90. Hunger is written into the conditions on which this economic system operates, claims Cavanaugh.

58. Ibid., 91.

59. See Charles Eisenstein, *Sacred Economics: Money, Gift, and Society in an Age of Transition* (Berkeley: Evolver Editions, 2011), 354.

60. Cavanagh, *Being Consumed*, 94–100.

61. Ibid., 93.

62. Timothy J. Gorringe, *The Education of Desire: Towards a Theology of the Senses* (Harrisburg, PA: Trinity Press International, 2001), 85.

rate industrial agriculture we have explored in this volume is one of its primary drivers. While making food available today in many parts of the world, the larger impact of the industrial food complex is over-consumption, waste, and the destruction of Earth's basic life systems. Deeply embedded in its goals are prosperity for a few and the espousal of values of control, manipulation, and exploitation of natural resources for the sake of greater production and profit. Among its marketing strategies is the enticement of individual consumers with greater and greater novelty—new products, new tastes, new flavors, new packaging—engaging those who have the means in an endless round of acquisition and competition but with no obligation toward those who cannot participate in this system. Natural resources needed for production are regarded as limitless, leaving Earth and generations to come with a seriously impaired future. True satisfaction on the part of consumers is never attained.

Eucharist, in contrast, holds out another paradigm, a different story about hunger and consumption, about satisfaction and happiness. It invites communities into an economy of gift and grace, of gratitude and reciprocity. We see this economy at work in stories of Jesus' feeding of the five thousand on the shores of Lake Tiberius. Jesus' hungry followers, already fed by his word but in need of physical nourishment, were invited to recline in a grassy place, even though there was no evident source for their satisfaction. In place of a market solution—purchasing two hundred denarii worth of bread—Jesus takes a few simple loaves and fish provided by a small boy, and, through his blessing and breaking, all those gathered were fed and *satisfied*; there was enough and to spare (John 6:10-30).

In the discourse following this event, Jesus places his presence at the heart of Eucharist: "I am the bread of life. Whoever comes to me will never be hungry" (John 6:35). The gift of Christ's life, offered to all, is not a scarce commodity: "Anyone who comes to me I will never turn away" (John 6:37). "Those who eat of me will never hunger" (John 6:35). To eat of Christ, as he invites, is not simply to consume nourishment in such a way that the eater remains detached from the food eaten, nor from others who likewise eat. Rather, those who partake of this bread become part of Jesus' body, their lives drawn into the larger life of God in Christ. Eucharistic food is not a commodity but an invitation to co-abide, to remain in active relationship, in deep mutuality not only with Christ but with all who are part of his body. This is the paradox at the heart of eucharistic eating: those who consume the life of Jesus, given as food and drink, do not appropriate it for their private use but are themselves assimilated into the larger body of Christ and his mission in the world. Consumption is turned inside out, and individually oriented market values are transformed communally.[63]

John's gospel tells us that eating has to do with abiding, abiding with Christ and co-abiding with all God's people and creatures. "Those who eat my flesh and drink my blood abide in me and I in them" (John 6:56). To eat the bread of life is not to absorb it into oneself and therefore abolish it but to be altered by it, to be consumed by what we consume and transformed for mission. "God is the food that consumes us," claimed Augustine.[64] Christ welcomed in the Eucharist becomes nourishment for body and soul so that those who eat the living bread live no longer by their own life but by his.[65] And his life continues within those who eat as a *mutual remembering*. Jesus lives on in them, not as deformed matter, but as food that in-forms and re-forms their lives from within. Eating becomes co-abiding.[66]

In Eucharist, communities are invited into something larger than themselves—drawn into an "act of cosmic love" (LS 236) that re-

---

63. Cavanaugh, *Being Consumed*, 95.

64. Augustine, *Confessions* 7.10.16, trans. Henry Chadwick (Oxford: Oxford University Press, 1991), 124. As noted in Wirzba, *Food and Faith*, 157.

65. Thomas Merton, *The Living Bread* (New York: Farrar, Straus & Cudahy, 1956), 114, as quoted in Wirzba, *Food and Faith*, 156.

66. Wirzba, *Food and Faith*, 157. See his longer reflection on eucharistic eating, co-abiding, and transformation, 154–65.

positions them in relation to others: the Earth community, other persons, and especially those who hunger and suffer deprivation. Consumption at the eucharistic table is an invitation to embrace others no longer as strangers but as part of one's self where exploitation of others and Earth is overcome with compassion and reverent care, where the drive for accumulation of goods is overcome with sharing and mutual service, and in which Christ's self-donation and self-emptying become the source and inspiration for acts of generosity, mercy, and justice.

Within a community of eucharistic eaters who abide in Jesus, the gift of his life implicates them, obligates them one to another to embrace the debt of tenderness, gratitude, and generous mutuality. In the eucharistic economy, the gift of food "relativizes the boundaries between what is mine and what is yours by relativizing the boundary between me and you. . . . [W]e participate in the divine life so that we are fed and simultaneously become food for others."[67] This is the world of complex co-abiding. "Inspired by Christ's own Eucharistic offering, people are invited to make themselves an offering to the world by attending to its hungers and needs. To do this in a Eucharistic way . . . requires us in some sense to be *eaten by Jesus*,"[68] to be consumed by his values, moved by his compassion, and converted by his hospitality. Eating and being eaten by Jesus invite a transformation of those who participate: to receive and embrace the world as given by God and to form their identities on the needs and joys, the hungers and struggles of others and of the body as a whole. The culture of consumption—of having—is replaced by an economy of giving and co-abiding.

Eucharistic eating announces the coming of God's kingdom now, already present by God's grace. "In Eucharist, God breaks in and disrupts the tragic despair of human history with a message of hope

67. Cavanaugh, *Being Consumed*, 97.
68. Wirzba, *Food and Faith*, 160.

and a demand for justice. The hungry cannot wait: the heavenly feast is now."[69] This in-breaking kingdom is driven not by human desire or satisfaction but by God's desire, God's great dream for the Earth, entrusted to eucharistic eaters. In the sharing of Jesus' Body and Blood, those who partake are missioned to be healers of Earth and lovers of all her creatures. In Eucharist, Jesus "comes not from above but from within; *he comes that we might find him in this world of ours*" (LS 236).

Questions for Reflection

1) Which of these orientations do you find most challenging and why? Which might be most important for your community to consider?

2) In the past, how have you thought about the connection between Christian social teaching, the ethical principles it holds out, and eucharistic practice? Has this assumption been challenged by these reflections, and if so, how?

3) How might an assembling community's embrace of a eucharistic economy challenge the consumer economy that is so dominant in affluent countries like the United States today? How might this choice bring a deeper experience of Christ's redeeming and life-giving love?

---

69. Cavanagh, *Being Consumed*, 98.

Bibliography

Ableman, Michael. *Street Farm*. White River Junction, VT: Chelsea Publications, 2016.

Alkon, Alison Hope, and Julian Agyeman, eds. *Cultivating Food Justice: Race, Class and Sustainability*. Cambridge, MA: MIT Press, 2011.

Anastopoulo, Rossi. "Where Have All the Apples Gone? An Investigation into the Disappearance of Apple Varieties and the Detectives Who Are Out to Find Them." *PIT Journal* (2014). Accessed June 11, 2019. http://pitjournal.unc.edu/article/where-have-all-apples-gone-investigation-disappearance-apple-varieties-and-detectives-who.

Armstrong, Donna. "A Survey of Community Gardens in Upstate New York: Implications for Health Promotion and Community Development." *Health and Place* 6, no. 4 (2000): 319–27.

Ayers, Jennifer R. *Good Food: Grounded Practical Theology*. Waco, TX: Baylor University Press, 2013.

Bahnson, Fred. *Soil and Sacrament: A Spiritual Memoir of Food and Faith*. New York: Simon and Schuster, 2013.

Bahnson, Fred, and Norman Wirzba. *Making Peace with the Land: God's Call to Reconcile with Creation*. Downers Grove, IL: IVP Books, 2012.

Balasuriya, Tissa. *The Eucharist and Human Liberation*. Maryknoll, NY: Orbis Books, 1980.

Barker, Debi. "Globalization and Industrial Agriculture." In *The Fatal Harvest Reader: The Tragedy of Industrial Agriculture*, edited by Andrew Kimbrell, 249–64. Sausalito, CA: Foundation for Deep Ecology, 2002.

Beiler, Andrea, and Luise Schottroff. *The Eucharist: Bodies, Bread, and Resurrection*. Minneapolis: Fortress Press, 2007.

Benjamin, Darryl. *Farm to Table*. White River Junction, VT: Chelsea Green Publishing, 2016.

Berry, Thomas. *The Dream of the Earth*. San Francisco: Sierra Club, 1988.

Berry, Wendell. *The Gift of Good Land: Further Essays Cultural and Agricultural*. New York: North Point Press, 1982.

———. "The Idea of a Local Economy." Accessed June 30, 2019. http://home2.btconnect.com/tipiglen/localecon.html.

Betto, Frei. "Zero Hunger: An Ethical-Political Project." In *Hunger, Bread and Eucharist*, edited by Christophe Boureaux, Janet Martin Soskice, and Luiz Carlos Susin, 11–13. *Concilium*, 2005/2. London: SCM Press, 2005.

Boff, Leonardo. *Ecology and Liberation*. Maryknoll, NY: Orbis Books, 1994.

Bouley, Allan. *From Freedom to Formula: The Evolution of the Eucharistic Prayer from Improvisation to Written Texts*. Washington, DC: The Catholic University of America Press, 1981.

Bowe, Barbara. "The Divine 'I Am': Wisdom Motifs in the Gospel of John." In *The Wisdom of Creation*, edited by Edward Foley and Robert Schreiter, 37–47. Collegeville, MN: Liturgical Press, 2004.

Bradshaw, Paul F. *Eucharistic Origins*. London: SPCK, 2004.

———. *The Search for the Origins of Christian Worship*. 2nd ed. Oxford: Oxford University Press, 2002.

Bradshaw, Paul F., and Maxwell E. Johnson. *The Eucharistic Liturgies: Their Evolution and Interpretation*. Collegeville, MN: Liturgical Press, 2012.

Brazal, Agnes M. "Church as Sacrament of Yin-Yang Harmony: Toward a More Incisive Participation of Laity and Women in the Church." *Theological Studies* 80, no. 2 (2019): 414–35.

Briola, Lucas. "Sustainable Communities and Eucharistic Communities: *Laudato Sí*, Appalachia, and Redemptive Recovery." *Journal of Moral Theology* 2, Special Issue 1 (2017): 22–33.

Britton, Bianca. "Climate Change Could Render Sudan 'Uninhabitable.'" December 8, 2016. Accessed July 8, 2019. https://www.cnn.com/2016/12/07/africa/sudan-climate-change/index.html.

Brown, Lester B. "Could Food Shortages Bring Down Civilization?" *Scientific American* (May 2009): 53.

———. *Full Planet, Empty Plates: A New Geopolitics of Food Security*. New York: W.W. Norton and Co., 2012.

Brown, Sandy, and Cindy Getz. "Farmworker Food Insecurity and the Production of Hunger in California." In *Cultivating Food Justice, Race,*

Class and Sustainability, edited by Alison Hope Alkon and Julian Agye-man, 221–46. Cambridge, MA: MIT Press, 2011.

Brueggemann, Walter. "Food Fight." *Word & World* 33, no. 4 (Fall 2013): 319–40.

———. "The Liturgy of Abundance, the Myth of Scarcity." In *Deep Memory, Exuberant Hope: Contested Truth in a Post-Christian World.* Minneapolis: Fortress Press, 2000.

Bruteau, Beatrice. "Eucharistic Ecology and Ecological Spirituality. *Cross Currents* 40 (1990): 499–514.

Bulgakov, Sergei. *Philosophy of Economy: The World as Household.* New Haven: Yale University Press, 2000.

Cambanis, Thanassis. "The Arab Spring Was a Revolution of the Hungry." *The Boston Globe*, August 23, 2015. Accessed June 30, 2019. https://www.bostonglobe.com/ideas/2015/08/22/the-arab-spring-was-revolution-hungry/K15S1kGeO5Y6gsJwAYHejI/story.html.

Campbell, Hugh. "Let Us Eat Cake? Historically Reframing the Problem of World Hunger and Its Purported Solutions." In *Food Systems Failure: The Global Food Crisis and the Future of Agriculture*, edited by Christopher Rosin, Paul Stock, and Hugh Campbell, 30–45. New York: Earthscan, 2012.

Cavanaugh, William T. *Being Consumed: Economics and Christian Desire.* Grand Rapids, MI: William B. Eerdmans, 2008.

Chauvet, Louise Marie. *The Sacraments: The Word of God at the Mercy of the Body.* Collegeville, MN: Liturgical Press, 2001.

Clapp, Jennifer, and Marc J. Cohen, eds. *The Global Food Crisis: Governance Challenges and Opportunities.* Waterloo, Ontario: Wilfrid Laurier University Press, 2009.

Congregation for Divine Worship and the Discipline of the Sacraments. *The General Instruction of the Roman Missal.* In *The Liturgy Documents.* 5th ed. Chicago: Liturgy Training Publications, 2012.

Consumer Reports. "Consumers Want Mandatory Labeling for GMO Foods." *Consumer Reports* (December 2, 2015). Accessed June 21, 2019. http://www.consumerreports.org/food-safety/consumers-want-mandatory-labeling-for-gmo-foods/.

Crouch, Martha L. "How the Terminator Terminates: An Explanation for the Non-Scientific of Remarkable Patent for Killing Second Generation

Seeds of Crop Plants." Edmonds Institute Occasional Paper, May 20, 2009. Accessed July 12, 2019. https://www.iatp.org/sites/default/files /How_the_Terminator_Terminates_An_Explanation_f.htm.

Cummings, Clare Hope. *Uncertain Peril: Genetic Engineering and the Future of Seeds.* Boston: Beacon Press, 2008.

Dahill, Lisa E., and James B. Martin-Schramm, eds. *Eco-Reformation: Grace and Hope for a Planet in Peril.* Eugene, OR: Cascade Books, 2016.

Daly, Robert. "Eucharistic Euchology." *Worship* 89, no. 2 (2015): 166–72.

Davis, Ellen F. *Scripture, Culture, and Agriculture: An Agrarian Reading of the Bible.* Cambridge: Cambridge University Press, 2009.

Dearie, James. "World Hunger Escalates, Says UN Report." *National Catholic Reporter.* September 28, 2017. Accessed June 22, 2019. https://www.ncronline.org/news/world/world-hunger-escalates-says -un-report.

Dempsey, Carol J. "Creation, Revelation, and Redemption: Recovering the Biblical Tradition as a Conversation Partner to Ecology." In *The Wisdom of Creation*, edited by Edward Foley and Robert Schreiter, 53–64. Collegeville, MN: Liturgical Press, 2004.

Denton-Daly, Margaret. *John: An Earth Bible Commentary.* London: T & T Clarke, 2017.

De Schutter, Olivier. "Report Submitted by the Special Rapporteur on the Right to Food." United Nations. December 17, 2010. Accessed June 22, 2019. http://www2.ohchr.org/english/issues/food/docs/A-HRC -16-49.pdf.

Doria, Corinne, ed. *Invisible Hands: Voices from the Global Economy.* San Francisco: Voice of Witness/McSweeny Books, 2014.

Duch Guillot, Gustavo, and Fernando Fernández Such. *Agro-Industry under Suspicion.* Barcelona: Christianisme I Justicia Booklets, 2011.

Earth Charter Initiative. *Earth Charter.* The Hague: June 29, 2000. Accessed July 7, 2019. https://earthcharter.org/discover/the-earth-charter/.

Edwards, Denis. "Celebrating Eucharist in a Time of Global Climate Change." *Pacifica* 19 (February 2006): 1–15.

———. *Deep Incarnation: God's Redemptive Suffering with Creatures.* Maryknoll, NY: Orbis Books, 2019.

———. *Ecology at the Heart of Faith.* Maryknoll, NY: Orbis Books, 2006.

———. "Eucharist and Ecology: Keeping Memorial of Creation." In *The Natural World and God: Theological Explorations*, 11–13. Adelaide: ATF Publications, 2017.

———. "'Sublime Communion': The Theology of the Natural World in *Laudato Sí*." *Theological Studies* 77, no. 2 (2016): 377–91.

Eichenwald, Kurt. *The Informant*. New York: Broadway Books, 2000.

Eisenstein, Charles. *Sacred Economics: Money, Gift, and Society in an Age of Transition*. Berkeley: Evolver Editions, 2011.

Finger, Reta Haldeman. *Of Widows and Meals: Communal Meals in the Book of Acts*. Grand Rapids, MI: Eerdmans, 2007.

Food Chain Workers' Alliance. *Guess Who's Coming to Breakfast?* (2013), film. https://www.youtube.com/watch?v=MHvU_xVIso8.

Fortin, Anne. "From the Depths of Hunger." In *Hunger, Bread and Eucharist*, edited by Christophe Boureus, et al., 46–53. London: SCM Press, 2005.

Forum for Food Sovereignty. Declaration of Nyéléni. Sélingué, Mali: World Democratic Forum, February 27, 2007.

Francis, Andrew. *What in God's Name Are You Eating?* Eugene, OR: Cascade Books, 2014.

Frawley, Acharya David. "The Power and Importance of the Seed: The Heritage of Nature's Intelligence." In *Sacred Seed*, edited by Vandana Shiva, 63–68. Point Reyes, CA: The Golden Sufi Center, 2014.

Fretheim, Terrance E. "Nature's Praise of God." Chapter 8 (pp. 249–68) in *God and World in the Old Testament: A Relational Theology of Creation*. Nashville: Abingdon, 2005.

Fuller, Thomas. "In a California Valley, Healthy Food Everywhere but on the Table." *New York Times*, November 23, 2016. Accessed March 20, 2017. https://www.nytimes.com/2016/11/23/us/in-a-california-valley-healthy-food-everywhere-but-on-the-table.html?_r=0.

Gálvez, Alicia. *Eating NAFTA: Trade, Food Policies, and the Destruction of Mexico*. Oakland: University of California Press, 2018.

Garcia, Deborah Koons, dir. *Symphony of the Soil*. Lily Films: 2012.

Gerety, Rowan Moore. "Buying the Body of Christ: How the Communion Wafer Arrived in the Capitalist Marketplace." Killing the Buddha. Accessed May 3, 2019. www.killingthebuddha.com/mag/dogma/buying-the-body-of-christ/.

Gorringe, Timothy J. *The Common Good and the Global Emergency: God and the Built Environment.* Cambridge: Cambridge University Press, 2011.

———. *The Education of Desire: Towards a Theology of the Senses.* Harrisburg, PA: Trinity Press International, 2001.

———. *Fair Shares: Ethics and the Global Economy.* New York: Thames & Hudson, Inc., 1999.

———. *Harvest: Food, Farming and the Churches.* London: SPCK, 2006.

———. *The Sign of Love: Reflections on the Eucharist.* London: SPCK, 1997.

Grahm, Mark E. *Sustainable Agriculture: A Christian Ethic of Gratitude.* Cleveland: Pilgrim Press, 2005.

Grassi, Joseph. *Broken Bread and Broken Bodies: The Lord's Supper and World Hunger.* Rev. ed. Maryknoll, NY: Orbis Books, 2004.

Gregersen, Niels Henrik. "The Cross of Christ in an Evolutionary World." *Dialogue: A Journal of Theology* 40 (2011): 192–207.

Grumett, David, and Luke Bretherton, Stephen R. Holmes. "Fast Food." *Food Culture and Society* 14, no. 31 (September 2011): 375–92.

Grumett, David. *Material Eucharist.* Oxford: Oxford University Press, 2016.

Habel, Norman C., ed. *Readings from the Perspective of Earth.* The Earth Bible Series. Sheffield: Sheffield Academic Press, 2000.

Hammes, Érico João. "Stones into Bread: Why Not? Eucharist—Koinonia—Diaconate." In *Hunger, Bread and Eucharist*, edited by Christopher Boureaus, et al., 25–35. London: SCM Press, 2005.

Hanh, Thich Nhat. *How to Eat.* Berkeley, CA: Parallax Press, 2014.

Hart, John. *Sacramental Commons.* New York: Rowman and Littlefield, 2006.

Hassett, Maurice. "Early Symbols of the Eucharist." In *The Catholic Encyclopedia*, vol. 5. New York: Robert Appleton Company, 1909. Accessed July 5, 2019. www.newadvent.org/cathen/05590a.htm.

Hauter, Wenonah. *Foodopoly: The Battle over the Future of Food and Farming in America.* New York: The New Press, 2012.

Hawken, Paul, ed. *Drawdown: The Most Comprehensive Plan Ever Proposed to Reverse Global Warming.* New York: Penguin Books, 2017.

Heaven and Earth Are Full of Your Glory: A United Methodist and Roman Catholic Statement on the Eucharist and Ecology. April 2012. Ac-

cessed June 15, 2019. http://www.usccb.org/beliefs-and-teachings
/ecumenical-and-interreligious/ecumenical/methodist/upload
/Heaven-and-Earth-are-Full-of-Your-Glory-Methodist-Catholic
-Dialogue-Agreed-Statement-Round-Seven.pdf

Hellwig, Monica K. *The Eucharist and the Hunger of the World.* Kansas City:
Sheed and Ward, 1992.

———. *Guests of God: Stewards of Divine Creation.* New York: Paulist Press,
1999.

Herlinger, Chris, and Paul Jeffrey. *Food Fight: Struggling for Justice in a
Hungry World.* New York: Seabury Books, 2015.

Hessel-Robinson, Timothy. "Requiem for the Baiji: Liturgical Lamentation
and Species Extension." In *Spirit and Nature: The Study of Christian
Spirituality in a Time of Ecological Urgency*, edited by Timothy Hessel-
Robinson and Ray Maria McNamara, 176–200. Eugene, OR: Pickwick Publications, 2011.

Hickel, Jason. "Regenerative Agriculture: Our Best Hope at Cooling the
Planet." (January 6, 2017). https://www.localfutures.org/regenerative
-agriculture-best-shot-cooling-planet/.

Hillel, Daniel J. *Out of the Earth: Civilization and the Life of the Soil.* New
York: The Free Press, 1991.

Holdrege, Craig, and Steve Talbott. *Beyond Biotechnology: The Barren
Promise of Genetic Engineering.* Lexington: University Press of Kentucky, 2008.

Holmgren, David. *Permaculture: Principles and Pathways beyond Sustainability.* Hepburn Springs, Victoria, Australia: Holmgren Design Services, 2002.

———. *Retrofitting Suburbia: The Downshifters Guide to a Resilient Future.*
Hepburn Springs, Victoria, Australia: Melliodora Publishing, 2018.

Holt-Giménez, Eric, and Raj Patel. *Food Rebellions! Crises and the Hunger
for Justice.* Oakland, CA: Food First Books, 2009.

Holt-Giménez, Eric. "Food Security, Food Justice, or Food Sovereignty."
In *Cultivating Food Justice: Race, Class, and Sustainability*, edited by
Alison Hope Alkon and Julian Agyeman, 309–30. Cambridge, MA:
MIT Press, 2011.

Howard, Albert. *The Soil and Health: A Study of Organic Agriculture.* Oxford,
UK: Benediction Classics, 2011.

Institute for Advanced Sustainability Studies. "Fertile Soils: Crucial in the Fight to Hunger and Climate Change." 2012.

Irwin, Kevin W. *A Commentary on Laudato Sí.* New York: Paulist Press, 2016.

Jasper, R. D. C., and G. J. Cuming, trans. *Prayers of the Eucharist,* edited by Paul F. Bradshaw and Maxwell E. Johnson. 4th ed. Collegeville, MN: Liturgical Press, 2019.

Johnson, Elizabeth. *Creation and the Cross: The Mercy of God for a Planet in Peril.* Maryknoll, NY: Orbis Books, 2018.

Karris, Robert J. *Eating Your Way through Luke's Gospel.* Collegeville, MN: Liturgical Press, 2006.

———. *Luke: Artist and Theologian.* New York: Paulist Press, 1985.

Kaufman, Frederick. *Bet the Farm: How Food Stopped Being Food.* Hoboken, NJ: John Wiley and Sons, 2012.

Kelly, Tony. *The Bread of God: Nurturing the Eucharistic Imagination.* Liguori, MO: Liguori Publications, 2001.

Kimbrell, Andrew. *The Fatal Harvest Reader: The Tragedy of Industrial Agriculture.* San Francisco: Foundation for Deep Ecology, 2002.

Klinghardt, Matthias, and Hal Taussig, eds. *Mahl und religiöse Identität im frühen Christentum (Meals and Religious Identity in Early Christianity).* Tübingen: Francke, 2012.

Kloppenburg, Jr., Jack John Hendrickson, and G. W. Stevensen. "Coming in to the Foodshed." *Agriculture and Human Values* 13, no. 3 (Summer 1996): 33–42.

Kobel, Esther. *Dining with John: Communal Meals and Identity Formation in the Fourth Gospel and Its Historical and Cultural Context.* Leiden: Brill, 2011.

Koons, Deborah, dir. *Symphony of Soil.* 2012, film.

Korten, David C. *Change the Story, Change the Future: Living Economy for a Living Earth.* Oakland, CA: Berrett-Koehler Publishers, 2015.

Kroese, Ron. "Industrial Agriculture's War against Nature." In *The Fatal Harvest Reader: The Tragedy of Industrial Agriculture,* edited by Andrew Kimbrell, 92–105. Sausalito, CA: Foundation for Deep Ecology, 2002.

Lappé, Frances Moore. *Eco-Mind: Changing the Way We Think to Create the World We Want.* New York: Nation Books, 2011.

———. *World Hunger: Twelve Myths.* New York: Grove Press, 1998.

Lavadiere, Eugene. *Dining in the Kingdom of God.* Chicago: Liturgy Training Publications, 1994.

Lederer, Edith M. "Rising Hunger Tied to Endless Global Warfare." *San Francisco Chronicle*, November 12, 2017.

LeVasseur, Todd, Pramod Parajuli, and Norman Wirzba, eds. *Religions and Sustainable Agriculture: World Spiritual Traditions and Food Ethics.* Lexington: University Press of Kentucky, 2016.

Lindsey, Robert. "Cesar Chavez Tries New Directions for United Farm Workers." *New York Times*, September 19, 1983.

Lymbery, Philip. *Dead Zone: Where the Wild Things Were.* London: Bloomsbury Publishing, 2017.

———. *Farmageddon: The True Cost of Cheap Meat.* London: Bloomsbury Publishing, 2014.

Lyson, Thomas A. *Civic Agriculture: Reconnecting Farm, Food and Community.* Medford, MA: Tufts University Press, 2004.

Macy, Joanna, and Molly Brown. *Coming Back to Life.* Gabriola Is, BC: New Society Publishers, 2014.

Mahon, Clare. "The Right to Food: A Right for Everyone." In *Food Systems Failure: The Global Food Crisis and the Future of Agriculture*, edited by Christopher Rosin, Paul Stock, and Paul Campbell, 83–97. New York: Earthscan, 2012.

Marglin, Stephen A. *The Dismal Science: How Thinking Like an Economist Undermines Community.* Cambridge, MA: Harvard University Press, 2008.

Matthews, Emily, and Allen Hammond. *Critical Consumption Trends and Implications: Degrading Earth's Ecosystems.* Washington, DC: World Resources Institute, 1999.

McClintock, Nathan. "From Industrial Garden to Food Desert: Demarcated Devaluation in the Flatlands of Oakland." In *Cultivating Food Justice: Race, Class, and Sustainability*, edited by Alison Hope Alkon and Julian Agyeman, 89–120. Cambridge, MA: MIT Press, 2011.

McDonald, Thomas. "We Did Not Make Ourselves." Wonderful Things. August 29, 2012. Accessed July 1, 2019. https://thomaslmcdonald .wordpress.com/2012/08/29/we-did-not-make-ourselves.

McDonagh, Sean. *Laudato Sí: With Commentary by Sean McDonagh.* Maryknoll, NY: Orbis Books, 2016.

McGowan, Andrew B. *Ancient Christian Worship: Early Church Practices in Social, Historical, and Theological Perspective.* Grand Rapids, MI: Baker Academic, 2016.

———. *Ascetic Eucharists: Food and Drink in Early Christian Ritual Meals.* Oxford: Clarendon Press, 1999.

———. "Dangerous Eating? Jesus, Inclusion, and Communion." *Liturgy* 20, no. 4 (2005): 13–20.

———. " 'Is There a Liturgical Text in This Gospel?' The Institution Narrative and Their Early Interpretive Communities." *Journal of Biblical Literature* 118, no. 1 (1999): 73–87.

———. "The Myth of the 'Lord's Supper': Paul's Eucharistic Meal Terminology and Its Ancient Reception." *The Catholic Biblical Quarterly* 77, no. 3 (2015): 503–21.

———. "Naming the Feast: The *Agape* and the Diversity of Early Christian Meals." *Studia Patristica* 30 (1997): 314–18.

———. "Rethinking Eucharistic Origins." *Pacifica* 23 (June 2010): 173–91.

McKenney, Jason. "Artificial Fertility: The Environmental Cost of Industrial Fertilizers." In *The Fatal Harvest Reader: The Tragedy of Industrial Agriculture*, edited by Andrew Kimbrell, 121–29. Sausalito, CA: Foundation for Deep Ecology, 2002.

McKibben, Bill. *Eaarth: Making a Life on a Tough New Planet.* New York: St. Martin's Griffin, 2011.

———. *Falter: Has the Human Game Begun to Play Itself Out?* New York: Henry Holt and Co., 2019.

McMinn, Lisa Graham. *To the Table: A Spirituality of Food, Farming, and Community.* Grand Rapids, MI: Brazos Press, 2016.

Méndes-Montoya, Angel F. *The Theology of Food: Eating and the Eucharist.* Chichester, UK: Wiley-Blackwell, 2009.

Merton, Thomas. *The Living Bread.* New York: Farrar, Straus & Cudahy, 1956.

Miller, Vincent J. "The Common Good and the Market." *America* (April 1, 2019): 32–37.

Millstone, Eric. "Beyond 'Substantial Equivalence.' " *Nature*, October 7, 1999.

Mick, Lawrence E. *Liturgy and Ecology in Dialogue.* Collegeville, MN: Liturgical Press, 1997.

Mitchell, Nathan. *Eucharist as Sacrament of Initiation.* Chicago: Liturgy Training Publications, 1994.

Moe-Lobeda, Cynthia D. *Healing a Broken World: Globalization and God.* Minneapolis, MN: Fortress Press, 2002.

———. *Resisting Structural Evil: Love as Ecological-Economic Vocation.* Minneapolis: Fortress Press, 2013.

Montgomery, David R. *Dirt: The Erosion of Civilizations.* Berkeley: University of California Press, 2007.

Montgomery, David R., and Anne Biklé. *The Hidden Half of Nature: The Microbial Roots of Life and Health.* New York: W.W. Norton and Co., 2016.

Montoya, Angel F. Méndes. *A Theology of Food: Eating and the Eucharist.* Oxford: Wiley Blackwell, 2009.

Mortimort, A. G. *The Church at Prayer: Principles of the Liturgy.* Collegeville, MN: Liturgical Press, 1987.

Murrow, Edward R. *Harvest of Shame.* Directed by Fred W. Friendly. 1960. CBS. Film.

Myers, Ched. *Binding the Strongman: A Political Reading of Mark's Story of Jesus.* Maryknoll, NY: Orbis Books, 1988.

———. "Prophetic Visions of Redemption as Rehydration: A Call to Watershed Discipleship." *Anglican Theological Review* 100, no. 1 (2018): 61–78.

———. *Watershed Discipleship: Reinhabiting Bioregional Faith and Practice.* Eugene, OR: Cascade, 2016.

———. *Who Will Roll Away the Stone? Discipleship Queries for First World Christians.* Maryknoll, NY: Orbis Books, 1994.

National Conference of Catholic Bishops, Committee on the Liturgy. *Environment and Art in Catholic Worship.* Washington, DC: USCC Publication Office, 1978.

Navdanya International. *Terra Viva: Our Soil, Our Commons, Our Future; A New Vision for Planetary Citizenship.* Navdanya International, 2015. www.navdanyainternational.it.

New World Encyclopedia Online. "History of Agriculture." Accessed June 20, 2019. //www.newworldencyclopedia.org/p/index.php?title =History_of_agriculture&oldid=100869.

Northcott, Michael. "Faithful Feasting." In *A Moral Climate: The Ethics of Global Warming,* 232–66. Maryknoll, NY: Orbis Books, 2007.

————. "Planetary Moral Economy and Creaturely Redemption in *Laudato Si'.*" *Theological Studies* 77, no. 4 (2016): 886–904.

O'Brien, David J., and Thomas A. Shannon, eds. *Catholic Social Thought: Encyclicals and Documents from Pope Leo XIII to Pope Francis.* 3rd rev. ed. Maryknoll, NY: Orbis Books, 2016.

O'Donnell, Hugh. *Eucharist and the Living Earth.* Rev. ed. Dublin: Columba Press, 2012.

Ofo-ob, Stephen, Victor M. "The Appropriateness of Rice Wine in the Celebration of the Holy Eucharist in the Episcopal Church in the Philippines." MTS thesis, Church Divinity School of the Pacific, Berkeley, CA, 2017.

O'Loughlin, Thomas. *The Eucharist: Origins and Contemporary Understandings.* New York: Bloomsbury T&T Clark, 2015.

Patel, Raj. *Stuffed and Starved: The Hidden Battle for the World's Food System.* Brooklyn, NY: Melville House Publications, 2012.

Paul, Helena, and Ricarda Steinbrecher. *Hungry Corporations: Transnational Biotech Companies Colonize the Food Chain.* London: Zed Books, 2003.

Paul, Katherine. "Organic Farming Explained." Organic Consumers Association, May 21, 2019. Accessed June 29, 2019. https://www.organic consumers.org/blog/organic-farming-explained.

Pfeiffer, Dale Allen. *Eating Fossil Fuels: Oil, Food, and the Coming Crisis in Agriculture.* Gabriola Island, BC: New Society Publishers, 2006.

Phan, Peter. *Being Religious Interreligiously.* Maryknoll, NY: Orbis Books, 2004.

Philpott, Tom. "New Research: Synthetic Nitrogen Destroys Soil Carbon, Undermines Soil Health." *Grist,* February 24, 2010. Accessed June 25, 2019. http://grist.org/article/2010-02-23-new-research-synthetic -nitrogen-destroys-soil-carbon-undermines/.

————. "Reviving a Much-Cited, Little-Read Sustainable-ag Masterpiece." *Grist,* March 2, 2007. Accessed June 25, 2019. http://grist.org/article /soil/.

Pohl, Christine D. *Recovering Hospitality as a Christian Tradition.* Grand Rapids, MI: William B. Eerdmans, 1999.

Pollan, Michael. *In Defense of Food: An Eater's Manifesto.* New York: Penguin Books, 2008.

Pope Francis. *Laudato Sí: On Care for Our Common Home.* Huntington, IN: Our Sunday Visitor Publishing, 2015.

Pope John Paul II. *Dies Domini: On Keeping the Lord's Day Holy.* In *The Liturgy Documents*, 36–85. 5th ed. Chicago: Liturgy Training Publications, 2012.

Pope Leo XIII. *Rerum Novarum: The Condition of Labor.* In *Catholic Social Thought*, edited by David J. O'Brien and Thomas A. Shannon, 12–40. 3rd rev. ed. Maryknoll, NY: Orbis Books, 2006.

Power, David N. "Eucharistic Justice." *Theological Studies* 67 (2006): 856–79.

———. *The Eucharistic Mystery: Revitalizing the Tradition.* New York: Crossroad, 1992.

———. "The Eucharistic Table: In Communion with the Hungry." *Worship* 83, no. 5 (September 2009): 386–98.

———. "Foundations for Pluralism in Sacramental Expression: Keeping Memory." *Worship* 75 no. 3 (May 2001): 194–209.

Pretty, Jules. *Agri-Culture: Reconnecting People, Land and Nature.* London: Earthscan, 2002.

Ramshaw, Gail. "A Look at New Anglican Eucharistic Prayers." *Worship* 86, no. 2 (March 2012): 161–67.

———. *Pray, Praise and Give Thanks.* Minneapolis: Augsburg Fortress, 2017.

Rasmussen, Larry L. *Earth Community, Earth Ethics.* Geneva: WCC Publications, 1996.

———. *Earth Honoring Faith: Religious Ethics in a New Key.* New York: Oxford University Press, 2013.

Rawal, Sanjay, dir. *Food Chains.* 2014.

Reese, Thomas. " 'Let's Not Wait for the Theologians,' Says Pope Francis about Sharing the Eucharist." *National Catholic Reporter*, June 6, 2019. Accessed July 5, 2019. https://www.ncronline.org/print/news/vatican /signs-times/lets-not-wait-theologians-says-pope-francis-about-sharing-eucharist.

Regenerative Agriculture Institute and The Carbon Underground. "What Is Regenerative Agriculture." Accessed June 29, 2019. https://regeneration international.org/2017/02/24/what-is-regenerative-agriculture/.

Roberts, Paul. *The End of Food.* Boston: Houghton, Mifflin, Harcourt, 2008.

Robin, Vicki. *Blessing the Hands That Feed Us: What Eating Closer to Home Can Teach Us about Food, Community, and Our Place on Earth.* New York: Viking Press, 2014.

Rodale Institute. "Regenerative Organic Agriculture and Climate Change." Accessed September 21, 2017. https://rodaleinstitute.org/wp-content/uploads/rodale-white-paper.pdf.

Rosin, Christopher, Paul Stock, and Paul Campbell, eds. *Food Systems Failure: The Global Food Crisis and the Future of Agriculture.* New York: Earthscan, 2012.

Rosset, Peter. "Small Is Beautiful." *Ecologist* 29, no. 8 (December 1999): 63.

Rossing, Barbara. "Why Luke's Gospel? Daily Bread and 'Recognition' of Christ in Food-Sharing." *Currents in Theology and Mission* 37, no. 3 (June 2010): 225–29.

Rowthorn, Anne, and Jeffery Rowthorn. *God's Good Earth: Praise and Prayer for Creation.* Collegeville, MN: Liturgical Press, 2018.

Ruether, Rosemary Radford. "Corporate Globalization and the Deepening of Earth's Impoverishment." In *Integrating Ecofeminism, Globalization and World Religions,* 1–40. Lanham, MD: Rowman and Littlefield Publishers, 2005.

Schlosser, Eric. *Fast Food Nation: The Dark Side of the All-American Meal.* New York: Houghton Mifflin, 2001.

Schneiders, Sandra M. *Written That You May Believe: Encountering Jesus in the Fourth Gospel.* New York: Crossroad, 1999.

Schut, Michael. "Why Food? Spirituality, Celebration and Justice." In *Food, Faith and Sustainability.* Seattle: Earth Ministry, 1997.

Science in Society Archive. "Paradigm Shift Urgently Needed in Agriculture." Science in Society Archive. September 17, 2013. Accessed June 17, 2019. http://www.i-sis.org.uk/Paradigm_Shift_Urgently_Needed_in_Agriculture.php.

Semedo, Maria-Helena. "Top Soil Could Be Gone in 60 Years if Degradation Continues." Address to forum marking World Soil Day, 2015. Accessed June 15, 2016. http://huffingtonpost.com/2014/12/05/soil-degradation-un_n_6276508.html.

Shaver, Stephen. "The Eucharistic Origins Story, Part I: The Breaking of the Loaf." *Worship* 92 (May 2018): 204–21.

————. "The Eucharistic Origins Story, Part 2: The Body and Blood of Christ." *Worship* 92 (July 2018): 298–319.

Shiva, Vandana. *Betting on Biodiversity: Why Genetic Engineering Will Not Feed the Hungry.* New Delhi: Research Foundation for Science, Technology and Ecology, 1999.

————. *Biopiracy: The Plunder of Nature and Knowledge.* Cambridge, MA: South End Press, 1997.

————. *Earth Democracy: Justice, Sustainability and Peace.* Berkeley: North Atlantic Books, 2005.

————. Keynote Address. Soil Not Oil Conference, Richmond, CA, September 4, 2015.

————. *Monocultures of the Mind: Perspectives on Biodiversity and Biotechnology.* New York: Zed Books, Ltd., 1993.

————. "The Rights of Mother Earth." Lecture, Berkeley, CA, October 20, 2014.

————. *Seeds of Suicide.* New Delhi: Navdanya, 2006.

————. *Seed Sovereignty, Food Security.* Berkeley: North Atlantic Press, 2016.

————. *Soil Not Oil.* Cambridge, MA: South End Press, 2008.

————. *Stolen Harvest: The Hacking of the Global Food Supply.* Cambridge, MA: South End Press, 2000.

————. "There Is No Reason Why India Should Face Hunger and Farmers Should Commit Suicide." Eco Watch, August 14, 2015. Accessed June 22, 2019. https://www.ecowatch.com/vandana-shiva-there-is-no -reason-why-india-should-face-hunger-and-farm-1882083425.html.

————. *Who Really Feeds the World? The Failures of Agribusiness and the Promise of Agroecology.* Berkeley, CA: North Atlantic Books, 2016.

Shiva, Vandana, ed. *Sacred Seed.* Point Reyes, CA: The Golden Sufi Center, 2014.

Shiva, Vandana, and Kunwar Jalees. *Why Is Every Fourth Indian Hungry? The Causes and Cures of Food Insecurity.* New Delhi: Navdanya, 2009.

Skelley, Michael. *The Liturgy of the World: Karl Rahner's Theology of Worship.* Collegeville, MN: Liturgical Press, 1991.

Smith, Dennis E. *From Symposium to Eucharist: The Banquet in the Early Christian World.* Minneapolis: Fortress Press, 2003.

Smith, Dennis E., and Hal E. Taussig, eds. *Meals in the Early Christian World: Social Formation, Experimentation, and Conflict at the Table.* New York: St. Martin's Press, 2012.

Smith, Jeffrey M. *Genetic Roulette.* Fairfield, IA: Yes! Books, 2007.

———. *Seeds of Deception: Exposing Industry and Government Lies about the Safety of Genetically Engineered Foods You're Eating.* Fairfield, IA: Yes! Books, 2003.

Snyder, Graydon F. *Inculturation of the Jesus Tradition.* Harrisburg, PA: Trinity International Press, 1999.

Society of Jesus, Social Justice and Ecology Secretariat. *Healing a Broken World.* Task Force on Ecology. 106, no. 2 (2011).

———. *Justice in the Global Economy: Building Sustainable and Inclusive Communities.* Special Report, Task Force on Economy. 121, no. 1 (2016). *www.sjweb.info/documents/sjs/pj/docs_pdf/pj_121_eng.pdf.*

Stone, Rachael M. *Eat with Joy: Redeeming God's Gift of Food.* Downers Grove, IL: InterVarsity, 2013.

Taussig, Hal. *In the Beginning Was the Meal: Social Experimentation and Early Christian Identity.* Minneapolis: Fortress Press, 2009.

Theokritoff, Elizabeth. *Living in God's Creation: Orthodox Perspectives on Ecology.* New York: St Vladimir's Seminary Press, 2009.

Tomczak, Jay. "Implications of Fossil Fuel Dependence for the Food System." Resilience, June 11, 2006. Accessed June 21, 2019. www.resilience .org/stories/2006-06-11/implications-fossil-fuel-dependence-food -system.

Tuckett, Christopher, ed. *Feasts and Festivals.* Leuven: Peeters, 2009.

Tweed, Thomas. *Crossing and Dwelling: A Theory of Religion.* Cambridge, MA: Harvard University Press, 2016.

Uhl, Christopher. *Developing Ecological Consciousness.* Lanham, MD: Roman and Littlefield, 2013.

United Nations Conference on Trade and Development. *Wake Up before It Is Too Late.* United Nations, 2013.

United Nations Environmental Programme. *International Assessment of Agricultural Knowledge, Science and Technology for Development.* United Nations, 2009. Accessed October 15, 2017. http://www.unep.org /dewa/agassement/report/IAASTD/EN?Agriculture%20at%20 a%20Crossroads_Synthesis%20Reports%20(english).pdf. Site discontinued.

United Nations Food and Agriculture Organization. "The Role of Soils in Ecosystem Processes." In *Status of the World's Soil Resources*. United Nations Food and Agriculture Organization, 2015. Accessed July 11, 2019. http://www.fao.org/3/a-i5199e.pdf.

———. "Soil Degradation." Accessed December 10, 2017. http://www .fao.org/soils-portal/soil-degradation-restoration/en/.

United Nations Human Settlement Programme. "The Challenge of Slums: Global Report on Human Settlements 2003." London: Earthscan, 2003. Accessed July 11, 2019. https://www.un.org/ruleoflaw/files /Challenge%20of%20Slums.pdf.

United Nations Office of the High Commissioner for Human Rights. "Fact Sheet No. 34: The Right to Adequate Food." Geneva: UN Office of the High Commissioner for Human Rights, 2010. Accessed July 11, 2019. https://www.refworld.org/docid/4ca460b02.html.

Uzukwu, Elochukwu E. "Food and Drink in Africa and the Christian Eucharist." *African Ecclesial Review* 22, no. 6 (1980): 370–85.

Vale, Robert, and Brenda Vale, eds. *Living within a Fair Share Ecological Footprint*. New York: Routledge, 2013.

Vandenberg, Katrina. "On Cold-Weather Vegetables." In *To Eat with Grace*, edited by Darra Goldstein et al., 19–21. Great Barrington, MA: Orion, 2014.

van der Zee, Bibi. "Why Factory Farming Is Not Just Cruel, But a Threat to All Life on the Planet: Interview with Philip Lymbery." *The Guardian*, October 4, 2017. Accessed June 10, 2018. https://www.theguardian .com/environment/2017/oct/04/factory-farming-destructive-wasteful -cruel-says-philip-lymbery-farmageddon-author.

Van Wieren, Gretel. *Restoration to Earth*. Washington, DC: Georgetown University Press, 2013.

Vatican II. "*Gaudium et Spes:* The Church in the Modern World." In *Vatican Council II: The Conciliar and Post Conciliar Documents*. Collegeville, MN: Liturgical Press, 2014.

———. "*Sacrosanctum Concilium*: Constitution on the Sacred Liturgy." In *The Liturgy Documents*. 5th ed. Chicago: Liturgy Training Publication, 2012.

Vidal, John. "Global Warming Causes 300,000 Deaths a Year, Says Kofi Annan Thinktank." *The Guardian*, May 20, 2009. Accessed June 22, 2019. https://www.theguardian.com/environment/2009/may/29/1.

Vincie, Catherine. *Worship and the New Cosmology*. Collegeville, MN: Liturgical Press, 2014.

Visser, Margaret. *The Gift of Thanks: The Roots and Rituals of Gratitude*. Boston: Houghton Mifflin Harcourt, 2009.

———. *The Rituals of Dinner: The Origins, Evolution, Eccentricities, and Meaning of Table Manners*. New York: Grove Weidenfeld, 1991.

Warshall, Peter. "Tilth and Technology: The Industrial Redesign of Our Nation's Soils." In *The Fatal Harvest Reader: The Tragedy of Industrial Agriculture*, edited by Andrew Kimbrell, 167–80. Sausalito, CA: Foundation for Deep Ecology, 2002.

Webster, Jane S. *Ingesting Jesus: Eating and Drinking in the Gospel of John*. Atlanta: Society of Biblical Literature, 2003.

Weinstein, Miriam. *The Surprising Power of Family Meals: How Eating Together Makes Us Smarter, Stronger, Healthier, and Happier*. Hanover, NH: Steerforth Press, 2005.

White, Courtney. *Grass, Soil, Hope: A Journey through Carbon Country*. White River Junction, VT: Chelsea Green Publishing, 2014.

Wilson, Julie. "Superbugs to Kill More People Than Cancer If Industrial Agriculture Doesn't Ditch Antibiotics and Pesticides." *Organic Consumer Association*, April 24, 2019.

Wirzba, Norman. *Food and Faith: A Theology of Eating*. New York: Cambridge University Press, 2011.

———. "Food for Theologians." *Interpretation: A Journal of Bible and Theology* 67, no. 4 (2013): 374–82.

———. *Living the Sabbath: Discovering the Rhythms of Rest and Delight*. Grand Rapids, MI: Brazos Press, 2006.

Wright, Jessica. "Biting the Hands Who Feed Us: Farmworker Abuse in the U.S." *Foodtank*, June, 2015. Accessed June 15, 2018. http://foodtank .com/news/2015/06/biting-the-hands-who-feed-us-farmworker -abuse-in-the-us.

Wright, Susan. *Molecular Politics: Developing American and British Regulatory Policy for Genetic Engineering, 1972–1982*. Chicago: University of Chicago Press, 1994.

Zeller, Benjamin E., Marie W. Dallam, Reid I. Neilson, and Nora I. Rubel, eds. *Religion, Food, and Eating in North America*. New York: Columbia University Press, 2014.

Zenner, Christiana. *Just Water: Theology, Ethics, and Fresh Water Crisis.* Rev. ed. Maryknoll, NY: Orbis Books, 2018.

Scripture Index

Genesis

1	27
1:3	27
1:20-21	27
1:26	180
2:15	180

Exodus

16	154
16:1-36	20
16:13	21
19–24	154

Deuteronomy

21:18-21	17

Ruth

3:3	31

Judith

10:3	31

Psalms

23:1	27
24:1	178
146	187

Proverbs

8:22-31	28
9:1-6	28

Song of Solomon

1:3	31

Wisdom

1:7	101
6:17-20	30
8:2-18	30

Sirach

14:20	29
15:1-3	29
24:8	28
24:17-21	29
24:19-21	28

Isaiah

16:3	179
25:6	26
25:6-8	26
25:7-8	26
40:11	27
52:4-8	26

Subject Index

Abundance
  and early Christian table ethics,
    49
  and scarcity, 6, 166
  earth's, xi, 6, 14, 129, 134, 140,
    145, 168
  Egypt's cuisine, 21
  eucharistic table of, 165–69
  future of Earth's, xii
  God as source of, 21
  gratitude for, 11
  illusion of, 9, 78, 198
  Jesus'/God's radical economy
    of, 16, 19, 22, 23, 26, 27,
    167, 168, 176,
  overabundance, 33
Accumulation, 7, 21, 22, 115, 154,
  190, 197, 201
Agriculture
  and climate change, 109
  and farmworkers, 118
  and justice, 140–45
  chemically intensive methods,
    61, 98, 99, 123–24
  Community Supported
    Agriculture, 130
  history of, 59

local, 129–33
organically sustained
  agriculture, 81–82, 109,
  133–36
regenerative, 137–40
small–scale, 126–29
sustainable, 123–46
urban agriculture, 131
U.S. Secretaries of, 61, 68
See also Corporate
  agribusiness; Farming
Agroecology, 135, 136–40, 141
Alternative economy, xi, 168, 177,
  188
  alternative food economy, 125,
    141
  alternative moral economy,
    167–68, 176
  alternative political order, 176
  in early Christian practice, 46,
    50
Apostolic Tradition, 41–42
Archer Daniels Midland
  Company, 191–92, 194
Assembling, 152
  around a common table, 157,
    159

and power distinctions, 158,
187
as body of Christ, 45, 152–53,
172
as eschatological assembly, 18,
48
as eucharistic community, 153,
155–56, 164, 169, 173, 186,
202
and ritualization of scarcity,
166
as political act, 153, 155, 159
in communion with Earth, 170,
173, 179
in early Christian communities,
44, 154–55

Banquets, 9, 35–53
and Eucharistic imagery, 167
Christian gathering as, 35–53
cosmic/messianic, 12, 16, 17,
18, 20, 26, 48–49
Eucharist as, 57
in Greco-Roman/Hellenistic
society, 39, 41, 46, 47, 48, 51
diepnon and *symposium*,
39–40
in Jesus' life and teaching, 17,
18, 19, 20, 25–26, 31–32,
33, 167
in portrayals of the Last
Supper, 160
wedding imagery, 26
See also Meals, early Christian;
Greco-Roman/Hellenistic
society

Beauty, 9, 93, 101, 138
charis, 47, 48
of creation in food and drink,
151, 168, 189
of vessels for food and drink, 161
Berry, Wendell, 3, 8, 47, 132
Biodiversity, 84, 106, 182, 184
in farming, fn. x, 124, 127, 128,
136
seeds and, 83, 85, 179
soil and, 96, 102
threatened by industrial food
system, 77, 85, 111, 179
Biofuels
and diversion of food crops/
cause of
and hunger, 79, 110, 144
Biotech corporations, 85, 88–92
and genetic modification of
seeds, 85
and GMO policy, 88–89
Blessing
of the cup, 37
of bread, 40, 199
of *eulogia*, 169
of other foods, 43
"cup of blessing," 40, 51
God, xi, 4, 20
in harvest rites, 173
in Jewish communities, 40, fn.
52, 189
Jesus', 199
Body and blood of Christ
and the poor, 161, 188
as new covenant, 47, 51, 171,
200